The Complete Urban Gardener

The Complete Urban Gardener

HOW TO GROW THINGS INDOORS AND OUT

Sonia Day

PROSPERO
B·O·O·K·S

For Sue Martin

Library and Archives Canada Cataloguing in Publication

Day, Sonia
        Complete urban gardener : how to grow things indoors and out / Sonia Day.

Includes index.
Originally publ. as The urban gardener and The urban gardener indoors.
ISBN 978-1-55267-555-7

        1. Indoor gardening. 2. House plants. 3. Balcony gardening. 4. Roof gardening. 5. Container gardening. I. Day, Sonia. Urban gardener. II. Day, Sonia. Urban gardener indoors. III. Title.
SB419.D39 2008   635.9'65   C2008-901332-8

This edition produced for Prospero Books

Key Porter Books Limited
Six Adelaide Street East, 10th floor
Toronto, Ontario
Canada M5C 1H6
www.keyporter.com

Text design: Peter Maher
Illustrations: Jock MacRae
Electronic formatting: Heidy Lawrance Associates

Printed and bound in Canada
08 09 10 11 12 5 4 3 2 1

The
Urban
Gardener

Contents

Introduction

Gardens are getting smaller. Only a few years ago, you needed a house with a front and back yard to qualify as a *real* gardener.

Not any more. People no longer confess in apologetic terms that "I just have a balcony." In fact, growing things on balconies —and rooftops, townhouse terraces, decks, and patios—has become North America's hottest gardening trend.

What's driving this change is, of course, demographics. More and more of us are living alone, and in cities. Many older couples are leaving family homes behind and buying condominiums. Younger twosomes, busy with careers and kids, are also coming to the conclusion that they don't have the time or the inclination to maintain a conventional garden, with an expanse of lawn and flowerbeds. While establishing a link with Mother Nature remains an ideal for most of us, we want that link to be small—and manageable.

Surprisingly, gardening magazines have been slow to recognize our changing attitudes to the great green world. Their features continue to focus on gardens around houses. Big gardens, mostly. There is very little material geared to the folks for whom the word "garden" means a collection of pots and planters grouped on a balcony or terrace. And while you can find plenty of books on container gardening, even these are often aimed at the "traditional" gardener—that is, they describe how to grow plants in containers around houses: on decks and patios, next to driveways, or on porches. The urban gardener who lives in a condo, apartment or townhouse tends to be forgotten.

Hence this book. It explains not only how to grow plants in containers, but also all the other nitty-gritty aspects of gardening off the ground. You'll learn how to get started when even the soil for your garden has to be hauled up elevators. There's advice on what will work on cold, windy balconies, where to buy plants when you don't have a car, how to create a quick and colorful instant garden, and how to help your little green oasis survive when winter comes. I've included money-saving ideas because so many condo and apartment dwellers don't have big budgets for gardening, particularly when they first move in. And there are lots of practical tips from real live city people who garden in small spaces.

An apartment dweller I met recently, Wendy Humphries, complained rather plaintively that "No one ever writes anything for us." After struggling for years with a balcony ten stories off the ground, she had finally managed to transform this space into her dream: a delightful urban retreat, overflowing with flowers and greenery, where she could sit with a glass of wine in the evening and feel surrounded by nature. Fulfilling this dream hadn't been easy, however. Wendy found many of her initial plant choices didn't survive—and she'd been ready, on occasion, to give up gardening.

"It would have been helpful to have a book for guidance," she mused, "because it is so different growing things above the ground."

It is indeed. Wendy, here is that book. Finally.

Those Bewildering Terms Gardeners Use

You won't find many in this book, but for the sake of brevity and clarity, a few horticultural expressions do pop up here and there. Here's what they mean.

Annual: A plant that grows from seed for only one summer, then dies.

Biennial: A plant that lasts two years. The first year, it usually sends out leaves, the second it produces flowers and seeds.

Bolt: When plants shoot up too quickly, they "bolt." Usually applied to leafy vegetables such as lettuce.

Cell paks: Little plastic trays, divided into compartments, in which pre-started plants are sold.

Deadhead: To snip off (or snap off with fingers) flower heads after they've bloomed. Done to encourage the plant to send out more flowers.

Double: Usually used in reference to flowers. Means two layers of petals, rather than one.

Hardy: Means plants can stay outside over the winter.

Mulch: A protective layer piled up around the base of plants to help them cope with winter or dryness.

Perennial: A plant that keeps coming up year after year.

Pinch: Remove buds. Usually applied to the little buds that form at the tips of plant stems.

Self-seed: When plants drop seeds at random, without any human help.

Single: Flowers that have only one layer of petals.

Spent: Has nothing to do with finances. Means a flower that has finished blooming.

Variegated: Usually used in reference to foliage. Means two (or more) different colors on the same leaf.

Weeping: Branches that hang downwards from a strong central stem. Usually used in reference to trees or shrubs.

Starting Out: Plan, If You Can

When it comes to gardening in small spaces, most of us do things back to front. We buy a condominium (or rent an apartment) and only start thinking about the outdoor space *after* we've moved in. Then we discover the drawbacks. That much-anticipated balcony (or terrace, or courtyard, or rooftop), which seemed so exciting at the outset, proves to have all kinds of inadequacies that we hadn't considered. It's too small, it gets no sun at all, it's windy, it faces an ugly air-conditioning shaft, there's no privacy, building management has all kinds of rules about what we can do there, and so on.

The way to avoid these kinds of disappointments is to think ahead. First of all, figure out why you want a little garden in the first place. Are you a serious gardener (or intending to be one)? Will you want to grow lots of plants out there? Or will you be content with a couple of flowerpots? Do you like sitting outside? Do you plan to relax quietly by yourself on the balcony—or do lots of entertaining? Then, before plunking down your hard-earned cash for the unit, check carefully that the exterior space is going to provide the amenities you want (or at least some of them).

That said, there's probably no such thing as a "perfect outdoor space." From a gardening point of view, however, some are much better designed than others. The most challenging kind of balcony is unfortunately all too common on many modern condominium and apartment buildings. It consists of a concrete pad jutting out from the building wall, with a railing running around three sides. The principal problem is that it's too open. There are no side walls on which to attach things, like trellises and hanging baskets. Often the difficulties are compounded by a solid wall of windows or glass patio doors directly behind the balcony. (You can't hang anything from those, either.) As well, most of these balconies are simply too small. There's hardly room for a chair, let alone flowerpots and planters. And it's often very windy.

Another important aspect that architects don't consider is watering arrangements. In condos and apartments, washrooms and kitchens are invariably situated far from the balcony or courtyard. Outside faucets never seem to be part of the deal, which means hauling heavy, clumsy watering cans over furniture, carpets, and hardwood flooring, often ruining everything in the process.

Not many of us have the financial wherewithal to shop around for a condominium or apartment with a custom-built balcony that's designed with gardening in mind. However, you can save yourself a lot of frustration by considering a few factors in advance.

What to look for in a balcony or courtyard

❀ **Space:** Good balconies (or townhouse courtyards) are roomy. An ideal size is 8 ft./2.5 m by 16 ft./5 m or bigger. A workable one is 6 ft./2 m by 6 ft./2 m.

❀ **Depth:** Avoid long, narrow spaces. It's difficult to fit chairs in them and awkward to move around them.

❀ **Surrounding walls:** Does the balcony or courtyard have any? The best type of balcony is partly inset into the sides of the building so you have solid walls on which to attach hooks and fixtures. (But it shouldn't have a roof overhanging the entire balcony, because that will stop the light getting in.) Townhouse courtyards are easier to work with if they have some kind of fence separating each unit.

❀ **Built-in planters:** Some buildings include them—and they are a tremendous plus because they make it possible to garden on different levels, instead of having to put everything on the floor of the balcony or courtyard.

❀ **Ground-floor lockers:** Does the unit have one, and is it accessible? Gardening in a small space inevitably involves finding space to stash a lot of stuff: bags of grow mix, planters, patio furniture, hoses. This storage area should be easy to reach.

❀ **Watering:** How far away is the nearest faucet? If you're buying a condo that hasn't been built yet, ask if it's possible to have a faucet installed on the balcony or in the courtyard as a custom feature. It will be worth every penny.

❀ **Building codes and bylaws:** Never presume that they won't affect you. Rules vary widely, and there are often restrictions on the type of gardening you can do. Some management boards forbid installation of any fixtures, like planters, trellises, and hanging baskets. Others don't allow residents to grow vegetables or certain kinds of vines and other plants. Always check that what you have in mind is going to be permitted.

❀ **Liability:** Add something to your balcony and you immediately become financially responsible for any damage that results from its installation. If your lovely new wooden planter leaks water onto the balcony below, staining the owner's posh white wicker chairs, you pay. Ditto if you install outdoor lighting in a courtyard and the wiring causes a fire in the unit next door. Always use qualified tradespeople if you make any structural changes—and first get permission to do the work.

> ## Hot tip
> "Carrying patio furniture down to lockers in the fall is back-breaking work. Buy tables and chairs that can stay outside all winter. Teak and lightweight cast aluminum are best, if you can afford them."
>
> —*Sue Martin, balcony gardener*

Let there be light (preferably lots)

You've moved in. You're dying to get started growing something. What to do first?

Look at the light outside. Carefully. Does your growing space have sun? Shade? A mixture of the two? It's important to find out. One of the biggest mistakes that beginning gardeners make is to march out and buy a lot of plants without working out how much light—and what *kind* of light—they have. When plant labels say, "Needs full sun," they generally mean at least six hours of unobstructed sunshine a day. If you don't have that much, it may be a waste of time and money to buy many sun-loving annuals and perennials. (However, there are lots of other things you can grow. See pages 55–56 and page 67.)

Before buying anything, observe carefully the time of day when the sun strikes your balcony, rooftop, or courtyard—and when it moves on. Also bear in mind that the sun shifts its position throughout the summer. By the end of June, it's going to rise and set much farther north than it does when you first venture outside after the winter.

Watch for obstructions that reduce the amount of light. Is your balcony (like so many) shaded much of the day by the balcony above? Do surrounding buildings or privacy fences stop the sun from reaching your courtyard terrace? And what about trees? Are they going to leaf out and cast shade once summer comes? It's crucial to consider all these factors because light—or the lack of it—will inevitably affect what you can grow.

Don't be discouraged, however, if your unit turns out to have more shade than you originally thought. Nowadays, people with shady balconies and courtyards are sometimes better off than those with supposedly "ideal" situations: unobstructed and facing smack south. With global warming becoming a reality, our summers are getting hotter. As a consequence, some high-rise gardeners are finding that a southern aspect is more of a hindrance than a help. Up high, the dry, searing heat becomes too much of a good thing for plants: they actually get sunburned.

There are no hard and fast rules about the best location for a balcony. It depends a lot on the local climate. Generally speaking, gardeners prefer balconies that face southeast or simply east. West is also good (but less so). However—here's the surprise—some balcony green thumbs, particularly those high off the ground, find their plants do surprisingly well on north-facing balconies. While they may not have any direct sunshine, there's still sufficient light up there—often bouncing off other buildings—for plants to flourish. Because pots and planters aren't baking every day in the sun's relentless rays, they don't dry out as quickly. The plants have a chance to establish healthy root systems and foliage.

Getting floored

Many balcony floors are made of concrete, which over time crumbles, flakes, and looks dreadful. One option is to paint the floor (if your building permits it). Use a paint designed specifically for concrete and a color that will blend in well with city dirt, such as gray. Avoid very dark colors; footprints and water stains will show, and you'll be forever wiping them off.

Some balcony gardeners find indoor-outdoor carpeting practical and comfortable (choose a muted shade, not that lurid rec room green), but don't make the carpet a permanent fixture. Left outside over the winter, this kind of floor covering will wreck the concrete. Also, be careful about water dripping from your plants onto the carpet. You don't want to be coping with mold and funny smells.

Another option is modular wooden or resin flooring that's made in squares. These sections are usually 2 ft./60 cm by 2 ft./60 cm and you simply slot them together on the floor. They're durable, look attractive, and come in all kinds of colors. They can also be custom-made to fit your space.

In courtyards and on rooftops you'll often get concrete paving slabs, which are functional but utilitarian. If the slabs aren't too big, swapping them for something else (like bricks, slate, or stone) can make a world of difference. On asphalt-covered rooftops, it's a good idea to lay a false roof on top—made from wooden crosspieces and raised on a framework of two-by-fours. Some gardeners also like to layer pebbles underneath planters and pots on rooftops to help drainage. Be sure to check with the management of your building, however, before doing any of these things. All kinds of restrictions are often imposed, usually for safety reasons. For example, some buildings won't permit the floor level on balconies and rooftops to be raised by even an inch because of concerns that someone may then topple over the balcony railing or rooftop parapet.

When you install wooden flooring or trellises, make all of it portable, lightweight, and easy to dismantle. Condo and apartment building bigwigs are fond of sending out edicts in spring announcing, "Everything must be removed from balconies and courtyards in order to carry out structural repairs." You don't want to be stuck with lugging a whole lot of heavy wooden planks and planters into your unit, and then keeping them indoors for months until the repairs are finished.

Tools to buy

One big plus of gardening on a balcony, terrace, or rooftop is that you don't have to invest in a lot of expensive equipment (unlike those poor suckers down below with their lawn mowers and string trimmers). You do need:

❀ Containers, of course (see pages 24–31).
❀ A hand trowel. Pick one with a narrow blade. If you want to remove a certain plant from a container, wide-bladed trowels tend to disturb other plants. The "slim Jims" are also best when making holes in growing mix in the spring for small plants.

❀ A fork or other small garden scratching tool. This is helpful for aerating impacted soil (so that water can get in) and for hooking out weeds. For really big planters, also buy a spade with a short handle. (If you don't have much storage space, camping stores sell spades with folding handles.)

* Lightweight pruners. There are all kinds on the market. Since you're unlikely to get into heavy pruning sessions, go for inexpensive ones. (On a balcony, buy a safety strap too. See page 120.)
* A big kitchen spoon, which is easier than a trowel for removing excess soil from pots or fitting soil around plants.
* A brush and dustpan to keep things tidy.
* A big plastic dishwashing bowl for potting up plants.
* A cheap plastic spray bottle for concocting bug deterrents.
* Thick-gauge garbage bags, which are great for storing excess soil, old plants, and discarded pots.
* Gloves, if you don't like getting your hands dirty.
* An out-of-sight storage area, if you have room for one. A chest with a lid is good: it can double as a bench.
* Watering equipment (see pages 42–45).

Should you do a design?

Nowadays, gardening gurus blather on about "design." Their insistence that we should always plan everything—and follow all kinds of rules—has taken a lot of the fun out of growing things.

The truth is, you don't have to care a fig about design—or make complicated drawings—to become a gardener. Just go out and get started: buy a couple of containers, a bag of growing mix, a few plants, and maybe some easy-to-grow seeds. Pot your purchases up and watch what happens. The thrill of seeing a seed sprout—or a tiny bundle of leaves evolve into a lovely flower—is what hooks most people on gardening in the

Cheapie tools are fine

Lightweight trowels and small garden forks made of a material called Nyglass are perfect for container gardeners. They cost peanuts, they're tough, and they won't rust if you leave them out in the rain. They come in colors like black, brown, and green and are sold everywhere.

first place. Agonizing endlessly about the style you want, the "right" things to buy, and where to put everything is tedious and often a waste of time because once you begin to garden, you'll keep changing your mind anyway.

Here are some tips for those who do like to work from a plan:

Do

✓ Position patio furniture first. Make room for at least one small chair so you can sit and admire your handiwork. If you like entertaining and the balcony is big enough, you'll need a proper seating area.

✓ Start small. Buy a few cheap plastic pots, all the same color. Fill them with plants that are carefree. It's easy to go overboard and come home with too much. Then gardening becomes a chore, not a pleasure.

✓ Create a potscape. Group containers closely together, rather than dib-dobbing them along the balcony. They generally look better in threes and fives, instead of twos. (However, by all means break the "rules." A pair of pots containing matching shrubs or trees can look great in certain situations.)

✓ Find ways to place pots on different levels. Elevate one on a box. Tuck two others of differing heights on the floor in front of those. Hang up a fourth above the group. Avoid putting pots all the same size in a long, boring row.

✓ Decide on an "anchor" color, then find ways to keep introducing it to your planting scheme. For example, using burgundy as the anchor, include at least one flower with petals or centers in burgundy (maybe pots too); add a vine with burgundy-colored leaves like sweet potato vine *Ipomoea batatas* 'Blackie' or tradescantia *T. pallida purpurea*. Then echo the theme again with a coleus that has a burgundy streak running through it.

✓ Create a focal point. On a small balcony, this could be: a flower that's scarlet, shocking pink, or orange (like a geranium); a foliage plant with striking leaves; an interesting container; a tall or colorful ornament; a mini-fountain.

✓ Have a focal point that's off-center. Smack in the middle of the balcony is not usually the best position. Place pots so they lead your eye to the focal point.

✓ Remember that cool colors recede, while warm ones pop out. To create a feeling of distance in a small space, place flowers and foliage in blues, cool pinks, purples, and blue greens at the back. Position the reds, yellows, and orangey pinks at the front.

Don't

✗ Feel you have to follow any design rules or master plan.
✗ Buy a certain type of container, garden furniture, or plant just because it's trendy. Put your own personality into what you do.
✗ Clutter the space up with too many itsy-bitsy doodads.
✗ Place anything where you—or visitors—will trip over it.
✗ Try to tackle everything in one day.

The problem of privacy

Homes are getting smaller; so are outdoor spaces. In cities, more and more of us now live cheek by jowl with neighbors. That can be both a pleasure and a pain in the neck. If nosy Neetha and garrulous Greg are getting on your nerves, consider putting up privacy screens. Don't, however make this partition into a Berlin Wall (that is, completely solid). On balconies and roof-tops—and even in ground-floor courtyards—the air needs to be able to pass through the screen, or gusts of wind will cause continual problems for you—and those annoying people next door.

Simple, inexpensive screens can be made with ready-made sections of lattice (sold at home renovation stores). If you install a wood fence (on each side of a courtyard, for instance), make sure there is some air space between the slats. The "blocky" appearance of such barricades can be softened by a variety of climbing vines (see pages 90–95) and tall shrubs (see pages 96–101).

(see pages 90–95)
(see pages 96–101)

Hot tip

"Take your time arranging—and rearranging—containers to get the look you want. The great thing about container gardening is that it's portable, not fixed."

—*Mary Lu Toms, rooftop gardener*

Hot to Pot: Choosing the Right Containers

When looking for pots, think "practical" rather than "pretty." Even though gardening is booming, good containers are often hard to find. The problem with many is that they simply aren't big enough. The pot may look appealing gussied up with a couple of fake gerberas in the garden decor shop, but take it home and you'll discover that there's hardly room to squeeze a couple of trowelfuls of soil into it.

How to shop for pots

Companies that service the landscaping trade are often good places to find practical containers. (Look in the Yellow Pages. You can sometimes persuade these places to sell retail too.) Hardware and home renovation stores usually have Plain Jane pots that work well with outdoor plants. The choice at garden centers, once dismal, is improving. Check out ads in gardening magazines and sites for gardeners on the Web: you can sometimes find splendid containers for sale by mail order. Artists at craft fairs can also be good sources, because they often garden themselves and know what makes a good pot.

Before buying, ask yourself these questions:

- ✿ What do I want to grow in this pot?
- ✿ Is it suitable for the purpose?
- ✿ Will it blend in with what's already on my balcony?

Do

✓ Look for *deep* pots if you plan to grow perennials, vines, shrubs, and trees. Most need room for roots to spread.

✓ Choose shallow pots for drought-tolerant, succulent plants like echeverias and sedums. Filled with soil, they'll be lighter than bigger pots (and the less heavy stuff you have to haul upstairs, the better).

✓ Make sure there's a drainage hole. Some potters have the annoying habit of producing lovely ceramic creations that don't have a hole in the bottom.

✓ Buy pots that you find appealing. You're going to be seeing a lot of each other on the balcony.

✓ Consider a pot's portability. Does it weigh a ton already? Will you be able to carry it into the elevator—and along building corridors? How heavy will it be full of potting mix?

✓ Stick to small pots if you have a tiny space. Big ones will make it seem cramped.

✓ Think about how the pot will look with something planted in it. (Jazzy designs and doodads on pots can be cute at first glance, but they often detract from the plants—and you'll tire of them quickly.)

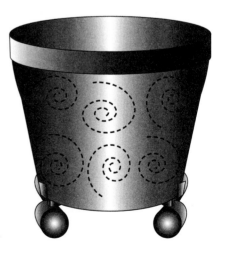

✓ Pick pots in several sizes. Some tall, some short, some wide make an attractive grouping. Mix oblong shapes with round ones.

✓ Put sets of wheels underneath big containers so you can move them easily. Many garden centers sell kits that consist of a frame on which to stand the pot, with castors underneath. If you're handy, attach some castors (the kind that are used on furniture) to the bottom of pots yourself.

✓ Investigate the possibility of having planters built in if you want to grow big trees or shrubs. It's expensive but worth it. Insulate the planter interiors with Styrofoam sheeting in colder climates— and be sure to include a drainage hole.

✓ Use offbeat containers. Old boots, olive oil and paint cans, or asparagus boxes from the greengrocer all can look terrific. A hot trend in Europe is to stand pots inside bags. Garden designers are using burlap sacks, old cloth shoulder bags, and even (yikes) grocery bags from the supermarket. These funky touches are fun, but don't overdo them.

✓ Be bold and original. Try painting your pots. Most containers—clay, plastic, wood, or synthetic materials—can take paint well. (Use a glossy oil-based paint that resists dampness. Paint before you put the plant in.) Try signal red, hot pink, canary yellow, Provençal blue, or purple, then choose plants that echo those colors. Bear in mind, though, that hot hues aren't restful. If you want a peaceful retreat, choose muted shades. Steel gray looks good with anything and is an excellent backdrop to many flowers, particularly pink and white ones.

Don't

✗ Buy pots that look great but have thick sides and tiny interiors. Inspect both the inside and outside. Pots that are wide at the top but very narrow at the bottom are a no-no. They'll cramp roots.

✗ Have too many styles and colors, especially if your balcony is small. Pots with a unified theme look best.

✗ Buy pots that have ornamental bits and pieces stuck on their sides. Soil and city dirt gets trapped in the raised areas, and they are difficult to clean. Remember also that white pots get grubby quickly.

✗ Go overboard. It's easy to buy too many containers and then find you don't have the energy, funds, or space to fill them with plants.

Which container works best?

Different materials suit different purposes. Ultimately, containers are also a matter of personal taste. Here are some pot pointers:

Ceramic and glass

Pluses: Often have great textures and colors. Show off plants nicely. Containers called "jardinieres" are usually made of ceramic. They don't dry out as quickly as clay.
Minuses: Heavy. Break easily. Many don't have drainage holes.
Recommendations: Avoid, but if you have a gorgeous ceramic jardiniere, nestle a plastic pot containing the plant inside it on a layer of gravel.

Clay

Pluses: Classic. Looks great, ages nicely, and is porous, so plants can breathe through it. Some gardeners swear that many plants, particularly herbs, grow better in clay—and they refuse to use any other kind of pot. Glazed clay pots won't dry out as quickly.
Minuses: Heavy. Breaks easily. Plants need watering more often. Cracks in frost, so you have to empty pots every fall.
Recommendation: For purists. Soak pots before planting. Skip strawberry jars (They have holes in their sides and dry out too quickly.) Look for clay pots that are fired at very high temperatures and are therefore less likely to crack. Skip clay if you want a low-maintenance garden.

Concrete and stone

Pluses: Formal. Elegant. Good for big things like trees and shrubs.
Minuses: Concrete can crack and crumble in frost. Heavy. Not portable.
Recommendations: Good for ground-floor courtyards only—unless they're already built into your balcony.

Metal

Pluses: Hip, contemporary. Also classic. (Aluminum florists' buckets and bronze or iron urns are hot in some circles.) Shiny surfaces look chic against brick walls, add sparkle to gloomy balconies, and show off some plants well.

Minuses: Expensive. Can rust. Corrodes. (Aluminum won't rust, but dents easily.) Can be heavy. Salts and minerals in water make sides look scummy.

Recommendations: If you like metal, use it for all your containers. Don't mix metal with other materials.

Plastic

Pluses: Lightweight. Cheap. Retains moisture. Terra cotta–colored plastic pots look as good as clay ones.

Minuses: Plastic can get too hot—and may fry plants in heat waves. Flimsy. May blow over in windy areas.

Recommendations: Best choice for budget gardeners. Pick light colors. Dark shades, like green and black, soak up more heat.

Resin, fiberglass, and other synthetic materials

Pluses: Lightweight. Tough. Durable. Terrific styles and sizes. Some now look exactly like "the real thing"—i.e., stone troughs, antique urns, terra cotta.

Minuses: Pricey. Expect to pay up to $200 for a big container. Tall ones can blow over in windy locations.

Recommendations: Best choice for balcony gardeners, if you can afford them.

Wood

Pluses: Nice appearance, natural looking, insulates plants well, keeps roots cool. Can be painted to a color you want or covered in materials like copper sheeting. Good for big, built-in planters. A group in redwood, cedar, or teak gives continuity, especially in a small space.

Minuses: Cheap ones are inclined to rot. Treated wood lasts longer but is toxic. Often leaks, unless seams are well sealed.

Recommendation: Raise wooden planters off the ground on supports or legs so air can pass underneath. Line wooden containers with plastic and nestle plastic pots containing plants inside.

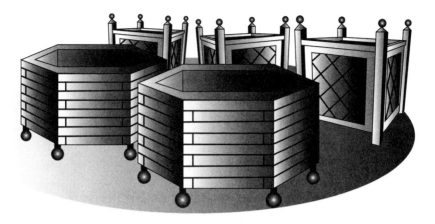

Go for good pots

It's worth investing in quality containers. Be selective. Wait till the fall, when the expensive resin ones go on sale, then add one to your collection every year.

Hanging basket hell

It happens. Hanging baskets usually look wonderful in stores (especially if they're ready planted), but bring them home and it's hassle city. Baskets require hooks to hang from, they rock in the wind, they dry out quickly, and water drips all over the place.

If you insist on using this type of container,

❀ Make absolutely sure the basket is suspended safely (see pages 120–21).
❀ Hang the basket above other plants so they can benefit from the excess water dripping out.
❀ Don't hang the basket too high. Make sure you can reach it easily for watering.

- ❀ Position it where runoff water won't dribble down and soak the people on the balcony below you.
- ❀ Avoid wire baskets lined with moss or cocoa fiber, especially in a windy, exposed area. (They need watering constantly.) Plastic pots will stay moist longer. They are also lighter.
- ❀ Use mostly trailing plants.
- ❀ Make sure the basket is big enough—at least 1 ft./30 cm wide. A small, shallow basket will need constant watering.
- ❀ Add hydrogel granules (sold in some garden centers) to the planting mix. They hold several hundred times their weight in water. One teaspoonful is sufficient per hanging basket. Soak the granules before adding to the mix.

Some words about window boxes

They're traditional. The first containers that gardeners used for plants raised off the ground were probably window boxes. But they can pose problems. If you have your heart set on some,

- ❀ Hang boxes inside the balcony, not outside, and use solid brackets to support them (see page 121).
- ❀ Check that box interiors provide enough room to accommodate plants. Many cheap plastic or wooden window boxes are dinky and useless. A good size is 3 ft./1 m long, 1 ft./30 cm deep, and 1 ft./30 cm wide.
- ❀ Wooden boxes often leak. Line them with plastic sheeting or garbage bags, then add pebbles and a bit of peat moss. Put flowers planted in plastic pots on top of the peat moss. The advantage of this setup is that you can keep changing the plants throughout the summer (see page 109).

A barrel of fun

Some of the best containers, if you have sufficient space, are old whiskey or wine barrels cut in half. They hold lots of plants, and because they're deep and roomy, perennials can often winter over in them without problems.

If you want to use a barrel for a miniature water garden, be sure to wash it out thoroughly before adding fish. (They can actually get drunk on that leftover single malt.)

The suitability of barrels for gardening comes with a price tag: they are getting absurdly expensive at garden centers. (After all, it's not as though you're buying a new container. Wine and whiskey makers discard them.) Look for barrels that aren't too dried out. Don't buy them if the bottoms are warped and twisted. Watch too for staves that have shrunk so much the metal hoops encasing the barrels have become loose.

And don't pay exorbitant prices for these fun containers. Shop around for the best buy.

Hot tip

"Ask at the supermarket for empty poultry boxes. They are wide, flat cardboard boxes with low sides. They make great temporary work benches for potting up annuals in spring."
—*Sue Martin, balcony gardener*

Get Growing: It's All in the Bag

Soil isn't found in the sky. Unfortunately. For a balcony or rooftop garden, every ounce of the stuff has to be hauled in. It's the most tedious aspect of creating a garden above ground, but there are some advantages.

People with regular gardens down on street level rarely have perfect soil. In its natural state, dirt is usually either too clayey or too sandy. Clay soil clumps together and bakes as hard as a brick in summertime. With sandy soil, water drains away too fast. Amending both with compost, manure, and peat moss into an ideal "friable loam" is backbreaking work, especially if you're restoring an old, neglected garden. It also means buying digging tools like forks and spades. As well, ordinary garden soil may contain fungal diseases or nasty nuisances like cutworms (which love shearing off stems of tomato plants, right after you've planted them).

By contrast, balcony gardeners can get it right the first time. When everything is grown in containers, providing that magical friable formula is a snap. There are usually no bugs to contend with, either. You simply buy bags of the right growing mix from a garden center or hardware store, pot up, and wait for results.

Note those three crucial words: *right growing mix*. Not "soil." Using ordinary garden soil is a definite no-no (however friable it is). Squeezed into the artificial environment of a pot, plants need more cosseting than Mother Earth can provide. Potted plants can't ramble anywhere they please (as they do in a regular garden), so air spaces must be trapped in their containers to help roots breathe. Also, because the space is unnaturally small, nutrients need to be replenished regularly. Finally, there should be good drainage; plants don't like to sit with wet feet any more than we do. Specially formulated growing mixes are designed to meet those needs.

What do growing mixes contain?

Visit a garden center and there's a bewildering variety of growing mixes to choose from. Labels on the big, shiny bags often make extravagant claims ("Perfect perennials in two weeks!"; "Grow tomatoes as big as baseballs!"), but they're vague and unhelpful about the actual ingredients of the mix.

Here's why: most of them contain the same thing—lots of peat moss. This natural ingredient, which is harvested from former bogs, is used for container-grown plants because it retains moisture well. However, peat moss doesn't have a lot of nutrients, so most mix makers supplement it with chemical fertilizers in different formulas. They also may add composted softwood bark, vermiculite (which looks like nubbly bits of Styrofoam), or perlite (which is usually also nubbly and is made from heated lava rock). Bentonite clay may be included too, to help retain water.

Because peat moss is the prime ingredient in virtually all mixes, "expensive" doesn't automatically mean "better." It pays to shop around and experiment with different products. A garden writer who conducted some tests found that mixes varied enormously. Some stayed too soggy. One had too much nitrogen (so flowering plants produced lots of leaves but few blooms). Another was so fluffy with vermiculite, water whooshed through containers in seconds and didn't stay long enough to give plants a drink. And in one test, the most costly mix performed the worst.

You'll also see bags labeled "potting soil." Often this is simply soil, but it may have peat moss, compost, sand, and vermiculite added. It can be excellent or poor, depending on the company that packaged it. Again, experiment. Also, remember that bags of potting soil weigh more than mixes made with peat moss, so they may be a bigger hassle to haul upstairs.

The advantage of using ready-made mixes is that they are (usually) sterile. Manufacturers heat them to 180°F/82°C to kill bacteria and weed seeds. However, convenience comes at a price. If you need to fill lots of pots and planters, mixes can get mighty expensive.

Making your own mix

Good cooks work from scratch, rather than using pre-packaged ingredients. So do experienced gardeners, because it's cheaper and they can control what goes into the mix. To do this, spread out a big piece of plastic sheeting on the balcony floor or use a plastic garbage bin. Wear gloves if you don't like to get messy.

Two mixes recommended by condo gardeners

Pauline Walsh suggests: "Buy equal parts of potting soil, peat moss, triple mix (which contains peat moss, soil, and manure), and vermiculite. Keep mixing them till they look nice and crumbly. Once you've filled the pots, sprinkle aquarium charcoal on top. This absorbs odors and helps keep the soil sweet and moist." Her herbs flourish on this formula.

Elsa Young, whose terrace is full of magnificent clematis and roses, makes this recommendation: "Combine a bag each of composted sheep manure, peat moss, and a soil-less mix that contains vermiculite. Add several handfuls of bone meal."

More mix tips

❀ Avoid composted horse manure (unless it's three years old). It's too salty for most plants.

❀ Add a smidgen of horticultural sulphur or aluminum sulfate (sold at garden centers) if you're growing acid-loving plants like rhododendrons.

❀ A scoop of builder's sand is good, especially for herbs and cactus. Buy it at home reno stores and builders' yards. Don't use beach sand, which is too fine.

❀ If you're buying a ready-made mix, add a handful of granular slow-release fertilizer before planting. (It's usually sold in plastic jars or boxes.) First, however, always read what's written on your bag of growing mix. If it says something like, "With special nutrients added," that means fertilizer and you shouldn't add any.

❀ Never be a cheapskate and get soil from a friend's garden. Besides offering inadequate nutrients, soil packs down too hard in containers and may harbor diseases and creepy-crawlies that will multiply like mad in your pots.

What is humus?

If you're puzzled by that funny word "humus," don't be. It simply means decomposed or decayed organic matter. Peat moss is humus. So are composted leaves. It often looks exactly like topsoil. If you see a bag labeled "humus" at the garden center, it may contain some kind of composted material, leaves, or tree bark (or all three.) It's all good stuff.

Fertilizer facts

Gardeners who worry about the environment usually don't like to do anything "artificial." However, the fact is, most container-grown plants need fertilizer. There isn't sufficient nourishment in pots for them to flourish long term without some kind of boost.

If you pot up in spring using a growing mix that has fertilizers included (or some granular stuff that you added yourself), plants will usually do fine for a couple of months. But by mid-summer, they're probably getting tired and have used up the nutrients in the mix. That's the time to start fertilizing. If, however, you've used a mix that contains no additives (they consist of pure peat moss, compost, or potting soil), begin a regime of fertilizing right after planting.

There are many good fertilizers aimed at home gardeners. Often, they are simply called "plant food." Some are crystals, others liquid, and you stir them into a jug of water. Whichever type you use, let the mix sit for a few hours before pouring on plants. (Avoid touching leaves). If you have a garden hose, fertilizer granules that go into a gizmo attached to the hose are even easier. Some gardeners swear by little fertilizer "sticks" that are pushed into the soil. If you use these, be careful not to overdo them, or plant roots may get burned.

Check the numbers

Confused by all those mysterious numbers on the bottle or package of plant food? Here's a brief explanation.

All fertilizers contain these three basic nutrients:

❀ Nitrogen (chemical symbol N) promotes growth of green leaves and stems.
❀ Phosphorus (chemical symbol P) helps roots, flowers, and fruit grow.
❀ Potassium (chemical symbol K) assists flowering and fruiting too, but also makes plants develop strong stems and resistance to disease.

The three symbols are listed as numbers on product labels, always in that order. When you see something that says 5-10-5, it means the product contains 5% nitrogen, 10% phosphorus, and 5% potassium.

What's best to use? It depends on your plants. A good all-round formula is 20-20-20 or 10-10-10. This works well with most houseplants and it's fine for flowers grown out of doors, particularly annuals. Leafy plants prefer a formula where nitrogen is emphasized, for instance 10-7-7.

Organic or chemical?

Which is best? Both have merits. So-called natural fertilizers—often composted manure, fish emulsion, bone meal, or blood meal—are more expensive, but take effect slowly and generally won't harm plants. Chemical products get results quicker, but can burn leaves and roots if used incorrectly. Ultimately, the choice is a personal one. Look for a product that suits what you're growing, and follow label instructions to the letter. More plants are killed by people being too generous with fertilizer than by anything else.

When to fertilize?

Most balcony gardeners do it every two weeks. Some swear by a weekly regime. Don't fertilize at all during a heat wave, because it stresses plants. Wait till the weather cools down a bit. Also, stop fertilizing in the fall.

How to plant

Do

✓ Plant in the evening, not during the heat of the day.
✓ Choose a day when rain is forecast. Plants seem to love a good soak right after being planted.
✓ Soak growing mixes thoroughly before filling pots. (If they're in bags, cut the bag open and pour a jug of water in. Let it sit overnight.)
✓ Add granular fertilizer if necessary and be sure to follow the manufacturer's instructions as to quantity.
✓ Fill containers two-thirds full with growing mix.
✓ Arrange plants on top of the mix (still in their little plastic pots, if possible). Keep moving them around until you get an arrangement that satisfies you.
✓ Use plenty of plants. They can be closer together than in a regular garden. Put plants that will grow tall in the center (or at the back of a long planter). Trailing ones are best around the edge.
✓ Loosen root balls with your fingers if they're tightly packed, then push them gently into the mix. (Make sure root balls aren't dried out when you do this. They should be damp.) Push a bit more soil in around the plants with your hands.
✓ Check that you haven't planted the root balls too high. They should not be sticking up above the surface of the mix. If they are, start again.
✓ If plants are already flowering, pinch their flower heads right off. (Yes, off. It may seem crazy, but plants will settle

in better and get bushier if you deflower them at the beginning.)

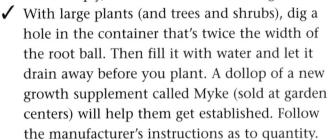

✓ Water deeply, so it comes out the drainage holes.
✓ With large plants (and trees and shrubs), dig a hole in the container that's twice the width of the root ball. Then fill it with water and let it drain away before you plant. A dollop of a new growth supplement called Myke (sold at garden centers) will help them get established. Follow the manufacturer's instructions as to quantity.
✓ If you're growing annuals, add broken up bits of Styrofoam or packing peanuts to the bottom of large containers before putting growing mix in. The containers won't weigh as much, and you'll spend less on growing mix. (But don't do this with big perennials, shrubs, or trees. Their roots need every inch of space they can get in containers.)

Don't

✗ Use dry mix. Peat moss needs to soak up water first. If it's too dry when you plant, it may stay that way forever. Your plants will never receive enough moisture.
✗ Fill pots too full. Leave at least 1 in./2.5 cm of head space so water and soil don't dribble over the top.
✗ Put bits of old pots or crockery in the bottom of the pot. Yes, it's accepted practice, but it's not necessary and it adds to the pot's weight. If you're worried about soil falling out the hole, put a cheap, lightweight sponge or coffee filter in the bottom of the pot.
✗ Pack the soil down hard.
✗ Put pots in direct sunshine right after you've planted them. Keep them in shade for a couple of days to settle in.
✗ Plant anything in really torrid temperatures. Wait for a cooler day.

Hot tip

"Put a piece of self-watering mat, sold at garden centers, in the bottom of your pots. It helps to wick moisture up into the soil."

—*Pauline Walsh, balcony gardener*

Townhouse troubles

If you're gardening on the ground in a townhouse courtyard, be prepared for extra work. Lots of it. The so-called soil around new townhouse developments is usually little more than construction debris, topped with a thin layer of earth (or sod) to prettify its appearance. Don't be tempted to plant in this miserable stuff; nothing will grow well. The only remedy is to dig everything out and replace it with real topsoil. Mix in some gritty sand, peat moss, and composted sheep manure too, if you intend to grow flowers. It's backbreaking work, but you will be starting off right.

Yes, you can compost

Composting will help the environment and your bank balance. Even on a tiny balcony, it's possible to recycle vegetable scraps—and produce that lovely, dark brown crumbly stuff that plants love. Here's how:

❀ In the fall, empty soil from some of your pots into a big garbage bag. Mix in a small bag of leaves gathered from the street. (Avoid oak leaves, which often take ages to break down, and cut the leaves up a bit, if you can.)

❀ Stand empty pots (which should be at least 15 in./40 cm wide) in an accessible place.

❀ Cut vegetable scraps into tiny pieces, add a bit of water, then keep mixing these scraps in your empty pots with trowelfuls of soil from the garbage bag.

❀ The veggie matter will quickly break down, so long as you keep introducing air to your mini-pile by working it with the trowel. As one pot fills up, put it aside and start on another pot.

❀ Use only plastic or fiberglass containers, because clay will crack during the winter. And don't worry about the stuff freezing. If it does, you can resume mixing once it warms up.

❀ Cover containers with lids if you're worried about flies and pests (though they are seldom a problem).

❀ Add tea bags and coffee grounds to your compost. But leave out the coffee filters. They take too long to break down.

❀ If you're brave enough, add a cupful of your own urine to the mix sometimes. It's full of nitrogen and really helps break things down.

Made-in-a-pot compost is ready to use the following spring when it feels crumbly. (If the texture isn't quite right, add a bit of peat moss.)

Alternatively, on a large balcony or rooftop, there may be room to squeeze in a mini-composter. These are boxy plastic contraptions with lids and aerating slats cut into the sides. Many municipalities give them out free, or at a reduced rate, to gardeners. If you use one, position it in the sun or shade

Mini-composter

(either works well) in a spot where the air can circulate freely. Then follow the three basic rules for creating compost quickly: cut everything you put into the composter into small pieces, mix wet and dry in layers, and keep turning the pile.

You don't need more growing mix

In spring, top up all your containers with a scoop of homemade compost. It's cheaper—and easier—than going out and buying fresh bags of mix.

Just Add Water (Often)

One big drawback to growing things in containers is often overlooked: watering. You can't escape it. Relying on the rain won't work. Any plant with its roots cramped into a container will dry out much more quickly than when it's growing in a regular garden. As well, many balcony gardeners are cursed with a concrete overhang, so rainwater can't reach plants.

Balconies, terraces, and rooftops can also be subject to non-stop winds that aren't even noticed on the ground. This dries things out even more. In summertime, your plants will usually need a drink once, sometimes twice, a day. If you neglect them for even twenty-four hours, they may give up the ghost.

Signs that you aren't watering enough include:

* Leaves shriveled, brown, or dried at edges
* Entire plant—or parts of it—drooping
* Flowers or leaves falling off prematurely
* Soil that's dusty, baked hard as a brick, cracking open, blowing out, or pulling away from the sides of pots

Wise ways to water

Do

✓ Water in the early morning, if you can. It's the best time. But if you have to wait till later, don't worry. That stuff about "wet foliage getting burned by the sun" is exaggerated.

✓ Install an outside faucet, if you can afford it.

✓ Invest in a hose that doesn't take up much space. Some are self-coiling (that is, they have springy tubing, like telephone cords). Other, more expensive ones flatten out after use, like firefighters' hoses. Check that you can attach such hoses to the kitchen tap.

✓ Fit the hose with a snap-on watering wand. Add the kind of adjustable nozzle that pokes directly into containers. (Avoid a wide "rose" nozzle.)

✓ Water deeply. Make sure the entire soil mass is wet.

✓ Be extra careful to regularly water anything you've just planted. Don't allow it to dry out.

✓ Put dishes (old saucers, pie plates, or made-for-the-job catch basins, sold at garden centers) under containers to catch the water. Raise the pots up a bit, on pebbles or broken bits of old clay pots, so air can circulate.

Don't

✗ Forget to water once the fun of spring planting wears off.

✗ Water late at night. Once in a while is okay, but a regular nocturnal routine is out. Plants that stay damp overnight get mildew and slugs.

✗ Use softened water, if you can avoid it. It's salty, and plants don't like it.

✗ Spray water on leaves, which can cause ugly spotting and fungal diseases. It's best to wet the soil and roots.

✗ Leave water sitting in dishes under pots for longer than a day. Stagnant water is a perfect breeding ground for mosquitoes. It will also stink. (It's not good for plants, either. Their roots may rot.) Tip the water out of small dishes; in bigger ones, suck it out with a turkey baster or mop it up with a sponge.

Try the tepid treatment

Buy a big plastic pail, not a pretty watering can. Keep this pail in an unobtrusive place, and fill it with water every morning. Let it stand for several hours. Then scoop the contents out with an empty yogurt container or plastic jug and pour directly onto soil around plants. This works particularly well because

- 🌸 Plants (especially newly potted ones) prefer tepid water.
- 🌸 You can direct the water where it matters most.
- 🌸 It doesn't wet everything else the way watering cans do.

How to cut down on watering

- 🌸 Grow plants in large containers. The bigger the planter, the slower it will dry out.
- 🌸 Don't use clay pots. Plastic or resin will hold water longer.
- 🌸 Group plants together in spots that aren't windy.
- 🌸 Forget hanging baskets. They fry quickly in the heat (especially those lined with moss).
- 🌸 Use a growing mix that contains moisture-retaining perlite or vermiculite.
- 🌸 Put a piece of landscaping cloth or a folded piece of newspaper in the bottom of pots before adding soil. This will help stop water from draining away too quickly.
- 🌸 Put mulch over the tops of all your containers. If you don't have any, use old newspapers, cut to fit.
- 🌸 Check labels at garden centers and don't buy anything that says, "Needs a moist location."

How to rescue dried-out plants

Fill the kitchen sink and dunk the entire plant into it. Water should be at least an inch over the top of the container. Leave

Grow things that can survive with little water
Annual flowers include coreopsis, gazanias, morning glories, nasturtiums, portulacas, some types of salvia, and the stubby orange marigold (Tagetes). Among perennials, try sedums, hens and chicks, grasses, yarrows, and tropical plants like echeverias, jade plants, and cacti. Some geraniums (usually the varieties called "ivies") are also drought-tolerant. Check their labels.

immersed until bubbles have stopped coming to the surface. Remove and keep out of the sun for a couple of days.

Pots too big to lift into the sink? Try soaking them thoroughly with a stream of water from a hose for ten minutes (but be careful of the poor souls on the balcony below).

Do you overwater?

Beginners are often guilty of this. If leaves are turning yellow, the stems are soft and transparent-looking, or the soil is sodden all the time, not simply moist, you may be overwatering.

Rescue routine: remove the plant from the pot carefully and let the whole thing dry out, sitting in a dish. Snip off moldy, mushy, or blackened bits of roots. Don't put the dish in sunshine. Place a sheet of newspaper or cloth over the plant so roots aren't exposed to light. Once the soil feels damp but not wet, restore the plant to its pot with fresh growing mix.

When you go on vacation

Group plants together. Move them to the shade, if they're in hot sun. Take hanging baskets off hooks and put them on the balcony floor. Give everything a good soak, then wad damp newspapers over the tops of containers, around the plants.

Then talk nicely to the neighbors. The smartest course of action is to have someone come in to water during your absence. If that's not possible, look into buying an automatic drip irrigation kit. Most require an outside faucet, a timer, and quite a bit of fiddling about with tubing and clamps to set up. They can also leak or clog and must be checked regularly.

You can also make a primitive self-watering system. Fill a bucket of water. Cut some long strands of thick wool or sisal twine. Put one end of the strands into the bucket and the other end into the soil in your containers. This will wick some (but not much) water into the plants.

Getting Started with Plants

Gardening has become the number one pastime of many North Americans. (Surveys consistently put it ahead of sex and watching television.) As a result, growers keep coming out with more and more varieties of plants to seduce us. Nowadays, you can easily go crazy looking at all those little pots with labels at garden centers. It's hard to know which ones to buy—and what to do with them.

Annuals and perennials: What's the difference?

If you've never grown anything before and wonder where to start, here's what you need to know: all garden plants (except shrubs, trees, bulbs, and tropical exotica, which we'll get to later) are classified for home gardeners as "annuals" or "perennials." In a northern climate, you plant annuals every spring, enjoy them for the summer, then ditch them in the fall (preferably on a compost heap) because they won't survive outside during the winter. Perennials are another matter. They can endure cold temperatures and keep coming up year after year. So you plant them once, and leave them to become permanent fixtures in the garden (or in pots and planters on your balcony).

Which are best for a balcony—or other small spaces—where they'll be confined to containers? Annuals and perennials have different attributes. Annuals are mostly easy to grow, and they provide continuous color throughout the summer. Their drawback is that you have to keep potting up new ones every spring. Perennials can be more interesting plants, but they have much shorter blooming periods. They may produce flowers in spring, summer, or fall, but rarely in all three seasons. That means they often take up valuable space in pots and planters when they aren't looking their best. You also have to give perennials special care in the winter (see pages 132–35), which can be a hassle in condos or apartments.

Beginners should try annuals first.

Understanding plant labels

Be sure to read those tags stuck into plant pots. Whether the plants are annuals or perennials, most tags carry symbols that will tell you the growing requirements. In the matter of sun versus shade, plant growers divide their offerings into three basic categories. These are:

- ○ A completely white circle means the plant needs full sun. This means at least six unobstructed hours of sunshine (with no shade from trees or buildings) every day.
- ◑ A circle split in two—one half white, the other black—means part sun. At least half a day of sunshine (i.e., three hours) is required. Most plants prefer morning sun. If your unit faces west, you'll need a bit more unobstructed sunshine in the afternoon—a total of, say, four hours —for plants in this category to flourish.
- ● A solid black circle means the plant prefers no direct sunshine at all. But we're not talking "total darkness" here. Remember that all plants need some light to grow. Just don't put anything with this kind of label where it will get direct sunshine in the heat of the day.

When labels carry two symbols
Confusingly, you'll sometimes see plant labels with two symbols. The tag might indicate "full sun" and "part sun." Or it says "part sun" and "shade."

What this means is the plant can grow in a range of conditions. It may prefer full sun, but will cope with some shade. Or it's a shade-loving plant, but it doesn't mind some sun.

What is "dappled shade"?

Once upon a time, poets waxed eloquent about "dappled" mares. They were talking about horses, of course, but now the horticultural world has taken over the term. In gardening books and catalogues, "dappled" means shade from surrounding trees. Buildings cast solid shade (the sun obviously can't penetrate through concrete), but with foliage, the shadows are less fixed. Some light filters through, particularly on a windy day, when leaves sway to and fro. That's dappled shade. Plants that carry tags with "part sun" or "part shade" circles are the kind to buy if your growing space gets this kind of light.

> ## Hot tip
> "Save plant tags. Write the planting date on the top, then file them in a photo album with transparent, peel-back pages. It's less time-consuming than keeping a gardening diary, and just as useful."
> —*Sue Martin, garden designer*

Know your hardiness zone

Experienced gardeners are fond of tossing around strange expressions like, "Ah, Zone 6," in reference to plants. This can be bewildering for beginners. Here are a few words of explanation.

All the regions of North America are divided up into hardiness zones for the purposes of agriculture and horticulture. The main factor in delineating these zones is how low the temperature dips in winter (because that determines whether or not a plant will survive until next spring). The warmer the weather, the higher the hardiness zone number. For example, Zone 1 is way up—brr—in the Arctic tundra. But by the time you travel south to Zone 11, you're down Mexico way.

It's important to know what hardiness zone you live in. Many beginner gardeners don't bother to find this out—and they wind up wasting a lot of money on expensive perennials, shrubs, and trees that promptly bite the dust once winter comes. Maps of hardiness zones are often published in gardening books. Examine them, but don't trust the information (frequently presented in a complex chart) implicitly. For clarification, ask at a local garden center, because various climatic influences in your area can skew your hardiness zone. The books may state that you live in Zone 5, but they won't take into account a local body of water, or the fact that you garden high off the ground, on a windy, exposed balcony. These kinds of factors can ratchet your zone up—or down—a notch or two.

Once you know your hardiness zone, always check that the plants you're buying match it. Don't try to overwinter a Zone 7 plant if you garden in Zone 5. It will almost certainly die. There is a lot of blather nowadays about "zonal denial"—that is, ignoring hardiness zones, planting what you please, and keeping your fingers crossed. While this can be fun, it's not recommended for people who grow things in containers, particularly on balconies or rooftops. Plants have a hard enough time surviving off the ground; we don't need to stress them any further.

Look on plant tags. Sometimes the hardiness zones are listed, but often they aren't. If in doubt, ask the garden center staff—and don't be fobbed off by some summer employee who isn't sure. Ask to see the horticulturist. This is crucial information. Make sure you get it before forking over your hard-earned cash for plants—particularly perennials, shrubs, and trees.

Ask your neighbors

They probably know better than anybody else what plants will work—and which ones to avoid. Before blowing a bundle of bucks at a garden center, get their input.

Moving houseplants outside: Is it wise?

Yes, but with caution. Houseplants are like people who live in northern climates heading south for winter vacations. Both need time to acclimatize to new surroundings. If you suddenly plunk plants outside on a hot, sunny balcony when they've been accustomed to life indoors, they may get as sunburned as we do on a beach in the Bahamas. However, unlike humans, plants may never recover from the shock.

Light levels inside our homes are invariably lower than out of doors. (This applies even if you have plants on sunny window ledges or under lights.) So it pays to break prized specimens into their summer environment slowly.

Hot tip

"We save money by putting our houseplants outside every summer. They look great, combined with annuals."

—*Ida Weippert and Dave Wilson, balcony gardeners*

Some gardeners prefer not to move their indoor plants outside at all. They insist that doing so weakens the plants and that they are better off staying in the same environment year-round. Other gardeners disagree. They find that, like humans, plants benefit from a dollop of the fresh air and sunshine after being cooped up indoors over the winter. The choice is yours. If you do decide to haul houseplants out onto your balcony or rooftop,

Do

✓ Put all houseplants (grouped together for protection) in a shady corner of your balcony that doesn't receive *any* direct sunlight for at least a couple of weeks.

✓ If the indirect light is fierce, gently cover the plants with an old sheet for the first week. Water really well.

✓ Keep the kind of houseplants that normally thrive in low-light conditions—philodendrons, Chinese evergreens, and spider plants—in shade all summer.

✓ Bring cacti, rosemary bushes, bay trees, amaryllis, and succulents like jade plants into the sun after an adjustment period. Give them only an hour of sunshine at first, then gradually increase it. (Grouping them on a trolley with castors is a good idea, if you have space.)

✓ Prune houseplants back at the end of summer. Then give them a bath before they come indoors again (see page 133).

Don't

✗ Subject plants to "reverse shock" in fall. It's foolish to leave things outside until the temperature plummets, then expect them to adjust instantly to hot, dry central heating. As in spring, plants need to acclimatize slowly.

✗ Immediately toss a plant out that got nipped by frost. It may be salvageable. Cut all the foliage off, water well, and wait to see if new shoots appear.

Exciting Annuals, New and Old

Out of fashion for years, annuals are back big time. There is, in fact, an extraordinary variety of single-season flowers and foliage plants available now. In warmer climates, it's possible to treat some of the following as perennials. But if you're a northern gardener, just enjoy their burst of glory for one summer.

How to buy annuals

Do

✓ Buy pre-started plants, in little cell paks. You usually get four or six small plants to a pak.

✓ Check out greengrocers and corner stores in your city neighborhood. They often have great selections of plants.

✓ Ask storeowners what works well locally. They're often very knowledgeable (and are frequently far more interested in helping you than summer students at garden centers).

✓ Buy early in the season, when there's more to choose from and plants are fresh.

✓ Choose small plants with lots of bud tips. They'll settle in better than those with stems and flower heads already shooting up everywhere.

✓ Check the undersides of cell paks. If a mess of roots is sticking out the bottom, the plants have been potted too long and may not be worth buying.

✓ After planting, pinch out the main flower buds on pre-started plants. This may sound crazy, but it will promote bushy growth.

Don't

✗ Buy anything that has yellowing leaves, is long and leggy, or is completely dried out.

✗ Trust all the labels. Shoppers often switch them!

✗ Leave plants sitting in cell paks too long. If you can't plant right away, be sure to keep them in a shady spot and slosh some water over them.

✗ Start annuals from seed (except nasturtiums). It takes too long.

Four foolproof flowers

In sun, the two Ps: Pansies and petunias

Pansies and petunias are a cinch in pots and window boxes. Both come in wonderful colors, and they always make a great show.

Pansies are cute little flowers with "faces" (which everybody loves) and are usually trouble-free. Plant them close together in pots as soon as the weather starts to warm up (if there's still frost, wait), but remember too that pansies are primarily cool-weather flowers. They can't take searing heat and will tolerate some shade. Most varieties are finished by July (unless you water constantly), and then you'll probably have to replace them with something else. Don't bother with the much ballyhooed Icicle pansies. While they are frost-tolerant, they are primarily of interest to people who plant pansies in ground-level flowerbeds and want them to stay there year-round. Some good pansy combinations:

❀ For pizzazz: three bright varieties, like purple, yellow, and orange

❀ For trendy Wendys: black and white

❀ For lovers of Provence: cobalt blue pansies (sans faces), on their own or with yellow

> ## Hot tip
> "Don't buy pre-started pansies with big, juicy leaves. You'll get more flowers if the leaves are smaller."
> —Jennifer Reynolds, gardening editor

❀ For old-fashioned elegance: luscious antique shades—apricots, creams, salmon, and orange. These are hard to find nowadays because they take longer to germinate than other varieties, so growers don't bother with them. Grab heirloom varieties if you can.

Petunias have been around for donkey's years and were considered ho-hum for a while. But now they are hot again, with many yummy shades and sizes. They need lots of sun (or they get straggly, with few flowers) and frequent feeding. They will die down in summer if you don't fertilize weekly (with a water-soluble plant food in a formula like 14-14-14). Most have showy, single blooms, but look for pretty doubles and coin-sized minis too. New Surfinia and Wave varieties and Balcon minis develop into wonderful, cascading mats of flowers that are great for window boxes and planters. A look-alike flowering annual called Calibrachoa Million Bells also works well. Wait till all frosts are finished before planting. One drawback to petunias: you must deadhead them or they won't continue to flower all summer, and most varieties feel horribly sticky. Keep gardening gloves handy! Some great petunia pairings:

❀ Two pink varieties: shocking pink with pale pink (but don't use against red brick walls)
❀ White with beet red or purple
❀ Scarlet with cream (beautiful against brick)
❀ Pink or red petunias with bidens (*Bidens ferulifolia*) and licorice vine (*Helichrysum petiolare*) in either silver or the yellow-green Limelight variety (but watch this vigorous vine: its roots may get too pushy in a pot and suffocate the petunias)
❀ Golden yellow *Calibrachoa* Million Bells, which comes in both upright and trailing varieties, with trailing purple lobelia

For shade, the two Cs: Coleus and caladiums

Coleus and caladiums are foliage plants, which means their leaves are the alluring part. While plants without blooms may sound boring to beginners, coleus and caladiums look as dazzling as any flower, particularly up against concrete. Their big asset? They won't sulk in shade.

Coleus is originally from Malaysia and has a correct name that's a real tongue twister: *Solenostemon scutellarioides*. It is treated as an annual in northern climates, and it's a snap to

grow. Victorians went nuts over its flamboyant foliage, but then it careened into oblivion (dismissed as "too garish"). Now it's back with a vengeance: there are dozens of varieties, with fun names like Cranberry Salad and Inky Fingers. Look for the Avalanche series, which comes in truly riotous colors. Coleus produce a nondescript spike of pale blue flowers. Some people pinch this off (because it detracts from the leaves), but lazy gardeners can ignore it.

Coleus tips:

❀ Perk up a dark corner with scarlet, magenta, and bronze varieties planted together.
❀ Purple- or maroon-leaved coleus look good with any pink, orange, or white flowers. (Begonias are a good bet if you have a shady balcony.)
❀ Mix green and yellow coleus varieties with something scarlet, like geraniums (in sun).

- Use the colors of coleus to "echo" the shades of other plants. For instance, combine a golden coleus that has red streaks with a scarlet monkey flower (*Mimulus* x *hybridus*).

Caladiums are from South America and are not as hassle-free as coleus. Keen gardeners with lots of space buy them as tubers in early spring and start them indoors. For a balcony, simply buy ready-potted caladiums. They have gorgeous, heart-shaped leaves, often as delicate as tissue paper, which unfurl like flags. Colors are striking pinks, reds, and greens, or white with veining in green and red. Their flower spikes should be cut off (they suck energy from the leaves). You can bring caladiums indoors for the winter, but they tend to be temperamental. It's easier to buy new ones every spring. How to use them:

- Combine caladiums with spiky houseplants (like *dracaena*) brought outdoors for the summer.
- Pair white varieties with brightly colored coleus in shady corners.
- Position next to a pond (they like it damp).

Twenty-five great annuals

- **Allysum:** Sold at just about every garden center. Considered ho-hum by hoity horts, but the white or mauve mats of flowers are a great edger in front of other plants. Easy. Needs sun to produce lots of flowers. Shear back after flowering and it will bloom again.
- **Bacopa (*Sutera cordata*):** Pretty little white flowers, with dark green leaves. Good if you have shade because it tends to wilt in full sun. Water regularly. There's also a lavender variety called Pink Domino or Mauve Mist.
- **Bells of Ireland (*Moluccella laevis*):** A novelty plant. In late summer, it produces stems of green "bells," in

which tiny white or pink flowers nestle. The bells turn white and papery and are great for fall floral arrangements.

Hot tip

"Plant your entire balcony in coleus if you're elderly and can't do much. I do. They're cheap, easy to grow, and it's fascinating to watch their colors develop."
—Jack Lieber, 82-year-old balcony gardener

❀ **Bidens** (pronounced bye-denz): A European annual, now hot with gardeners everywhere. Produces pretty small trailing flowers in yellow, with bright green foliage. Try it with scarlet geraniums. Bidens takes time to get established, but is otherwise easy and drought-tolerant. It self-seeds everywhere, but you can yank out the "volunteers."

❀ **Blue fan flower (*Scaevola aemula*):** Another trendy trailer. Blooms are an interesting shape (they fan sideways), and the divine blue-violet color goes well with anything.

❀ **Brachyscome:** Also known as the Swan River daisy. Flowers come in a variety of colors: white, pink, yellow, purple. Good mixed with trailing plants. It grows about 1 ft./30 cm tall and needs sun.

❀ **Browallia:** A garden stalwart with star-shaped blue or white flowers that grows to about 1 ft./30 cm and does well in semi-shade. Looks good with any other annual.

❀ **Cosmos:** Cheap and cheerful, mostly with white, pink, or magenta flowers and pretty feathery foliage. Try the offbeat Sea Shells, with peculiar pink petals rolled into tubes. Most cosmos are tall and floppy (put them behind something shorter), but the dwarf Klondike series reaches only 1 ft./30 cm high and is great in containers. They need sun. Deadhead regularly.

❀ **Fuchsias:** For balconies without much direct sun. Most have flowers that droop downwards. Best in hanging baskets or raised containers where you can see blooms up close, because their shapes are fascinating. Some look like frilly skirts on ballet dancers.

❀ **Gazanias:** Zingy yellow, red, or orange daisy-like flowers offset by grey-green foliage. Truly drought-tolerant. (Forget to water and gazanias don't give up.) Needs full sun and heat to flourish. One drawback: flowers on some varieties stay closed on cloudy days. Look for the less reclusive

Daybreak kind. The compact Chansonette blooms earlier than the rest.

- **Heliotrope:** Out of style for years, now back. Purple flowers and nice green foliage. Its smell is supposed to be like cherry pie, but that's debatable. Will grow in semi-shade; don't let it dry out. Combine with any flower in white, pink, or magenta, and green-leaved trailers like licorice vine and Plectranthus.

- **Lantana:** A tropical plant that grows into a big, beautiful bush in the Bahamas. Less pushy in containers in northern climates. Interesting multicolored flowers in yellow, orange, and red. Will bloom all summer if you deadhead it diligently. Needs sun.

- **Licorice vine (*Helichrysum petiolare*):** A hot container item because its trailing leaves—like silver velvet—harmonize with anything. Try the Limelight variety too. Its yellow-green leaves are a knockout with scarlet. Be careful, though: this is a pushy plant that loves squeezing out the competition. A thin-leaved variety, Spike, is less likely to suffocate other plants.

- **Lobelia:** Another garden mainstay, with small flowers in an intense blue or purple. Backs up flowers of any color well. Prefers cool weather. In torrid temperatures, lobelia will languish. Shear it back; it'll bloom again. The Cascade kind is a trailing plant, best for containers. Tolerates some shade.

- **Monkey flower (*Mimulus* x *hybridus*):** Bright orange, red, or yellow flowers with funny purple spots. Definitely an acquired taste. Pair with a leafy plant in dark green. Likes lots of water.

- **Morning glories (*Ipomoea*):** Climbers with spectacular but short-lived flowers, long a garden mainstay. What's hot nowadays are two variations: *I. alba* (moonflower vine), with heart-shaped leaves and white flowers that smell gorgeous at night, and *I. batatas* (sweet potato vine), a non-climbing variety grown for its foliage. The latter comes in vivid yellow-green (called Terrace Lime)

Hot tip

"Don't bother to drive out to garden centers in the suburbs if you live in a city neighborhood. I buy all my annuals at local greengrocers and convenience stores."

—Athina Smardenka, window box gardener

or deep purple (called Blackie). Both look sensational with most flowers. While regular morning glories need sun, sweet potato vine prefers some shade and will wilt in hot sunshine or wind.

- ❀ **Nasturtium (*Tropaeolum majus*):** Easy-to-grow trailing mainstays, with orange, red, and creamy-colored flowers and juicy green leaves. Avoid the types with variegated foliage (it looks like a viral disease). Nasturtiums prefer poor soil. If the growing mix is nitrogen-rich, you'll get lots of leaves but few flowers. Difficult to transplant. Works best from seed. Plant seeds right after frosts are over, or blooms won't appear till late summer. The flowers and big seedpods taste good. (Sort of peppery. Gourmet chefs love them.)

- ❀ **Nicotiana:** Flowering tobacco. Small varieties, called Nickis, sold everywhere, produce prolific flowers in red, pink, or white and grow about 1 ft./30 cm tall. Mix with trailing plants. Sometimes they are faintly scented, but only true wild tobacco, *N. sylvestris*, has the magical evening fragrance that many gardeners go gaga over. Not for small spaces, *N. sylvestris* grows over 6 ft./2 m tall, with white flower clusters and enormous leaves. Pre-started plants are scarce at garden centers (even though it's easy to grow from seed). In a container, it will send up only one flower spike. Position it in sniffing range. All nicotianas prefer sun (but cope well with part shade) and are prone to attacks by aphids.

- ❀ **Oxalis:** Looks like shamrock and is often called the "good luck plant." The purple variety *O. triangularis* has dainty lavender-pink flowers. Does well in sun or shade.

- ❀ **Pentas:** A pretty import from Africa, becoming big as a container plant. Produces clumps of dainty flowers in lavender, pink, or red. Grow in full sun. It can be bothered by aphids. In warmer regions, pentas can be wintered over outside.

- ❀ **Plectranthus:** Mostly trailing plants, often with fuzzy foliage. Related to coleus, they are great for containers, because—like coleus—they grow quickly and combine well with flowers. One popular variety is Mintleaf

(*P. madagascariensis*), which is green edged with white. Keep moist. They don't mind a bit of shade.

❀ **Portulaca:** Out of fashion for years, but hot again—and perfect for containers. For dry, sunny spots. Pretty rose-like flowers in red, orange, yellow, purple, pink, or white, with spiky foliage. Dries out easily. Likes a bit of sand in the growing mix. Look for the Sundial and Sundance varieties, which don't stay closed on cloudy days.

❀ **Snapdragons (*Antirrhinum*):** Available everywhere, easy to grow, many colors. Dwarf varieties are great, but try the Rocket series at the back of a tall planter. Black Prince, with rich red flowers and purple foliage, is lovely (mix it with yellow and violet flowers and gray foliage plants). One plus: you can plant snaps early (they don't mind cool weather) and they keep on blooming till the fall.

❀ **Wishbone flower (*Torenia*):** From Africa and Asia, unknown till a few years ago. Good in semi-shade. Snapdragon-like flowers in white, with pink, blue, and mauve markings. The Clown multicolored varieties are delightful.

❀ **Zinnia:** Pooh-poohed for years by hoity horts, now hot. Produces daisy-like flowers in sunny yellows, oranges, or reds. Its layered petals feel papery when they age. The dwarf Thumbelina series is good in small pots, but tall *Elegans* zinnias will give zip to bigger planters. Needs full sun.

A few to avoid

❀ **Ageratum:** Produces pretty, tufty flowers in violet, pink, purple, or blue, but dries out at the drop of a hat. Then the tufts turn brown and ugly.

❀ **Diascia:** A trendy, unusual plant with pretty little pink flowers. Does best in early spring, but doesn't like wet soil. Tends to turn temperamental in summer. There are both annual and perennial kinds.

- **Osteospermum:** Funny name, fashionable flower, like an exotic daisy. A fave of gardening gurus, but often hard to grow. It dries out too quickly and needs constant deadheading to flower.
- **Verbena:** Vibrant flowers, sold everywhere, but without full sun and excellent air circulation, all varieties invariably get mildew. *V. bonariensis,* an import from Brazil, is one of the hottest annuals around, sporting gray-green spiky stems topped by tufty violet flowers. Undeniably charming, it grows up to 4 ft./1.5 m high. Try only if you have space and a sheltered but well-ventilated location.

Forget this popular plant

Don't buy impatiens, also known as "busy Lizzie," for pots on balconies. Its flowers and leaves drop everywhere and make a dreadful mess. They will stain wood and concrete. Everyone loves impatiens because they're cheap, tough, and easy to grow, but these flowers are best planted in regular flowerbeds, on the ground.

Perennials:
A Pleasure, but Picky Too

Ask most gardeners what they prefer to grow nowadays and they'll probably say perennials. This category of plants has never been more popular—and it's hardly surprising. There are so many wonderful perennials to choose from. With careful planning, you can have different flowers from spring to fall, coupled with all kinds of perennial foliage plants. And the big plus of this category of plants is that they'll perform all over again next year. There's no need to plant every spring (as you do with annuals).

However, perennials aren't all as trouble-free as garden centers often claim. They also present special problems to people who garden on balconies (or other small spaces). If you want to grow perennials, be aware that

❀ Most perennial flowers have brief blooming periods, lasting a few weeks at most (unlike annuals, which bloom all summer). When they're not in bloom, the foliage of these flowers may look pretty blah on your balcony.
❀ Squeezed into containers, some perennials sulk. Others grow so vigorously they'll need constant dividing. You'll have to keep taking them out of their pots, whacking the root balls in half, and repotting.
❀ Many perennials are not hardy enough to stay unprotected in their containers, above the ground, all winter. If you live in a northern climate, this will mean going through the rigmarole every fall of either wrapping containers in some kind of insulation or hauling them indoors (see pages 132–35).

How to use perennials

Do

✓ Combine perennials and annuals together in containers. That way, you get a colorful show all summer. You'll get the knack of making these combinations as you go along.

✓ Plant perennials in the same growing mix as annuals. Add a slow-release granular fertilizer to the mix. A teaspoon of a new growth supplement called Myke, put into the bottom of each container, will get them off to a good start (but don't overdo it).

✓ Contrary to advice from many experts, try plants that are labeled "invasive." They're often tougher than other perennials and can survive better in containers.

✓ Pot your purchases quickly, especially if you've bought bare-root perennials. Never let them dry out. If you can't plant right away, cover them with sheets of damp newspaper, put them in a shady spot, and sprinkle water on the paper daily.

✓ Tease out roots with a small tool or your hands before planting. If roots are tightly bound together, cut into them with a knife.

✓ Plant perennials more densely in containers than in a regular garden.

✓ Look for "dwarf" and "compact" varieties of perennials. Always ask if a perennial that interests you is suitable for growing in a container (but expect blank looks from many garden center staff).

Don't

✗ Ignore plant labels. It's a waste of time to put a perennial that "needs a moist location" on a hot, dry balcony.

✗ Pick too many perennials at once. Experiment with them a couple at a time.

✗ Add any plant food to the watering can for the first two weeks. Let perennials settle in.

✗ Be discouraged if perennials die. There are plenty more to experiment with.

✗ Grow perennials from seed. It takes too long in containers.

Try these in containers

In sun

❀ **Catmint (*Nepeta*):** Also called catnip. Many kinds. Cats like munching and rolling on some varieties. *N. subsessilis* forms clumps, with pretty fetching upright blue flowers. Good at the front of containers.

❀ **Creeping phlox (*P. subulata*):** In flowerbeds, this multiplies into immense mats a yard across. Containers keep it under control. The mini-mats of little green leaves drape nicely over the edge of pots (mix them with a weeping sedum) and produce little mauve flowers in spring. If it becomes too much of a good thing, it's easy to pull out.

❀ **Daylilies (*Hemerocallis*):** Smaller varieties like Stella D'Oro and a mini relative, Stella D'Oro Lemon Drops, are best in containers. Both keep cranking out golden blooms, which last only a day, well into the fall. If you have a roomy planter, try a daylily that landscapers love, Bonanza. It's tough as old boots. Has limey yellow blooms, blotched with purple. For fragrance, plant lemon yellow *Hemerocallis citrina* (but watch out: it multiplies like crazy). Don't even think of trying daylilies if you have any shade.

❀ **Donkey tail spurge (*Euphorbia myrsinites*):** A curiosity plant, this looks tropical, with funny twirly stems and blue-green leaves, topped by little acid yellow leafy bits in spring. Combines well with other things and doesn't mind dryness. Easy to grow.

❀ **Feverfew (*Tanacetum parthenium*):** This herb, often used to ease headaches, tends to be too much of a good thing in regular gardens, but in containers it's cheery and easy to grow. Has small daisy-like flowers and lovely bright green foliage. Varieties called Golden Moss and Aureum have goldish green leaves.

❀ **Fountain grass (*Pennisetum setaceum*):** Many gardeners can't get enough of ornamental grasses. This one, a beauty, is a perennial in southern climates. In the

> ## Hot tip
> "If your perennials are getting too cramped, scoop some soil out of their containers in spring. Then, with an old bread knife, hack a section of the roots off. Remove those bits and top up with new potting soil, mixed with blood meal or bone meal."
> —*Sue Martin, balcony gardener*

ELEGANCE PERSONIFIED: Statues make great focal points, even in small spaces. Position them before adding containers and plants. A trellis helps to create privacy.

CAPTIVATING COMBOS: Pink and white geranium Freckles (foreground) harmonizes nicely with plain pink Horizon, blue pimpernel (Anagallis) and (rear right) an echeveria and magenta mini petunias.

INEXPENSIVE ELEGANCE: Four varieties of coleus and Tradescantia flumensis in a plastic urn.

IMPACT STATEMENT: Don't be afraid to mass containers in big groups. The glorious display in this ground-floor court-yard includes geraniums, herbs, succulents and several shrubs.

PLANT PROGRESS (left): A tiny city balcony is dense with glorious greenery; Above: How the same space looked before the perennials and Clematis fargessioides (top left) filled out.

*TALL TREAT: Weeping 'Red Jade' crabapple (right), underplanted with licorice vine (*Helichrysum petiolare*), takes well to containers. Behind the chair, ornamental bunch grass (*Calamagrostis acutiflora *'Karl Foerster') and white *Aster novi-belgii *'Kristina'.*

CLIMBING CAVALCADE: Vines like purple Clematis jackmanii *and pink-flowered* Mandevilla *(right) need deep, roomy pots. Grow them up obelisks if you have nowhere to hang a trellis.*

SHELVE IT: Show off ornaments and fave plants on simple wooden shelves attached to fence dividers.

GREEN GROUPING (left): On dry, sunny rooftops, position plants close together to conserve moisture; PLANTER PIZAZZ (below): Scarlet geraniums, shocking pink petunias, blue fan flower, marigolds, trailing euonymus and cascading Calibrachoa Million Bells.

ANNUAL ELEGANCE: Three varieties of geraniums intermingle with white bacopa and yellow dwarf snapdragons.

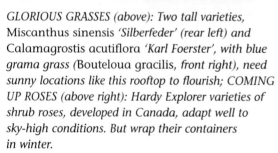

GLORIOUS GRASSES (above): Two tall varieties, Miscanthus sinensis 'Silberfeder' (rear left) and Calamagrostis acutiflora 'Karl Foerster', with blue grama grass (Bouteloua gracilis, front right), need sunny locations like this rooftop to flourish; COMING UP ROSES (above right): Hardy Explorer varieties of shrub roses, developed in Canada, adapt well to sky-high conditions. But wrap their containers in winter.

TURN TO URNS: When fall comes, ornamental kales and cabbages, combined with trailing vinca, are a great easy-care pick-me-up.

Clockwise from top: SERENE GREEN BACKDROP: Shrubs, ornamental grasses and columnar cedars set off (from left) Stella d'Oro daylilies, spiky white Yucca filamentosa, a red and yellow croton and violet-pink torches of Liatris spicata; WINDOW BOX WOW: Pansies, scarlet geraniums, white and red impatiens, calla lily leaves, and trailing licorice vine are colorful and easy to grow; COOK'S DELIGHT: Tight groups of herbs suit small sunny spaces. Counter-clockwise from left: oregano, chives, mint, bush basil, bay. Behind the cherub, patio rose Red Cascade.

*KNOCK-OUT COLOR: Three Cs—caladiums (foreground),
different kinds of coleus, and tall burgundy-leafed cannas
(rear)—give a big bang for the buck, as do nasturtiums
(center); PASTEL PERFECTION (inset): Lavender spikes
with rock daisies* (Brachysome multifida), *yellow*
Lysimachia congestifolia, *trailing mintleaf*
(Plectranthus madagascariensis) *and a leafy azalea.*

north, treat it as an annual (though it can sometimes be wintered over). It produces purplish fuzzy plumes, with lovely spiky leaves in purple and brownish green that look super with other plants. Grows about 2 ft./60 cm high. If you have a sheltered location and plenty of space, try taller grasses like maiden grass *Miscanthus Gracillimus* 'Silberfeder'—also sometimes called 'Silver Feather'. It grows 8 ft./2.5 m tall, with gorgeous silvery seedheads in fall, and winters over well on rooftops. But remember that all ornamental grasses need *lots* of sun.

❀ **Gardener's garters (*Phalaris arundinacea v. picta*):** Don't plant this terror (also called ribbon grass) in a courtyard flowerbed. It will take over. But the stripy green leaves can be kept under control in containers—and they look great with most flowers. Plant it in front of something tall, like annual cosmos.

❀ **Gayfeathers (*Liatris spicata*):** Fun flowers, with bottle-brush blooms in (usually) a pale purple. Terrific in containers. Their shape contrasts well with rounded flowers, like cosmos or daisies, and with ornamental grasses.

❀ **Phormiums***:* Tropical foliage plants with big strappy leaves in exciting colors. Very fashionable. Their bold shapes look great in containers, but one drawback is that they must be brought indoors in the fall. A relative, the striking Adam's Needle (*Yucca filamentosa*) is tougher: it can sometimes be wintered over on a balcony.

❀ **Purple coneflowers (*Echinacea purpurea*):** Misnamed (they're pink, not purple), these are like droopy daisies: petals hang downwards from a big, beehive-like seedpod. No matter. They're pretty and easy to grow. Said to be drought-tolerant, but they wilt in dry spells. There's also a white variety.

❀ **Shasta daisies (*Leucanthemum superbum*):** Everybody loves these flowers, but some kinds are too tall and bossy in containers. Try the dwarf Silberprinzesschen, which grows 1 ft./30 cm high, with dainty white flowers. Pinch back in spring, and deadhead flowers.

❀ **Tickseed (*Coreopsis verticillata*):** Frilly little flowers in hot chrome that look great with annuals. A variety called Moonbeam is fashionable: it has soft, butter yellow blooms. Tends to sprawl. Plant at the back of containers. The common name "tickseed" is rarely used.

Part sun

❀ **Bethlehem sage (*Pulmonaria saccharata*):** One of the first perennials to bloom in spring. Always a delight, it somehow performs the feat of producing pink, violet, and pale blue flowers all on the same stem. The green foliage with white spots looks good too, when flowers have finished. Easy, grows about 1 ft./30 cm high. If leaves get ratty-looking, cut them off; more will quickly appear.

❀ **Cranesbills, or hardy geraniums:** True geraniums (not to be confused with window box geraniums, which are really pelargoniums. See pages 68–71). Dozens of varieties, mostly with tiny flowers. Will tolerate complete shade but you'll get more blooms with a bit of sun. Try Max Frei (*G. sanguineum*), which forms mounds, with bright magenta flowers, and dwarf *G. cinereum,* with gray-green leaves and white or pale pink blooms. Steer clear of Johnson's Blue. Its flowers are a divine color, but the plant gets straggly and messy.

❀ **Heuchera***:* A few years ago, you could only get one variety, with little red flowers and nondescript leaves, called Coral Bells. Now heuchera are so hot a new kind appears every few months. They have metamorphosed into foliage plants, in all shapes and colors, to combine with other plants. Particularly pretty are Palace Pier, Pewter Veil, and Chocolate Ruffles.

❀ **Stonecrop (*Sedum*):** The plant-naming people insisted on saddling this huge family of plants with the monstrous new moniker *Hylotelephiums* a few years ago. Yikes. Fortunately, everyone still calls them sedums. The most forgiving plants on the planet, they tolerate dryness, shade (though they love sun), and all kinds of abuse. Try Gold Moss stonecrop (*S. acre*), which grows only 2 in./5 cm tall, with little

> **Hot tip**
>
> "If you're leaving a family home behind, bring along a favorite perennial and grow it in a pot on your balcony. It will help you settle in."
>
> —Denis Flanagan, gardening show host

yellow flowers. Another dinky variety is *S. spurium*, with fuzzy pinkish blooms. Autumn Joy grows 2 ft./60 cm tall, with bright pink clumpy flowers in late summer; and Vera Jamieson, another tall variety, has oh-so-elegant purply pink leaves.

Shade

❀ **Ferns:** So many to choose from. Go for varieties that won't get too big for their boots. Try shield fern (*Polystichum aculeatum*), which stays reliably evergreen; maidenhair fern (*Adiantum*), which has gorgeous delicate foliage; and Japanese painted fern (*Athyrium nipponicum* 'Pictum'), which is silver-gray and purple. The last one tends to self-seed in gardens, but usually isn't a problem in containers.

❀ **Hostas:** Another fave foliage plant. Many small varieties that suit containers are being introduced. Look for Stiletto and Bitsy Green. They have narrow leaves and won't hog too much space. If you're bothered by creepy-crawlies, there are also slug-resistant hostas (see page 124). Although touted as a shade plant, hostas do fine in sun too (but their layers of leaves spread like mad). In a very shady court-yard, a bed of hostas looks terrific.

❀ **Lady's mantle** (*Alchemilla mollis*): Fascinating leaves, which collect the dew and open like little umbrellas. Grown primarily for its foliage. Produces fuzzy yellow flowers in late spring that can get messy. Often invasive. You may need to divide it after a year or two. Easy to grow.

Hosta

Pick small perennials

Big isn't necessarily a good thing when you're shopping for plants. Small perennials often settle in better than bigger ones, because they go through less transplant shock. What matters more is that plants are healthy-looking, with fresh shoots.

The Joy of Geraniums

Hoity horts hate geraniums, because they're so universally popular and they have brash colors. Ignore the snobs. Geraniums enjoy a justifiably deserved reputation as the "classic window box flower." Europeans have adored their blobs of brightness for centuries. Visit villages in Germany, Greece, and Italy in summertime and they overflow with eye-popping displays of geraniums, mostly in containers. These icons of summer are, in fact, perfect choices for pots and planters, because they provide plenty of oomph without hogging too much space.

Geraniums can be mighty confusing, however. As any gardener in the know will take delight in telling you, the flowers we know as "geraniums" aren't really geraniums at all. Their true name is pelargoniums. You can blame the seventeenth-century botanist Linnaeus for the blooper. He lumped true geraniums—which are perennial plants with small, inconspicuous blossoms (see page 66)—in with their brash tropical cousins. Both belong to the big *Geraniaceae* family, but they're actually different species of plants.

Don't worry about this historical stuff at a garden center. It's quite acceptable to carry on calling them geraniums; no one will dismiss you as a rube. What's worth knowing, however, is that geraniums (or, if you prefer, pelargoniums) don't all look the same. Believe or not, there are 230 kinds of geraniums, in all shapes and sizes.

Types of geraniums

Here are the five kinds you'll see in garden centers most often:

❀ **Zonals:** Traditional geraniums. Easiest to grow. Big show-off blooms, often double. Rounded leaves, frilly at the edges. They reach up to 2 ft./60 cm high. Also called Uprights because of their straight stems. They look good in either a window box or flowerpot, with trailing annuals around their bases. Once, these flowers were used in a tedious triumvirate: you always saw fire engine red zonals combined with white allysum and trailing blue lobelia. It was patriotic, all right, but that look is now considered passé. Instead, gardeners are getting adventurous and combining zonals in knockout planting schemes.

❀ **Regals:** Also called Martha Washingtons. Similar to zonals, but with pointier leaves and less flamboyant flowers. Use them in the same way as zonals.

❀ **Cascading:** Spikier flowers. Develop quickly into big, bushy plants that trail prettily over the edges of pots. Good on their own in hanging baskets. Popular in Europe. Best bet for lazy gardeners, because garden centers often sell them ready-planted.

❀ **Ivy-leafed:** Pretty pointy leaves, like ivy, with spiky flowers. They can be cascading or have a more compact growth habit. Often more heat-tolerant than other varieties. Work well in both planters and smaller pots.

❀ **Scented:** Mostly ho-hum flowers, but the plants smell divine. Interesting foliage, often fuzzy-textured and fun to stroke. Good for semi-shady spots: the only geraniums that don't insist on full sun. Combine them with colorful annuals, in sniffing range and in spots where you can brush up against them to release the scent. Varieties to look for:

  ❀ *P. odoratissimum:* Known as the "apple geranium." A fave with Victorians. Fragrance of both apple and cinnamon.
  ❀ *P. capitatum* or Attar of Roses. Scent is just like roses. Needs a big pot.

> ## Hot tip
> "Even if you love white flowers, don't bother with white geraniums. When their petals drop, they go brown. These cling to the flower heads and look awful."
> —*Martin Knirr, geranium grower*

- ❀ **P. quercifolium 'Chocolate-Mint':** Pretty, minty, with purple-streaked leaves. Some people swear they can also detect chocolate.
- ❀ **P. citrosa:** Strong citronella scent. Said to repel mosquitoes, but that's debatable.
- ❀ **P. 'Frensham':** Truly divine scent of lemons that's better than the real thing.
- ❀ **P. tomentosum:** The peppermint geranium. Velvety purplish green leaves. Good in hanging baskets. Nice minty smell.

Do

- ✓ Keep geraniums (except scented ones) in full sun. They won't flower well in shade.
- ✓ Water, but don't overdo it. Geraniums hate wet feet.
- ✓ Look for heat-tolerant varieties (check the labels).
- ✓ Nip off spent flower heads.
- ✓ Fertilize weekly with 20-20-20, starting in mid-summer.

Don't

- ✗ Don't pot up geraniums dry. Make sure the soil mass surrounding the roots is damp before transplanting into a bigger pot.
- ✗ Put geraniums outside in spring if the temperature is going to drop below 50°F/10°C.
- ✗ Expose young plants to cold winds.
- ✗ Feel you must rush them indoors before a light fall frost. Tough, mature plants can take a little bit of freezing (but not much).

Colorful combos

- ❀ Orange geraniums (preferably zonals) with a burgundy-colored coleus, a tall phormium in green and purple, and white impatiens or white browallia.
- ❀ A stellar geranium called Vancouver Centennial (which has orangey red flowers with exquisite brown and gold leaves) with trailing nasturtiums in red and chrome, the yellow-green foliage of *Helichrysum petiolare* Limelight, and spiky spider plants.

- Shocking pink geraniums with violet verbena, purple heliotrope, and dwarf white snapdragons (*Antirrhinum hispanicum*).
- A geranium variety called Freckles, which has rose-pink flowers daubed with white and deep pink, with silver-leaved licorice vine (*Helichrysum petiolare*) and purply blue pimpernel (*Anagallis monellii*) or blue fanflower (*Scaevola aemula*). Terrific in a gray pot.

Can I winter geraniums over outside?

Probably not. Geraniums are tropical flowers, originally from South Africa. They're generally hardy to about 35°F/2°C. Scented geraniums can sometimes be wintered over, in pots against a sunny wall, if you live where nighttime temperatures don't dip below 23°F/–5°C.

As for other varieties of geraniums, the best thing is to winter them over, still in their pots, in a cool, dry basement or garage. Prune the plants back to a few inches and don't water during this dormant period. However, since this procedure is out of the question in most condos and apartments, it's often best to simply buy new started geraniums every spring.

Try recycling geraniums

Here's a way to save money: every November, cut back your geraniums to 1 ft./30 cm high. Dig them out of window boxes and pack them tightly together into a plastic pot. Soak the pot thoroughly on the balcony. Then bring it in and store it on a dresser, away from the window. Water a bit, but not much.

In spring, cut back leggy new growth to 3 in./8 cm high and repot in fresh potting soil (three or four plants to each window box). Put them out on the balcony again.

Note: Gardening gurus consider this formula highly irregular. They take a different tack. Their suggestion:

Make stem cuttings 4 in./10 cm long several weeks before frost hits. Pot these up in new soil. Throw the mother plant out. Grow the babies on a sunny window ledge throughout the winter. Come spring, introduce them to the great green world.

The choice is yours.

How to Have Everything Coming Up Roses

Roses are romantic, but they tend to be finicky. While many balcony and rooftop gardeners dream of having lots of luscious roses tumbling over arbors and trellises, that dream can be hard to translate into reality. The unfortunate truth is, many roses aren't suitable for containers. They require full sun, heavy soil that drains well, and lots of room. Certain types of roses also don't take kindly to being left outside, with their roots above the ground, throughout the winter. However, you don't have to miss out on the undeniable elegance of these classic flowers. The trick is to pick the "toughies" that will adapt well to difficult conditions.

Resilient roses for balconies, rooftops, and courtyards

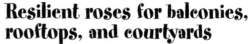

❀ **Hardy shrub roses**, especially those labeled "Parkland" or "Explorer." These types were developed in areas of Canada where winters are harsh (Winnipeg and Ottawa) and they're bred especially to cope with adverse conditions. For planting in containers, pick smaller varieties. Worth trying are Morden

Blush, which has lovely peachy blooms; Henry Hudson, with pinkish white flowers; and Champlain, which is dark red. To train up a trellis, try the shrub rose Alchymist.

- ❀ **Old-fashioned climbing roses** are great in a ground-floor courtyard. You can train them up trellises—they grow tall and will help make the place seem private. Worth trying are *Rosa* 'Alba', an ancient white rose; York and Lancaster, a fragrant damask that's white streaked with pink; and Evelyn, a David Austin climber. Their blooming period is, unfortunately, brief.

- ❀ **Ballerina,** a hybrid musk rose. Many balcony gardeners find this one takes to a container like a charm (but make sure the container is big). An import from England (first introduced in 1937), it forms a rounded shrub about 4 ft./125 cm in height, and its biggest plus is that it keeps on producing clusters of delightful pinkish white single blooms, edged with pink, for weeks on end. Ballerina is also somewhat fragrant.

- ❀ **Polyantha roses** perform particularly well on rooftops. They're low-growing and less affected by winds than taller roses. They bloom continuously all summer. The Fairy and Orange Triumph varieties are hardy and disease-resistant.

- ❀ *Rosa rugosa,* both the Alba (white) and Rubra (pink) varieties, are the toughest roses around. They grow wild along the eastern seaboard of North America and produce lovely bright orange hips the size of cherry tomatoes. Their delicious scent can be detected yards away. The drawback of *R. rugosa* is that the blooming period is often disappointingly short—and the rest of the year the bushes take up a lot of space and look quite homely. They also need big containers, as they spread rapidly.

- ❀ *Rosa gallica* is one of the few roses that will tolerate a bit of shade. It comes in several varieties; pick a compact one for a small space.

Making roses flourish

Do

✓ Buy roses from a reputable specialist rose nursery in your area and ask for advice on varieties that are suitable for containers or courtyards.

✓ Use big, roomy containers. The French Versailles type of planter (a big squarish box standing on legs) is ideal. So are old whiskey barrels. Fill them with a good, rich growing mix (see pages 33–35), and add several handfuls of bone meal to the mix. Be prepared to replace the soil every few years.

✓ Plant in early fall. That way, roses have a chance to settle into their new surroundings before winter freeze-up—and as a result, they will often adapt better to summer's heat the following year.

✓ When planting roses in cold climates, always position the crown (the lumpy bit, where the stem meets the roots) 1 to 2 in./2.5 to 5 cm *below* the surface of the soil. This applies equally whether you're planting in the ground or in containers. (Misleading advice is sometimes given on plant tags and in garden center catalogs.)

✓ Mound up the soil around the stem right after planting. (This applies whether you're planting in a container or the ground.) Leave the soil mounded up all winter.

✓ Water thoroughly after planting. Not once, but twice. One condo gardener (who is an expert at growing roses) recommends positioning the rosebush in its hole, filling with soil halfway up the sides, then watering. Once the hole is filled to the top, water again.

✓ Come summer, prune off dead flowers right after they've finished blooming. Don't leave them on the stems.

Don't

✗ Buy hybrid tea roses. They're sold everywhere and often make a promising start, but they develop problems later on. These roses are notoriously prone to diseases such as mildew and black spot and usually require constant fussing.

✗ Leave container-grown roses outside all winter, unprotected, and expect them to survive (see page 134).

Plant miniature roses

Also called "patio roses," minis are inexpensive and surprisingly tough. Many garden centers sell them ready-planted in pots. Their small, dainty double blooms come in shades like pink, cherry red, and salmon and they look charming mixed with annual flowers of a similar size. Minis will grow like gangbusters in an environment that suits them and often winter over happily on a balcony. But they are so reasonably priced, some gardeners find it simpler to just buy new ones every spring.

Summer Bulbs: Exotic and Different

For years, the only bulbs grown by most gardeners were the kind you plant in the fall: tulips, daffodils, crocuses, and so on. But now summer-blooming tropical bulbs are all the rage, and that's good news for people gardening in condos, apartment buildings, and other small spaces. These types of bulbs are perfectly suited to cultivating in containers. Most start producing gorgeous flowers quickly and will continue to put on a show all summer.

Buy summer bulbs in spring. They're sold at most garden centers. Some look bulb-like; others are elongated tubers or hard little rhizomes in green or brown. Most come packed in sawdust shavings in net bags. Press the bulby and tuberous ones with a finger; they should be firm and full, with no squashy or dried-out bits. (You can also buy from specialist nurseries by mail order. They tend to be more expensive, but the selection and quality is better.) Plant early in spring in a light, soil-less mix (follow instructions as to depth and spacing), and keep them indoors on a sunny window ledge for a few weeks. Don't put them outside until all frosts have finished. If you have no indoor facilities, it's a good idea to look for pre-started plants; otherwise, you'll wait till mid or late summer for flowers. Fertilize every two weeks. In the right kind of conditions—they like heat, with plenty of moisture—many summer bulbs grow with gusto.

Bulbous beauties to try

❀ **Achimenes** (pronounced *ack-im-en-EES*): Produces pretty, jewel-like 2 in./5 cm blooms in red, pink, or apricot for weeks on end. Slow to get started. Will tolerate a bit of shade.

❀ **Begonias:** Dismissed as "old ladies' plants" for years, begonias are back in a big way. Most garden centers sell pre-started tuberous kinds in pink, yellow, orange, or red. Buy these if you want quick results (replant in bigger pots). They will bloom non-stop all summer. For hanging baskets, look for small trailing begonias and picotee varieties (which means petals with a contrasting color

Picotee begonia

around the edge—very fetching). But what's even hotter are non-tuberous begonias, which often have interesting flowers *and* fantastic foliage. Look for Dragon's Wing, Angel Wing, and Holly Leaf kinds. The biggest plus of all begonias is that they thrive in shade.

❀ **Calla lilies (*Zantedeschia*):** Fashionable, but often finicky. Large, shiny blooms shaped like trumpets and exotic dark green foliage, often spotted with white. Good on balconies because they can cope with windy locations. They don't produce as many flower heads as other summer-flowering bulbs, but are spectacular when they do unfurl themselves. Don't confuse callas with cannas.

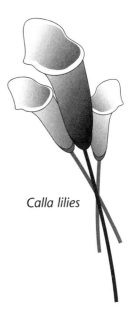

Calla lilies

- ❀ **Canna lilies:** Oh-so-trendy right now, these knockout plants grow huge, with whacking great leaves and brilliant flowers, usually in reds or oranges. Pick the ones with striped foliage, not plain green, and give them lots of room. Cannas can be frustrating, because they take a while to develop. (Start them indoors, if you can.) They can reach 6 ft./2 m high and need sun.

- ❀ **Dahlias:** Consigned to the compost heap for decades, but now gardeners are drooling over dahlias again. In containers, skip the huge, showy blooms (which need propping up with ugly sticks) and go for smaller varieties like Bonne Esperance, which has pink daisy-like flowers, or Kasagi, deep orange and red. Dahlias with burgundy foliage, such as Japanese Bishop, are in vogue (combine them with the leaves of canna lilies). They all like sun and won't bloom till late summer.

- ❀ **Ismene (*Hymenocallis*):** Don't confuse this one with *Hemerocallis*, which are daylilies. You see *Hymenocallis* a lot on Caribbean islands. They have flaring, fragrant blooms in white or yellow that look a bit like daffodils and make a fantastic display in mid-summer. They prefer light, filtered shade.

- ❀ **Pineapple lily (*Eucomis*):** An underrated curiosity plant. The huge bulbs send up sturdy stalks, about 1.5 ft./45 cm tall, enveloped in little star-shaped flowers. A fluffy crown of leaves develops on top, making the whole thing look rather like a pineapple. Autumnalis has white flowers, and Comosa is pinkish white. A snap to grow. Gets going early. Doesn't mind a bit of shade.

When winter comes

Bring summer bulbs indoors and store them— still in their containers—in a cool, dry place. Centrally heated condos and apartments get too hot. An unheated garage or locker is good (but never

Eucomis

expose bulbs to freezing temperatures). Let the containers dry out, then next spring add a bit of fresh potting soil, water thoroughly, and put out on the balcony again.

If you don't have a cool storage space, forget trying to winter over summer bulbs on a window ledge or in a cupboard. They probably won't do well. Unfortunately, it's best to throw them out and simply buy new bulbs next year.

Hot tip

"Look for big begonia and dahlia tubers. They'll produce more flowers."

—*Dugald Cameron, bulb expert*

Herbs Make Great Scents for Beginners

Ask experienced balcony gardeners what they grew first and most of them say the same thing: herbs. They're perfect container plants. Mostly hassle-free, they look and smell good—and they don't take up too much space. It's also fun to have fresh herbs close at hand to use in cooking.

If you have a hankering for herbs, however, remember that nearly all of them like sun. Lots of it. Many originate in Mediterranean countries like Greece and Italy, and they don't take kindly to shady locations. If your balcony, courtyard, or rooftop doesn't get sunshine five or six hours a day, forget herbs. They'll look lousy and leggy (and are also prone to attacks by bugs or fungal diseases).

Here are a few tips for success with herbs:

Do
✓ Buy a growing mix that contains perlite or vermiculite, because herbs need good drainage.
✓ Add a scoop of coarse, gritty sand (get it at a builder's yard) to your growing mix, if you can. Most herbs like sandy soil.
✓ Buy herbs as started plants. All of them (except dill) take too long to raise from seed.
✓ Water regularly and position herbs in the sunniest spot.
✓ Grow herbs together in the same pot. Combine different textures and colors. Gray-leaved sage, for instance, looks great with parsley and lemon thyme.
✓ Mix herbs with other plants. The trailing ones, like thyme, make a great mulch around the base of pots.

✓ Experiment. Herb growers keep coming out with amazing variations on tried and true stalwarts.

✓ Position herbs where you can bury your nose in them and brush legs and arms up against them.

✓ Crush herbs between your thumb and forefinger. It's the best way to release the scent.

✓ Snip young leaves off for salads and cooked dishes. Old ones get tough.

Don't

✗ Let herbs flower if you want to use them in the kitchen. Keep pinching the flower heads off.

✗ Grow mint and oregano in the same container as other plants. Both are bossy, with roots that spread everywhere. (Plant mint in a ground-floor courtyard and you will never get rid of it.)

Eight easy herbs

❀ **Basil:** This fave comes in more than thirty-five varieties now. There's Thai basil, Greek basil, African blue basil, Genovese basil—the list goes on. Confused? Then opt for plain old sweet basil (*Ocimum basilicum*), which is still one of the best. If you intend to dry it, get the smaller-leaved variety *O. basilicum minimum*. Basil is an annual: it will turn black when frost hits.

❀ **Chives:** Pretty plant, great for cooks. Pick a few long strands at a time and snip them into dishes. Include the violet flowers: they taste surprisingly good. Try flat-leaved garlic chives (*Allium tuberosum*), which have a stronger flavor and aren't as invasive as regular chives. In fall, prune chives back hard, dig up a section of the roots, replant them in a new pot, and bring indoors. You'll soon have fresh new leaves to snip off throughout the winter.

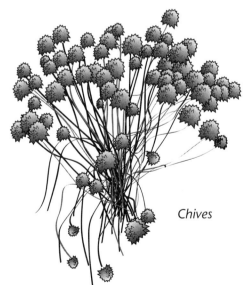

Chives

❋ **Dill (*Anethum graveolens*):** Annual, grows tall, and can look untidy on a balcony. It also self-seeds everywhere. To avoid a dilly deluge, pick leaves early, before the big flower heads develop (they taste best when they're small, anyway).

❋ **Italian parsley (*Petroselinum crispum neapolitanum*):** This flat-leaved variety is said to have better flavor than the common curly-leaved kind (though that's debatable). Parsley is a biennial, but it's best to buy new plants every spring, as older plants get tough and taste bitter.

❋ **Oregano:** A perennial and a must in Italian cooking, but there's a lot of awful oregano around. Make sure you buy the variety *Origanum* Kaliteri, which the Greeks grow. Can be wintered over indoors, but tends to get straggly. Try leaving it outside, with a protective mulch.

❋ **Rosemary**: Beautiful fragrant herb, with gray-green spiky leaves and violet flowers. Shear it back in the autumn and winter it over indoors, preferably in a cool, dry place. (It often gets mildew inside homes that are too warm or where there is insufficient light.)

❋ **Sage (*Salvia officinalis*):** Good-looking container plant that can grow 2 ft./60 cm high. Try variegated sages too, which have pretty lime green edges. (Russian sage, *Perovskia atriplicifolia*, a recent hot herb, is ornamental too, but not really a sage.) A perennial, sage can winter out of doors in many locations. Don't prune it too fiercely in spring. Leave the old woody bits on the plant. Just cut off the dead stems.

❋ **English thyme (*Thymus vulgaris*):** The compact form is best for containers. But if you have space, try lemon

Start small

Grow only a few favorite herbs that you know you'll use. It's easy to get carried away at the garden center and buy ten different kinds of basil. Then you get home and wonder what to do with them.

thyme and orange spice thyme (with gorgeous scents; use them fresh, not dried, in soups and fish and chicken dishes) and woolly thyme (*T. pseudolaginosus*).

Unusual herbs to try

❊ **Beefsteak plant (*Perilla frutescens*):** Misnamed (it has nothing to do with tomatoes), this tall purple-leaved annual is the "shiso" of Japanese cuisine (served fresh or pickled to accompany sushi or sashimi). It makes a lovely backdrop to many flowers, and is very easy to grow.

❊ **Bergamot (*Monarda didyma*):** The secret "scent" in Earl Grey tea. Pretty red or pink tufty flowers, which attract bees and look lovely in containers. Delicious fragrance. Perennial. Grow where there's good air circulation. It often gets mildew and is best planted behind a shorter flower (so its affected stems are hidden). Winter outside, covered in mulch.

❊ **Hyssop (*Agastache*):** A pretty herb, with fronds of flowers in purple (also other colors). Easy to grow, but dislikes it wet. Attracts butterflies. Grow as an annual in northern climates.

❊ **Sweet herb of Paraguay, or sugar leaf (*Stevia rebaudiana*):** Nothing special to look at, but a novelty. It contains steviaside, which is a hundred times sweeter than sugar. Soon, stevia may replace those little pink packets of Sweet'N Low found on fast-food counters. In the meantime, dry the leaves and crumble them into coffee or add them to pies. They taste faintly of cinnamon and certainly are sweet. Bring indoors for the winter.

❊ **Vietnamese coriander (*Polygonum odoratum*):** Not a pretty herb, but a great alternative to regular coriander (*Eryngium foetidum*), which is tedious to grow. (You have to keep planting new seed all summer.) The Vietnamese version gives the same zip to Mexican and Indian dishes as those bunches of regular coriander sold in supermarkets. It's a tropical plant, related to a common weed found in North America. Grows easily, with a trailing habit. Plant in a wide container. Cut back and bring indoors in the fall.

Yes, You Can Grow Veggies

There's an undeniable thrill in eating something that you've grown yourself. A plain tomato, picked fresh off the vine and sliced while it's still warm from the sun, tastes better than the most exotic, expensive vegetable or fruit sold at the supermarket. Crisp, just-pulled greens, rinsed clean and added to a salad or a stir fry, are also hard to beat.

Many people with small gardens miss out on this experience because they presume that their balcony, terrace, or courtyard isn't big enough for vegetables. They're probably mistaken. You can usually squeeze in something—even if it's just one tomato plant or a bit of Swiss chard. And who wants to be drowning in zucchini as big as baseball bats anyway? Traditional vegetable gardens, with everything planted in rows, may yield a lot to eat, but they're a huge amount of work, and their owners usually wind up giving most of the stuff away at the end of the summer. By contrast, a few veggies cultivated in containers are fun. The taste treats may be few and far between, but that makes them all the more delectable. And don't worry about the aesthetic aspect of vegetables. Contrary to popular opinion, most aren't plug ugly. Some veggies can look surprisingly decorative, intermingled with flowers.

Does the sun shine in?

If it doesn't, forget virtually all vegetables. Their one essential requirement is full, unobstructed sunlight for at least six hours a day. A balcony or courtyard that faces south-east with no concrete overhang is the best location, because vegetables want to bask in the glow of that big, round orb the moment it appears over the horizon. A southern aspect is fine too (though, in some areas, it can get too hot and dry). If you face west, and the sun doesn't swing around to your condo or apartment until noon, some veggies are probably still a possibility—so long as you have uninterrupted sunshine until the evening.

Then there's the wind...

Constant breezes can actually be a plus, because most vegetables benefit from good air circulation. However, very high winds will damage and burn plant stems and leaves—and may prevent some veggies from growing at all. If you have a windy balcony or rooftop, consider putting up screens to protect your plants (see pages 22–23).

...And the water

Most vegetables get thirsty quickly. Without sufficient moisture, leafy ones (like lettuce) will taste bitter when they mature, and those that produce tubers (like beets) won't develop properly. You need to water often—and deeply. It also helps to put mulch around the base of plants to conserve moisture.

...And the soil

You can't get away with so-so soil, because veggies are greedy: most gobble up more nutrients than flowers. Buy a bagged growing medium that's formulated for vegetables (it will have fertilizers added). If you can't find one, get a mix that contains peat moss, vermiculite, and perlite, with some composted manure. Then be prepared to juice up this concoction with fertilizers regularly. Look for a fertilizer that's designed for the vegetables you are growing. Use it every week. (Tomatoes require a different formula from leafy vegetables because they set fruit.)

You also need big, deep containers for most vegetables. Planters at least 2 ft./60 cm long are terrific (you can mix some herbs in too). So are whiskey barrels.

Eight veggies to try

❁ **Beans:** The bush variety (which we buy in stores) won't work in containers. But Scarlet Runner beans do—and their red flowers provide lovely dabs of color. Give them a trellis or strings to climb up and they're as eye-catching as any clematis. Soak the bean seeds in tepid water for twenty-four hours before planting and you'll get quicker results. Be sure to pick Scarlet Runner bean pods early. They get stringy and tough if they're are left on the vine too long. Blue Lake, another climbing bean, is less fibrous, but not as pretty. It has white flowers.

✻ **Beets:** Will grow in a deep container. One of the few veggies that tolerates a bit of shade. Scatter the seeds on the top of your pots. Add just a smidgen of soil to cover them. Lots of seedlings will come up. Keep thinning these to just two or three plants; otherwise, the beet bit under the soil won't get a chance to expand. (The easiest way to do this is with a pair of nail scissors. Yanking out unwanted seedlings with your fingers will disturb the seedlings you want to leave behind.) The crimson-edged leaves and magenta stems are colorful in a container. You can also pick the young leaves and eat them (in salads or steamed) while the rest is developing.

✻ **Garlic:** A conversation piece on a balcony, because garlic stems can grow 8 ft/2.5 m high, and they develop incredibly curly flower stalks. (Plant them behind something else.) People think garlic is too fiddly, but it's easy—and fun. Simply plant single cloves, with the skin still attached, 4 to 6 in./10 to 15 cm below the soil in a deep planter, *during the fall*. They need good, rich soil. (Buy a garlic variety that's grown in your area, not the supermarket kind.) If you have long freezing winters, wrap the container (see pages 134–35). Wait till spring. The corn-like way that garlic shoots up is astonishing. Harvest the mature bulb late that summer, when the stems are turning brown. But in a windy location, forget garlic—its tall stalks may snap.

✻ **Lettuce:** Does well for some people, poorly for others. In containers, it prefers a bit of shade (a too sunny location will make it bolt). A variety called Grand Rapids keeps producing leaves instead of maturing into a heart, so you can keep picking it. Use started plants rather than seed.

※ **Onions:** Can be picky about soil and moisture—and slow to mature. Green onions are easiest. Buy started seedlings, trim them back by one-third, and plant early in the spring, with the top bit of the bulb sticking up above the soil surface.

※ **Swiss chard:** A truly super veggie. Much better for balconies than spinach because it will carry on growing all summer, whatever the weather. It's also highly decorative. Try a variety called Bright Lights, which boasts stems in an amazing array of colors: white, red, yellow, pink, or orange. Plant chard early in spring (but it won't sulk if you don't get around to it until early summer) and thin to a couple of plants. They're ample for several people. Just cut leaves off as you need them and steam or stir fry with onion and butter. Eat the stems too. They're surprisingly tender and actually taste as good as the leaves. A trailing herb (like thyme) looks pretty growing around the base of a chard plant.

※ **Tomatoes:** For container growing, the cherry kind work best. (Big beefsteaky types of tomatoes need lots of space and don't usually produce many fruits in containers.) A variety called Tiny Tim is sold everywhere, but look for Sweet 100, a prolific provider of yummy little fruits. Buy started tomato plants rather than seeds (which take too long to develop for most condo and apartment dwellers). Put only one tomato plant in a pot at least 1 ft./30 cm in diameter and provide a stake or a wire cage for support. Plastic protective sleeves (which you fill with water) are a good idea in areas with late spring frosts.

You can also train tomatoes up a trellis. Tie the central tomato stem to the trellis with something soft like panty-hose or strips of rag. Then keep nipping out the side shoots to stop the plant getting bushy.

Leave tomatoes on the vine as long as you can. When frost is threatening, harvest right away or cover with a blanket at night. While tomatoes appreciate fertilizer, be careful of any product that's high in nitrogen. (It's the first number in fertilizer formulas, for instance, 20-10-10.) You'll wind up with a big leafy plant—and few fruits. And leave *Lycopersicon esculentum* (the lovely Latin mouthful of a name for tomatoes) off your gardening list if you have any shade at all. This is one veggie that demands a front and center situation in the sun.

🌼 **Zucchini:** If you have lots of space on a rooftop, try one. (But only one. They grow huge.) In a whiskey barrel or big planter, zucchini leaves can look as decorative as any expensive shrub—and they make an impact quickly. Plant three seeds. Thin to a single plant when it's about 4 in./ 10 cm tall. Look for compact varieties with interesting "fruit." Jaguar produces shiny dark green zucchinis. Those of Golden Dawn are a yummy yellow (and they're fun to watch, spiking out from the plant). Pollination may be a problem on very tall high-rises. If you get leaves but nothing else, you may be too high in the sky for pollinating insects to fly in and work their magic.

Three to avoid

🌼 **Corn:** Grows too tall. Tends to blow over. Try only if you have a sheltered position and tons of space.

🌼 **Spinach:** Bolts when weather turns hot. Swiss chard tastes better anyway.

🌼 **Squash:** Fall varieties, that is. (Zucchini is a type of squash.) They ramble everywhere and need a long growing season. (But if you have a rooftop where it can spread, try a variety called Cream of the Crop in a *very* big container.)

When summer's over

Remove the leftover veggie stalks, haul them off to a friend's compost heap, and put ornamental kale and cabbages on the menu instead. Both are delish as new decorative plants in your containers.

Pre-started ornamental kale plants come in yummy colors—pale greens, violets, pinks, purples—with fantastic, frilly shapes. Cabbages are usually smaller, with smooth, rounded leaves, and their centers often resemble delicate pink or cream roses.

Buy plump specimens with lots of healthy-looking leaves. Position them at an angle in the containers so you can see their showy flower heads from the front. (Some growers are now producing ornamental cabbage and kale with curving stems so gardeners don't have to do this.) Add a few pansies. Enjoy the display for weeks. All these plants can take a bit of frost and may last a long time, depending on the climate. (But don't be tempted to eat the kale and cabbages. They taste like shoe leather.)

Try rhubarb

Rhubarb is getting pricey (and hard to find) in supermarket produce sections. If you love this spring fruit and have lots of sun, try growing your own in a big container. The leaves are very decorative—and you can make a pie from the stalks to impress your friends.

Rhubarb

Grow Up: Make Maximum Use of Your Space

Think about growing up—that is, choosing vines that climb vertically. This kind of greenery is especially useful in a tiny space, but it can look wonderful in any outdoor area, large or small. North American gardeners tend to overlook vines, yet in Britain, they clamber everywhere—over gates and archways, up walls, fences, and drainage pipes. They look terrific too. The Brits, a nation of savvy gardeners crowded together on an island, undoubtedly learned long ago that if you have no room to spread outwards, you can always go upwards.

Aside from the aesthetic aspect, there are many pluses to vines. Plants that creep, weave, twine, or cling are often easy to grow; they send forth plenty of greenery (and hence add oxygen to the air); they muffle sound from the street; they provide a sense of enclosure. But their most appealing feature in our crowded cities is that they make great privacy screens. Your little oasis will seem less open and unprotected (and neighbors less intrusive) if you include a couple of vines. It's definitely worth the effort to grow them.

Vines do take a bit of effort. While a few will cling unassisted to walls and balcony railings (or trail nicely out of window boxes), most need some kind of support. And on balconies or rooftops high off the ground, watch out for the wind. It can be so fierce it will rip vines with slender, fragile stems (like clematis) right off trellises.

Honeysuckle

How to grow vines

Do

✓ First check that they are permitted. Some buildings forbid residents to grow certain types of vines on the grounds that the clinging foliage may wreck masonry or ramble everywhere and upset neighbors. (These fears are often unfounded, but it can be hard to convince people otherwise.)

✓ Inform your neighbors. Don't just go ahead and plant.

✓ Before buying, consider if you have space to attach a trellis. On open balconies, particularly those backed by big plate glass windows, there's often nowhere to hang up anything, not even one hook—in which case, you'll probably have to settle for vines grown on free-standing supports (or skip them entirely).

✓ Make all supports portable, in case you move. Simple trellises, fashioned from crisscrossed slats of wood, are sold at home renovation stores everywhere. Look for one called Double Six. It's recommended by many balcony gardeners. Hang the prefabricated sections, which usually measure 6 ft./ 2 m by 4 ft./125 cm, from walls on big hooks. Make sure hooks are firmly screwed into the wall. Use wall plugs in concrete and masonry. Also in vogue: trellises made from metals like copper and iron, fashioned into squiggly shapes.

✓ Make inexpensive free-standing supports from bare tree branches, gathered in spring. (They should have plenty of twiggy bits.) Press branches firmly into pots and train vines up them. Some people pull the branches together at the top, and tie them together. This makes a pleasing obelisk shape. You can also buy wrought-iron obelisks, which look elegant but are expensive.

✓ Prune vines back if they get too unruly.

✓ Check out tropical vines, which must be brought indoors during the winter in northern climates. Some inspired choices: winter jasmine (*Jasminum polyanthum*); mandevilla (sometimes known by an older name, *Dipladenia*); and passion flower (*Passiflora*), which can be annual or perennial.

Don't

✗ Bother with wisteria. It's beautiful, but frustrating. Many of these vines never flower, even after years of TLC.

✗ Scrimp. All vines do best in big, roomy containers filled with good growing mix. For flowering vines like clematis, add generous handfuls of bone meal to the mix (but don't do it if you live in an area where squirrels are a nuisance. See page 130).

✗ Wait till a vine is rambling everywhere before putting up something to support it. Hang up trellises in advance. You'll damage the plant doing it afterwards.

✗ Grow invasive vines. Many factors play a role in determining how big a plant will grow, but in areas with long, hot summers, you may be wise to avoid

    ❀ Boston ivy (*Parthenocissus tricuspidata*)
    ❀ Common hops (*Humulus lupulus*)
    ❀ Kudzu (*Pueraria lobata*)
    ❀ Dutchman's pipe (*Aristolochia durior*)
    ❀ Silver lace vine (*Polygonum aubertii*)
    ❀ Trumpet vine (*Campsis radicans*)
    ❀ Virginia creeper (*Parthenocissus quinquefolia*)

String your beans

Buy some jute string in a natural color. Lengths of it, stretched from hooks, provide a cheap support for many light annual vines, such as Scarlet Runner beans. Avoid plastic string in lurid colors. Take down the string in fall.

Pretty perennial climbers

Most perennial vines need something substantial to climb on. If the support isn't solid enough, they are liable to collapse after a few years' growth. Remember too that you'll have leave these vines outside in their containers all winter, and that most need some protection (see pages 134–35).

- **Bittersweet vine *(Celastrus scandens)*:** In gardens this can ramble everywhere, but it's well mannered in a container. The spring flowers are nothing special, but come fall, golden foliage and clusters of scarlet berries are to die for. Be sure to buy a female plant (look for 'Diane' on the label) or you won't get that spectacular fruit. ('Hercules' is the male version. He does not produce berries.)

- **Clematis:** An oh-so-fashionable vine that comes in more varieties than Heinz. A good bet for balcony gardeners because it doesn't mind a bit of shade and usually isn't a rampant grower. (But there are exceptions. If you want a quick privacy screen, try clematis varieties called *tangutica* or late-summer-flowering *fargesioides*. They grow quicker than others, often into huge tangles of greenery. Whack them back if they get out of hand.) Experts invariably claim that clematis is easy to grow, but it often isn't. Most varieties do best in a protected location with early morning sun. If you're high on an exposed balcony that faces west, you may find that the fragile stems get ripped off trellises by the wind. Always shield the roots of clematis with another plant, give them some kind of support, and keep them moist. Entire books are written about clematis varieties and their peculiar pruning requirements. If you're a beginner, stick to a classic variety, *C. jackmanii*, which produces pretty purple blooms in mid-summer. Cut the stick-like stems back to 1 ft./30 cm high every spring.

Clematis

- **Climbing hydrangea (*Hydrangea anomala petiolaris*):** This is a great vine if you have shade, but don't use it as a privacy screen: it takes too long to get going.

Some keep their owners in suspense for years before producing their first flowers. Has dark leaves with pretty, lacy white flowers, which are more prolific in sun. On a brick or concrete wall, it will cling without any means of support. (A relative, Japanese hydrangea vine (*Schizophragma hydrangeoides*) gets going quicker, but is hard to find at garden centres).

❀ **English ivy (*Hedera helix*):** A classic climbing plant with shiny green leaves. Beloved by the Brits, who cover walls with it. Be warned, however: ivy can be hard to grow in areas of North America that get long, cold winters. It often dies off (even though plant catalogs claim it's "hardy").

❀ **Euonymus:** There are climbing varieties (see pages 99–100).

❀ **Five-leaved Akebia:** Originally from Asia, it's often called "the chocolate vine" because of its brown stems. Has fragrant purplish flowers in spring, but grow this one for its pretty, semi-evergreen leaves, which have five segments. Akebia can be too pushy, but shouldn't be a problem in containers—and it makes a good privacy screen.

❀ **Honeysuckle (*Lonicera*):** The glorious scent of honey-suckle flowers in mornings and evenings is one of gardening's delights. Hummingbirds love it. Be sure to pick a variety called Gold Flame if you want fragrance. Another popular variety, Dropmore Scarlet, is prettier, with scarlet flowers, but has no scent. Position in full sun and don't grow honeysuckle unless you have lots of space.

❀ **Porcelain berry (*Ampelopsis brevipedunculata*):** No one had heard of this vine a decade ago. Now you see it everywhere, with good reason. It has unusual foliage in green, white, and pink and its berries, produced in fall, are an extraordinary electric blue-purple. It can be difficult to grow.

Easy annual vines

The best way to grow most of these is from seed. Started plants will produce flowers quicker, but the seedlings of annual vines often don't take kindly to being transplanted. They all prefer full sun.

- **Black-eyed Susan vine (*Thunbergia alata*):** Has delightful orange flowers with black centers. Needs support on a wall, but can also be used in hanging baskets.
- **Cup and saucer vine (*Cobaea scandens*):** Deserves to be better known. A Mexican native, with pretty purple flowers. Climbs by tendrils that push out everywhere. Give it a trellis for support. (Don't try to start this one from seed unless you have a nighttime temperature of at least 70°F/20°C.)
- **Morning glories (*Ipomoea*):** Garden mainstays, perfect for containers. They twine themselves nicely up strings. Flower colors range from white to pale pink to a lurid turquoise. A relative, moonflower vine, produces white flowers that open at night—and have a glorious scent. Plant it in sniffing range. It's okay to buy moonflower vine pre-started. You'll get flowers quicker.
- **Red bean (*Dolichos lablab*):** A fast-growing annual vine that produces gorgeous pinkish purple flowers. Needs some kind of support. You can also eat the beans.
- **Scarlet runner beans (*Phaseolus coccineus*):** See pages 85–86.

See pages 85–86.

> ### Hot tip
> "In cold climates, plant vines several inches deeper than gardening books say, and mound earth up around them before winter. This works particularly well for clematis."
> —Elsa Young, condo clematis grower

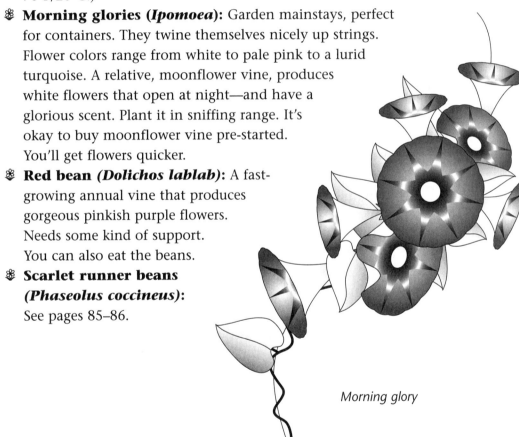

Morning glory

Shrubs: Great Shapes, Great Styles

Many people overlook shrubs because they presume "bushes" are boring. They aren't. Planted in containers, the blocky shapes of shrubs will add symmetry and style to your balcony. Shrubs also function well as backdrops to displays of perennials and annuals—and some of them, particularly flowering ones, are outstanding showpieces grown on their own.

The other wonderful advantage of shrubs is that most are low maintenance. In the fiddling and fussing department, shrubs win hands down over most flowers, perennial or annual. In many cases, you simply plant shrubs, water deeply—and that's it.

However, these kinds of plants do have drawbacks, particularly for balcony gardeners. Most shrubs have a bushy growth habit. They shoot out stems that (usually) turn into woody branches as they age, and these branches keep on multiplying. So, over time, shrubs will outgrow containers. They also require pruning to keep their shape. If you're looking for a suitable shrub, always seek out those two magic words, "compact" and "dwarf." And remember that if shrubs do get too big, you may have to divide them.

Many popular shrubs also can't take long cold winters in containers, especially in exposed locations. Be sure to ask at the garden center if the shrub you are thinking of buying will be hardy in a container in your area. If they tell you it's "borderline hardy," be sure to wrap the shrub up in some protective insulation for the winter (see page 135).

Some shrubs to try

- **Anthony Waterer spirea (*Spiraea* x *bumalda* 'Anthony Waterer'):** One of the easiest shrubs in the world to grow. Bursts forth with bubble gum pink flowers and lime green leaves in early spring. Use a big container; it spreads rapidly and can grow to about 3 ft./1 m or taller. Tolerates some shade, but needs sun to flower prolifically. When it's getting too big for the container, simply tip it out and hack it in half. It is as tough as old boots and tolerates all kinds of abuse. Look also for a relative, Gold Flame spirea. It's easy to grow, too.

- **Deutzia:** A durable, attractive shrub that doesn't get enough recognition from gardeners. Try a compact variety, *Deutzia* x *lemoinei* 'Compacta', which produces scads of pretty white flowers in spring and grows to about 4 ft./125 cm high, or the smaller Nikko Slender deutzia (*Deutzia gracilis* 'Nikko').

- **Hydrangeas:** Can be difficult in containers, because they like it damp and are fussy about soil. The fashionable lace-cap varieties, *Hydrangea macrophylla*, seem particularly picky. Try instead Pee Wee oakleaf hydrangea, *Hydrangea quercifolia*, which blooms late in the summer, or another Pee Wee, *Hydrangea paniculata* 'Pink Diamond'. In locations they like, these shrubs can grow huge, with long-lasting decorative flowers (which look good in winter too).

- **Miss Kim dwarf lilac (*Syringa patula* 'Miss Kim'):** Most lilacs grow too tall and wide for balconies. This one will reach about 6.5 ft./2 m, and it tolerates cold well. It has fragrant bluish flowers. Prune off dead flower heads immediately after flowering, or blooms will be sparse next year.

- **Purple leaf sand cherry (*Prunus cistena*):** Reddish purple foliage with white flowers in spring. A good background shrub to other plants. Tough and easy to grow.

- **Royal Purple smoke tree (*Cotinus coggyria*):** Deep purple foliage from May to September, with yellow-gray flower heads that resemble puffs of smoke. It looks sensational combined with *Weigela florida* 'Variegata'.

- **Seven-son flower (*Heptacodium miconioides*):** A hot new import from China, this is well worth trying in a big container. It has some big pluses: creamy white fragrant flowers that bloom in late summer (when other bushy shrubs are looking blah), spectacular fall color, and attractive bark (which peels off). It's also hardy in northern climates. Needs watering often.
- **Shrubby cinquefoil (*Potentilla fruticosa*):** Some gardeners turn their noses up at this garden stalwart because of its itty-bitty leaves and unremarkable chrome or pale yellow flowers. However, if you don't have much space, potentillas are perfect: unlike many other shrubs (and perennials), they keep on blooming merrily all summer. Another advantage is that potentillas are tough and hardy in most regions. They grow slowly, up to 4 ft./125 cm high, and need full sun to flower well. For a variation on the usual yellows, try Abbotsford, with pretty white flowers and bluish green leaves; Red Ace for reddish yellow flowers and a low growth habit; and Pink Beauty for clear pink flowers.

- **Weigela:** Many gardeners despise weigela (pronounced wee-GHEEL-a) because the beet red flowers of a variety called Bristol Ruby look lurid. Try instead *W. florida* 'Variegata', which has lovely pale pink flowers and green leaves edged with white; *W. florida* 'Wine and Roses', whose leaves are a spectacular burgundy purple, offsetting the rosy pink flowers; or a new dwarf variety, *W. florida* 'Midnight Wine', which looks similar to Wine and Roses.

Shrubs that stay green year round

The shrubs listed above are deciduous, which means they lose their leaves (and admittedly look pretty boring) in winter. That's why many gardeners like to include some evergreen shrubs. There are two different kinds of evergreens: conifers (which include spruces, pines, cedars, and junipers; most have spiky gray-green needles) and broadleaf evergreens (which are shrubs with regular-looking leaves that stay on the plant year-round). Many evergreens do well in containers. When buying any kind of evergreen, be sure to check if it is hardy in your area. Some are surprisingly sensitive to frost damage and may require winter protection (see page 135–36).

Conifers

❀ **Cedars** (*Thuja occidentalis*): A variety called Little Giant Globe grows to about 2.5 ft./75 cm high and a perfect globe shape. There are also taller kinds, if you have space.

❀ **Junipers:** Popular with landscapers, these are used around public buildings everywhere because they withstand rough treatment, spread nicely, and look good in winter. There are many choices, but on a balcony, go for small, slow-growing varieties like Blue Star (*Juniperus squamata*), which has dense steel-blue foliage; 'Compact Andorra (*Juniperus horizontalis* 'Plumosa Compacta'), which is gray-green; and Dwarf Japanese Garden (*Juniperus procumbens* 'Nana'), with unusual tufty foliage that's blue-green. Sniff junipers closely before buying them. Some have an unpleasant smell, like cat spray.

❀ **Spruces:** Spruces are primarily trees, but some have a shrubby growth habit. One good choice is Little Gem (*Picea abies*), which develops into a nice, globe-shaped mound. Tree-sized conifers are covered on pages 105–7.

Broadleaf evergreens

❀ **Daphne (*Daphne cneorum*):** A pretty, low shrub with rose pink flowers that are fragrant. Very hardy, but keep it moist. It doesn't like to dry out. A relative, *Daphne burkwoodii* 'Carol Mackie', is even prettier, but not as hardy.

❀ **Euonymus (*Euonymus fortunei*):** These spreading shrubs are also loved for their toughness by professional landscapers. (If you live in a high-rise with landscaping around it, take a hard look. There's probably euonymus growing somewhere.) They also look colorful year round and don't mind shade. On a balcony, plant euonymus at the front of a big container and put something taller behind it. Compact varieties are good as edging plants in ground-floor courtyards. If you like things neat, don't be afraid to prune euonymus. Cut off the straggly "spikes" that shoot out from the center and give the rest of the shrub an occasional haircut. Caution: Euonymus is sometimes attacked by scale (see page 126).

These euonymus varieties are all good in containers:

- ❀ Emerald Gaiety: Very popular, with green and white leaves. Goes with anything.
- ❀ Emerald 'n' Gold: Similar to Emerald Gaiety but more colorful. Narrow, bright green leaves tipped with yellow edges (which look pinkish in winter.) A fave with shrub fanciers.
- ❀ Sarcoxie: Also used everywhere, with shiny dark green leaves. Put the container up against a wall and you can train this one to climb.
- ❀ Wintercreeper (*Coloratus*): Green in summer, purple in winter, this will also train well up a wall. A dense grower, it may eventually outgrow its container.

❀ **Holly (*Ilex meserveae*):** If you hanker after the look of traditional holly, try varieties called Blue Princess or Blue Girl. They are hardy in cold climates, have lustrous blue-green leaves, and produce red berries in fall. In hot, dry locations, *Ilex cornuta* x *I rugosa* varieties such as China Girl may be a better bet.

❀ **Oregon grape (*Mahonia aquifolium*):** The name is misleading, as there nothing's "grapey" about this shrub. Instead, it resembles holly. It has similar shiny, prickly leaves, but is easier to grow than red-berried Christmas holly. Mahonia produces decorative bright yellow flowers in spring and blue berries later on. It doesn't mind some shade. Keep it in a sheltered area, away from cold winds.

❀ **Pieris (*Pieris japonica*):** A gorgeous shrub, but not for beginners because it requires an acid soil. Its container growing mix should be supplemented with lots of peat moss, acid humus (like chopped-up oak leaves), and a bit of garden sulphur (sold at garden centers). The Forest Flame variety is sensational. In spring, it sends out brilliant red foliage that turns green by summer.

Privacy screens

If you want to block out an undesirable view, the quickest way to do it is with container-grown shrubs. Position a group closely together in front of the area that you want to block out. Buy mature shrubs with dense vegetation. Some ideas:

❀ **Bamboo:** There are many types of bamboo, but the *Phyllostachys* varieties are most common. They grow vigor-ously, make great privacy screens, and are unlikely to get out of hand in containers. Their drawback in northern climates is that they must be brought indoors in the fall. Don't buy bamboo if you have limited indoor space. Before hauling indoors, prune them back hard.

❀ **Columnar cedar (*Thuja occidentalis* 'Holmstrup'):** Lovely emerald green foliage in a pyramid shape. A great screener, but it grows at a snail's pace. Buy large specimens.

❀ **Hick's upright yew (*Taxus media* 'Hicksii'):** Grows fast in acidic, sandy soil. Add peat moss or composted leaves to the growing mix (and, if possible, a bit of coarse builder's sand). Shape it by pruning in summer or early fall.

❀ **Japanese knotweed (*Polygonum cuspidatum*):** A shrubby "weed" with reddish, bamboo-like stems. Banished from most gardens because it's too invasive, but it often makes a great privacy screen in containers. Will grow virtually anywhere.

Large houseplants like *Ficus benjamina*, philodendron, and schefflera can also be pressed into service as privacy screens.

It's Worth Trying Trees

Don't let any garden center salesperson fool you. Persuading trees to flourish on a balcony or rooftop takes persistence. The majority of trees hate the wind and dry atmosphere up in the sky. An equally big deterrent is having their feet cramped into a container. Even the biggest planters don't provide sufficient space for the roots of most trees. Contrary to popular belief, tree roots don't extend downwards, in a fan shape. They ramble outwards, just below the surface of the soil, and after a few years, they may extend 30 ft./9 m from the tree's trunk. It's obviously tough to duplicate that kind of an environment in a planter. What usually happens is a container-grown tree will perform well for about three years, then, as it expands and runs out of rambling room, it will simply give up.

If you have your heart set on trees,

Do

✓ Research trees that grow in your area. Find someone who's already grown some on a balcony. Ask what worked.
✓ Seek out "dwarf" or "compact" varieties at garden centers. (Check labels carefully.)
✓ Plant trees in big—really big—planters, at least 2 ft./ 60 cm deep and as wide and long as you can make them. (Usually, the best option is to have some built.)
✓ In northern climates with long cold winters, use wooden beams several inches thick for planters, then line them with Styrofoam and plastic sheeting before filling with soil. Make sure there are drainage holes.

✓ Tell the garden center you want trees with compact root balls bound in burlap, rather than trees ready-planted in pots. (They'll be easier to carry.)

✓ Consider the height of the tree when it's being brought back from the garden center. (Will it fit into the elevator—or your car, if you're hauling it home yourself?)

✓ Use good growing mix (see page 33–34). Top it up every spring.

✓ Plant early in spring, when it's cool. Avoid planting when summer heat has hit.

✓ Tease out the roots with a small garden tool before planting.

✓ After planting, water every day in summer, without fail. Never let the tree dry out.

✓ Fertilize once a month until late summer. Then stop.

✓ Group trees together, for protection.

✓ Before winter freeze-up, water extra deeply. Then, if you can, provide some kind of protection (see page 135).

Good trees are expensive

Be wary of "bargains" sold off in the heat of the summer. If they are dried out, with dead branches or shriveling brown leaves, they probably aren't worth planting. Look for strong, healthy specimens with plenty of buds.

Don't

✗ Position trees where they'll bake in hot sunshine all day. Some afternoon shade is preferable.

✗ Prune container-grown trees too fiercely. Just snip off brown bits in spring. If it's a flowering tree, prune after the blooming period has finished.

✗ Bother with trees if you have dense shade. Most do require some sun to flourish.

✗ Dig up trees at a friend's place in the country and expect them to adapt well to growing in a container.

Seven deciduous trees that may work

Generally speaking, shrubby trees adapt better to container growing than those with tall slender trunks. Trees with a weeping habit (i.e., their branches cascade downwards, instead of reaching outwards or upwards) are also a good choice on balconies, where you have another balcony floor directly above yours. Try:

❀ **Amur maple (*Acer ginnala*):** Grown in the ground, this can be a rampaging nuisance. Confined to a container, however, this tough, bushy type of maple sometimes performs admirably. It can reach 20 ft./6 m high, but seldom does in a planter. Several amur maples in a row make a good privacy screen for a large terrace, courtyard, or rooftop. They turn brilliant red in fall.

❀ **Crabapple *(Malus)*:** There are over 800 varieties of crabapples and most grow too big for containers. But try a weeping variety called Red Jade. It grows only about 10 ft./3 m high and produces deep pink or red flowers in spring and gorgeous fruit (which look like bunches of cherries) in fall. The hanging branches are graceful throughout the summer.

❀ **Dogwoods *(Cornus)*:** Strictly speaking, dogwoods are shrubs, but some grow tall enough to be considered trees. Try Bud's Yellow, which has a bushy, rounded shape with long yellow twiggy branches, or Silver Leaf (*C. alba elegantissima*), which has pretty green foliage with white edges, plus lovely crimson branches in winter. They can grow about 8 ft./2.5 m tall, but probably won't in containers.

❀ **Dwarf Korean lilac (*Syringa meyeri* 'Palibin' [*velutina*]):** This has pretty lavender pink flowers and can grow about 6.5 ft./2 m tall. It looks striking in a container. Needs full sun. Prune dead flower heads off, right after they finish blooming, or you won't get lots of flowers the following year. Be sure to ask for the "standard" (or tree) variety, rather than the shrub version.

❀ **Japanese maple (*Acer palmatum*):** Graceful trees—currently hot with gardeners—that have arching branches and delicate foliage in red, golden red, green, or purple.

With plenty of mulch and moisture, they can do well in containers. They prefer a bit of shade in the afternoon. Weeping varieties like Crimson Queen are best for small spaces.

- ❁ **Weeping birch (*Betula pendula*):** Birches tend to succumb to bugs and diseases, but some balcony gardeners have success with this type. It has fine, dark green foliage and, in perfect conditions, can reach about 15 ft./4.5 m high. If you buy a top-grafted variety (ask at the garden center), it can be kept to half that size. On a rooftop, clump birches are also a possibility, because they're less inclined to topple over than their cousins, which have slender trunks.
- ❁ **Weeping pea shrub (*Caragana arborescens* 'Pendula'):** This gets the thumbs up from many balcony gardeners. It copes admirably with city pollution, produces yellow flowers in late spring, and its cascading, bright green leaves look pretty in planters. It grows from 3 to 6.5 ft./1 to 2 m tall. Another weeping pea shrub, *Caragana arborescens* 'Walker', is less dependable but may work in some locations.

Evergreens to experiment with

Evergreens (also called conifers) are often recommended to gardeners on the grounds that they supply welcome greenery all year round (unlike the deciduous trees listed above). In reality, however, you won't see much of your evergreen trees in a northern climate during the winter, because most need to be swaddled in burlap or plastic netting in fall to stop heavy snow breaking their branches (see page 135).

Container-grown upright evergreens are actually at their best in summertime, when their lush new growth provides a pleasing backdrop to other plants on balconies. Try:

- ❁ **Cedars (*Thuja occidentalis*):** Slow-growing varieties, with columnar shapes, are best for containers. Balcony gardeners report success with De Groot's Spire (very narrow, a good accent tree) and Holmstrup (a wonderful emerald green pyramid). Both may reach 10 ft./3 m high.

Cut dead brown bits off in spring. If you prefer a cedar with a rounded shape, try a compact "globe" variety. There are many on the market.

❀ **Euonymus**: Shrub forms of euonymus are hugely popular (see pages 99–100) because they're so tough and easy to grow. Thanks to tinkering by experts, you can also now find varieties grown as trees. Try *Euonymus alata* 'Compacta' (be sure to ask for the tree form), which has spectacular red foliage in fall. Its odd zigzagging branches can also be beautiful in winter. Coated in ice, with the sun behind them, they look like stained glass.

❀ **Firs (*Abies*)**: Firs are iffy in containers. If you want one, try a dwarf balsam variety like *Abies balsamea* 'Nana'.

❀ **Pines (*Pinus*)**: Mugo pines are a fave with many gardeners—and indeed they are fun, with mounded shapes and big, spiky needles. Pick a dwarf variety and don't be afraid to keep pruning new growth back to keep the nice shape. Also worth trying is a native Scots pine (*Pinus strobus*) called White Mountain, from the mountains of New Hampshire. Avoid Austrian pine (*Pinus nigra*). Its needles are too open and spindly in containers.

❀ **Spruces (*Picea*)**: Skip spruces that grow enormous. Pick a tough, native variety if you have long cold winters. Good bets in cold areas: white North American spruce (*Picea glauca*), which has a pyramid shape, and blue spruce (*Picea pungens*) in compact varieties called Hoopsi Blue, Kosters, or Moerheim. They have pretty blue or silver-blue needles.

❀ **Yews (*Taxus*)**: If you have a ground-floor courtyard with absolutely no sun, try yews. They're the only evergreens that will tolerate complete shade. Generally tough, they also don't sulk in city pollution. Varieties like Hicks or Upright Japanese look good on either side of a door. Spreading varieties like Dense or Runyan are good for flowerbeds, but need to be pruned to keep their shape. Many yews are slow growing (be patient!). In shade, don't bother with the new so-called golden varieties. (These need sun for the colors to develop properly, and the green-leaved yews look more fetching anyway.)

A taste of topiary

Disliked for many years, trees trimmed into topiary shapes are back in fashion. They make striking accents on balconies and are also easy, because someone else does all the barbering in advance. Buy an evergreen— cedar, spruce, juniper —that's already been trained into a "pom pom," or "poodle," topiary design. Then simply keep on giving the tree a light haircut to keep its shape.

Be warned, however, that evergreens turned into topiary are expensive. (Understandably so. It often takes years for tree nurseries to fashion plants into those fascinating twists, twirls, and mounds.) Also, topiary tends to be short lived in containers. Stick to regular trees if you're on a tight budget.

The Instant Garden: For People with No Time

Mother Nature is bountiful, but she doesn't like to be rushed. That can be both a benefit and a drawback when you're gardening on a balcony (or in any kind of small space). Waiting for plants to develop and flowers to start blooming teaches us two great virtues: patience and humility. It's also relaxing. The more we garden, the more we become aware of the rhythm of the seasons—and of the fact that human beings can't control everything.

However, when opportunities to introduce flowers and foliage are limited, the pace of nature can be mighty frustrating. Many annuals don't start putting on a show until late in the summer. Perennials sometimes take years before strutting their stuff properly, as do some shrubs. That's fine in a garden around a house, where there's usually something else green (like a lawn and trees) to provide an outdoorsy feeling in the meantime. But what about when you're stuck with a bare, boring balcony or courtyard surrounded by concrete?

The solution is to buy big pre-started plants instead of small ones. Most annual flowers are sold at garden centers in plastic cell paks, four or six plants to a pak. Instead of choosing these diminutive specimens, look for individual plants in plastic or fiber pots at least 4 in./10 cm wide. They aren't hard to find nowadays. Follow the same routine with perennials and shrubs. Go for gallon- rather than pint-sized. Then put those in your containers instead. They'll produce results quicker.

Start with spring-flowering plants. Use them for a couple of months. Then, once their flowers are finished (or start to look less than their best), remove those plants and buy some replacements that will bloom throughout summer. When fall's coming, move on to plants that will provide a splash in late summer and fall. Finally, select some evergreens to brighten up the balcony in winter. An instant garden is that simple.

Drawbacks to hurry-up gardening

The "instant" style of growing things is undeniably easy, but it's not all a bed of roses. First, there's the cost: bigger plants are more expensive. Second, the hurry-up plants probably won't survive long, for two reasons: they were probably pampered in perfect conditions in greenhouses (and your balcony, rooftop, or courtyard won't provide the same environment), and if you transplant them, bigger plants, especially annuals, go through more shock than small ones. Third, it's wasteful. You wind up throwing a lot of plant material out, because you keep changing the display throughout the growing season. (Be kind to the environment; look for a friend with a compost heap where you can dump the discards instead of putting them in the garbage.)

That said, if you simply want a quick, colorful show, have limited space to grow things, and aren't particularly interested in the rituals of gardening, the quick, no nurturing method works well.

The best way to do it

Any kind of container can be used for an instant garden, but the easiest is a window box or big planter. Select a deep one, line it with plastic sheeting (sold at hardware stores; big garbage bags also work fine), then spread a layer of peat moss on the bottom of the box. Make sure there's a drainage hole.

Look for established, healthy plants with big flower heads. Nestle them, still in their original plastic pots, inside the window box or planter. (It's not necessary to transplant them if the pots are a fair size.) Cram in as many as you can. Change the pot groupings with the seasons. Keep them moist. You can grow all kinds of plants, annual and perennial, in this fashion.

Some plant suggestions

In spring

In sun or part shade: Start off with spring-flowering bulbs: narcissus, tulips, hyacinths. When they fade, swap them for pansies, primulas, *Arabis* (commonly known as rock cress), *Aurinia saxatile* (often called Cloth of Gold), lobelia (trailing varieties).

In summer

In sun: Petunias, geraniums (which will need big individual pots), bidens, gazanias, Dusty Miller, marigolds, salvias, trailing plants like periwinkle *Vinca major* and *Helichrysum* 'Spike', fountain grass (*Pennisetum alopecuroides*) and purple fountain grass (*P. setaceum* 'Rubrum').

In shade or part shade: Begonias, nicotiana, hardy geraniums, periwinkle *Vinca major*, houseplants like *dracaena* and Chinese evergreens. (Bring yours outside: see pages 49–51.)

In fall

In sun, part shade, or shade: Ornamental kales and cabbages in pinks, greens, and yellows; Icicle pansies; periwinkle *Vinca major*; miniature pumpkins and a hot new decorative item, osage oranges (get them at florists and garden centres), impaled on bamboo skewers, for accents.

In winter

Miniature conifers (spruces, cedars, junipers, cypresses), trailing varieties of euonymus (see pages 99–100); twigs of corkscrew hazel and bright red dogwood (sold at florists) for height; miniature outdoor lights twined around branches, if you have an electrical outlet on the balcony.

Turn to urns

The instant treatment outlined above also works well, on a smaller scale, in urns. Fashionable among many gardeners, these classic containers are an inspired choice if you like a formal, elegant style. They're available in clay, copper, and concrete, but come in lightweight resin too, which is preferable, as it's easy to move around. Go for metal if your balcony is very windy. Avoid clay and concrete if you want to leave the urns outside all winter.

Do

✓ Position a single urn front and center, where it's visible from indoors, if your space is small.

✓ Remove plants from their plastic or fiber pots and transplant them into the urns. Don't try cramming pots in. There won't be enough space.

✓ Pack plants tightly together. You'll be replacing this collection with something else soon, so they don't need room to expand.

✓ Cut sides of fiber pots open with a knife when plants won't come out easily.

✓ Use a knife to make slashes into the sides of big plant root balls before planting. It won't hurt the plants and helps them settle in.

✓ Pour in packaged potting soil, but don't fill the urn so it's overflowing. Dirt dribbling down the sides isn't pretty.

Don't

✗ Work on a new instant arrangement after soil freezes in fall and winter. Soil that isn't frozen is essential. If you have no time to plant before frost hits, remove 5 in./ 13 cm of soil and store it indoors until you're ready.

> ### Hot tip
> "Avoid using florists' oasis to position plants and branches in containers. It flies out during windy weather. Tuck them firmly into the soil instead."
> —Ann Dobec, garden designer

Mums aren't the word

Potted mums (botanical name Chrysanthemum *or* Dendranthema*) are cheap in the fall. They come in wonderful colors—yellows, russets, purples—and pots of them look great on a balcony. But once mums get nipped by the frost, their flower edges go brown and look lousy. Don't mix mums in with other fall arrangements. Use them on their own. Ornamental kales and cabbages are more economical because they last longer.*

Difficult Sites: How to Transform Them

Some balconies, terraces, courtyards, and rooftops seem like disaster areas where nothing will grow. However, with a few cunning moves, you can persuade Mother Nature to cooperate. Here are some ideas for transforming inhospitable spaces:

The windy, cold balcony

Often found high in the sky, on the north sides of high-rises. It gets no direct sun, feels freezing cold most of the time, and is constantly buffeted by winds.

Solution: Skip flowers and deciduous greenery. Go for a minimalist look with two hardy conifers, an arrangement of gray pebbles, and a stone statue or interesting large rock. Use heavy planters in stone or wood (covered with copper sheeting). Put rocks in the bottom of planters to weigh them down, then add plain potting soil. (Don't use lightweight growing mixes containing vermiculite. It will blow out.) Position the display where it's visible from indoors. Conifers to consider: junipers (*J. horizontalis* 'Compact Andorra' and *J. chinensis* 'Golden Pfitzer'), native white spruce (*Picea glauca*), and Siberian cypress (*Microbiota decussata*).

The dark, damp courtyard

Usually at the back or sides of townhouses. It's small, surrounded by high walls or fences, never gets sun, and is gloomy all day.

Solution: Lighten things up. Paint surrounding walls or fences white (if that's permitted). Add a small white table and chairs—and plastic planters, which you paint in white or hot hues (yellow, orange, fire engine red). Include a trellis on one wall, or a pottery "sun" that picks up the colors of your pots. Avoid sun-loving flowers. Grow evergreens and light-leaved foliage plants that survive in shade. Try columnar Hicks yews, climbing wintercreeper (*Euonymus fortunei* 'Coloratus' or *E. fortunei* 'Sarcoxie'), and potted white caladiums and coleus. In flower-beds, try *E. fortunei* 'Emerald Gaiety', shrubby Oregon grape (*Mahonia aquifolium*), periwinkle *Vinca minor*, deadnettle (*Lamium maculatum),* hostas, and that old garden standby, impatiens.

The fried egg balcony (or rooftop)

All too common. Usually faces south, on tops or sides of buildings. Hot, exposed, and windy, so plants keep drying out.

Solution: Put up windbreaks. (Cheap bamboo blinds, turned on their sides, can be effective.) Install a water feature, if possible. A small pond or a trickling fountain will make it seem instantly cooler. Grow drought-tolerant plants: yarrows (*Achillea*), milkweed (*Asclepias tuberosa*), portulaca, daylilies (*Hemerocallis*), Cloth of Gold (*Aurinia saxatile),* gaillardias, gazanias, Russian sage (*Perovskia atriplicifolia*), sedums, snow-in-summer (*Cerastium tomentosum*), and ornamental grasses (pick dwarf varieties, such as fountain grass, *Pennisetum alopecuroides* 'Hameln'; tall varieties will probably get flattened in winds).

> **Hot tip**
> "Be proud of your new gardening endeavor, whatever it is. Don't refer to it as 'just a balcony.' It sounds unimportant. This is your garden—and that's what you should call it."
> —*Denis Flanagan, gardening show host*

Conserve moisture in your containers by putting a "living mulch" of herbs around the base of shrubs and flowers. Lemon thyme, woolly thyme, oregano, and savory work well. Put containers on castors so you can wheel them out of hot sunshine into the shade.

When all else fails, try a new craze: trough gardening with alpine plants. Fill troughs (low-sided containers) with a mix of one part compost, one part potting soil, and one part coarse, gritty sand. Add some crushed slag on top. (Buy the latter two at builders' yards.) Super-tough plants to try: hens and chicks (*Sempervivum*), sea pinks (*Armeria maritima*), saxifrages, low-growing sedums, lemon thyme, woolly thyme, and donkey tail spurge (*Euphorbia myrsinites*). The troughs can be left outside over the winter.

The concrete bunker balcony

Usually set deep into the sides of buildings. Has a low ceiling, three solid walls, and another half-wall of concrete, facing the outside. Dark and gloomy.

Solution: Paint the balcony ceiling white. (Use a paint roller. *Don't* climb up a ladder if you live in a high-rise.) Raise plants off the balcony floor, close to the light source, in window boxes or hanging baskets. Buy containers and outdoor furniture in light colors. Hang a mirror on one wall, and a light-colored piece of art on the wall opposite. Don't clutter the place up. Go for flower and foliage plants in white and warm colors that will tolerate some shade. Try begonias, browallia, mimulus, torenia, snapdragons, white caladiums, and coleus in reds, oranges, and golds. Offset the flowers with trailing plants like periwinkle *Vinca major* 'Variegata' and sweet potato vine Blackie or Limelight.

The truly tiny balcony (or deck)

There's barely space for even a chair, and it's often surrounded by a high railing, blocking most of the view.

Solution: Buy a folding patio chair that you can stash indoors. Hang a half-basket from the railing, facing into your unit. Fill it with small flowering annuals, particularly trailing varieties. In sun: regal or ivy geraniums, mini petunias, Swan River daisies (*Brachyscome*), licorice vine (*Helichrysum petiolare*). In shade: small trailing begonias, browallia, fuchsias, scented geraniums, nicotiana, sweet potato vine Blackie, coleus with small leaves, periwinkle *Vinca major* 'Variegata'. See if there's space for a mini-trellis on either side of the balcony door. Grow easy-to-grow annual vines up it (see pages 94–95). Look for triangular containers that can be tucked into corners of the balcony.

Grow a bit of grass

If you love lawns, here's an inexpensive way to have a tiny one: buy a big tray (or ask at a garden center for a shallow wooden planting flat) and line it with plastic. Punch some drainage holes. Lay a piece of sod in the tray. Water regularly and trim with scissors. It won't last more than one summer—and you need a very sunny location—but it will give you a nice, green taste of turf.

The non-existent balcony

Nothing more than a concrete ledge, with a window or sliding screen door opening on to it. Usually has a high railing.

Solution: Hang a half-basket from the railing and fill it with flowers (see above). Underneath it, if there's room, place a long window box filled with eye-catching upright annuals: zonal geraniums in red or shocking pink, salvias in several shades, snapdragons, a purple foliage plant, *Perilla frutescens*. Or go minimalist with three narrow, columnar evergreens in individual containers. Try cedar *Thuja occidentalis* 'De Groot's Spire', or juniper *Juniperus virginiana* 'Blue Arrow'. If the window opening on to the ledge isn't tall, try a container of hens and chicks (*Sempervivum*). They're tough-as-nails plants that you can leave to fend for themselves year-round.

When Gardening Is a Pain

Growing things is good for us. Experts have found that gardening can produce endorphin "highs" similar to those experienced by joggers. Simply looking at greenery has been proven to reduce stress, lower blood pressure, and relieve muscle tension. Alzheimer's patients do much better in residences with gardens than in those with nowhere to get a taste of the great outdoors. In fact, there are so many remarkable benefits to being around plants—and taking care of them—horticultural therapy is a growing field. It's being used to successfully treat patients with a variety of mental and physical problems.

That said, gardening can also be a pain in the neck. And the back. And the knees. And the wrists. The list goes on. The older and creakier we get, the harder it is to handle those activities associated with gardening: bending down, digging, lifting heavy plants and pots. According to condo developers, the main reason why many older couples decide to quit the family home is that they don't want to get aching backs maintaining the front and back yard anymore.

However, if you've gardened all your life, it's often hard to give it up. That's why, for many people, a balcony or courtyard garden proves to be such a plus. It keeps us connected with nature, yet is small and manageable. There's no lawn to cut, no big flowerbeds to weed and fuss over. You can grow a bit of this and a bit of that, and not feel overpowered.

How to avoid sore joints

If you have arthritis or other mobility problems, here are ways to ensure that gardening is a pleasure, not a pain:

Do

✓ Keep gardening projects small. Just one flowerpot is enough for some people.

✓ Get rid of heavy metal tools. Plastic trowels and watering cans are easier to handle.

✓ Paint tools yellow, so you can spot them easily. (Many manufacturers now sensibly produce tools in this color.)

✓ Hang a basket at waist height, on a balcony railing or wall. Store tools in it.

✓ Garden in raised containers. Window boxes attached to balcony railings work well if you can stand up. If you prefer to sit—or are in a wheelchair—get a sturdy wooden bench built 2 ft./60 cm off the ground, and put flowerpots on it. Make the bench wide enough so your knees can slide underneath it comfortably.

✓ Always have a stool or chair close by so you can take a rest.

✓ Use lightweight resin containers (see page 28) and soil-less mix (see page 33).

Don't

✗ Bend down to do anything. Sweep up garden debris with a long-handled broom and dustpan. Grow plants vertically (see pages 90–95).

✗ Put containers in places where you have to stretch to reach them.

✗ Garden in the hot midday sun. Always wear a hat.

✗ Buy "difficult" plants. Stick to kinds that are easy to grow. Planting things that will cause you stress defeats the whole purpose of gardening.

Don't haul stones upstairs

Cheap lightweight sponges, sold at dollar stores, are excellent as drainage in the bottom of containers. Buy a package of them. They're easier and lighter than bits of crockery or stones.

Tools to try if you ache

Stiff joints or sore back? Buy "enabling" tools. Some mail order garden product companies, aware that Boomers are getting older and creakier, sell them. (Look in gardening magazines.) Among the options are:

❀ **Ergonomic hoes, trowels, and cultivators:** Often weird-looking (shaped like bicycle handlebars with pistol grips), they're designed to keep hands and wrists in a natural position while you dig. Rheumatologists recommend them.

❀ **Telescoping tools:** Made of lightweight aluminum with cushioned handles. Usually hoes, rakes, and brooms.

❀ **Kneeler benches:** Sold in many garden centers, they have cushioned kneeling pads and handles. (But on a balcony, gardening in raised containers is your best bet.)

> **Hot tip**
> "Wrap tools like scissors and pruners in thin pieces of foam rubber to cushion joints—and wear cotton gloves."
> —*Karen York, horticultural therapist*

❀ **Wrist wraps:** Like the protectors worn by roller bladers. They make wielding a trowel easier.

❀ **Long-handled picker-uppers:** Make it possible to lift things from the floor without bending over.

Safety in the Sky

It can be downright dangerous gardening on a balcony—especially if you're high in the sky. Most condominium and apartment buildings now have regulations stipulating what gardeners can and can't do. Often these prohibitions can seem unnecessary, but they are usually introduced for safety reasons.

How to avoid accidents

Do

✓ Hang window boxes inside the balcony.

✓ Buy sturdy, well-made supports for the boxes. (Cheap ones are often absurdly flimsy.) They should attach to both the balcony railing and the window box with long screws.

✓ Take careful measurements before going out to buy boxes and supports. Get a professional to install them if you aren't sure how to do the job yourself.

✓ Make sure the wires of hanging baskets are heavy enough to cope with strong winds. Attach these wires firmly to the baskets and to hooks, not nails, screwed into the balcony ceiling, using concrete plugs. (Or put up brackets on balcony walls.)

✓ Wrap lengths of wire completely around hanging baskets and run them to hooks on balcony side walls.

✓ If you aren't sure what your balcony ceiling and walls are made of (and what type of screws to use), ask the building management for guidance.

✓ Buy safety straps that go around wrists for pruners and scissors. It's all too easy to drop tools over the edge.

✓ Use a watering wand to reach pots.

Don't

✗ Place any containers on concrete ledges of balconies.

✗ Suspend baskets so high up you need to climb on to a chair to water them or tidy up plants.

✗ Buy hanging baskets that are bigger than 15 in./40 cm in diameter. Also avoid ready-planted ones with flimsy plastic hangers that aren't strong enough to support baskets filled with wet soil and plants.

✗ Let climbing plants ramble all over the place, so you have to lean far over the balcony edge to prune.

Be a happy hooker

Not a hazardous one. All kinds of ingenious hooks are available that will stop hanging plants from crashing to the ground. Look for these at garden centers and home renovation stores and always follow the manufacturers' instructions.

❀ **Ceiling hooks:** Cup hooks, often with a screw attached, or a toggle bolt (a winged bit for fastening into hollow ceilings).

❀ **Swivel hooks:** Rotate so that the plant can be turned to get sun on all sides.

❀ **Hanging container brackets:** Usually L-shaped or resembling decorative scrolls, for fastening into walls. The best ones are made from a heavy metal, such as wrought iron. (Avoid cheap, lightweight aluminum ones.) Some have pulleys attached so you can raise and lower hanging baskets.

❀ **Planter brackets:** They have solid metal arms that hook over balcony railings or screw into walls. The best ones are adjustable: there's a sliding section that expands or contracts to accommodate the width of both the balcony railing and planters. Smaller brackets are available for individual pots.

> ## Hot tip
> "Build a simple wooden work bench, with a window box on top. Store messy gardening stuff underneath the bench, hidden by some short, dark green curtains. It's easier to garden safely if you keep things tidy."
> —*Dave Wilson, high-rise balcony gardener*

Bugs (Blech!): Ways to Banish Them

One big advantage to growing things in containers on balconies is less bugs and diseases. Insects and creepy-crawlies mostly multiply down at ground level, in the soil, and don't tend to travel too high up. The same can be said of soil-borne infections and diseases. People with regular gardens down on terra firma have to cope with many more problems in this department than do balcony gardeners.

That said, your pots and planters are unlikely to be sitting pretty, unblemished and unbothered, all the time. Mother Nature is actually a bit of a sadist. She likes to ensure that we endure a bit of pain along with all that pleasure that her offspring give us. Sooner or later, all gardens, irrespective of their location, are likely to get visited by something vile and annoying.

In the live critter department, be on the watch for SEAS of problems—that is, slugs, earwigs, aphids, and scale. Where plant diseases are concerned, watch out mostly for downy mildew.

Slugs

If you're being bugged by slugs, chances are it's rained a lot recently, or you've overwatered your plants. Slugs love it damp. To get rid of them,

Do
✓ Try beer. Yes, it does kill slugs. But this precious liquid costs so much nowadays, why treat the slimeballs to a blissful, boozy end? Here's a cheaper alternative: mix two tablespoons of brewer's yeast (sold at health food stores) with a teaspoon of sugar in a 16 oz./500 ml yogurt

container of water. Pour the concoction into beer traps sunk in the ground to soil level. Use old saucers, empty sardine cans, or ready-made traps with lids (pretty ones are sold everywhere). Slugs drink themselves silly, fall in, and drown. Replace when it rains.

✓ Use copper tape—a good choice for container gardeners. Wrap a strip of this tape around the outside of each pot. Slugs don't like crawling across it. Copper tape is sold at some garden centers (one brand is called SureFire Slug and Snail Copper Barrier), but it's unfortunately pricey. Also, once the tape gets dirty, the nocturnal nuisances tend to come back—and it won't deter slugs already inside the pot, lurking under the soil.

✓ Try diatomaceous earth. Sold at garden centers, this is made from the ground-up skeletons of sea crustaceans. Touted as environmentally friendly, it kill slugs by puncturing holes in their sides (but unfortunately does the same to bees). Pour a pile of the razor-sharp crystals into the toe of old panty hose (or two layers of cheesecloth), tie a knot, then hit your plants with this weapon, coating all the stems, flowers, and foliage with dust (paying particular attention to the undersides of leaves). Repeat after rain.

✓ Enlist Fido's help. Some people say encircling affected plants with dog (or human) hair keeps slugs away. So does a ring of ash (from cigarettes or wood fires), diatomaceous earth, crunched up egg shells, or salt.

✓ Dig into planters in spring and look for slug eggs. They resemble tiny pearls, laid in clusters. You can easily pick them out.

✓ Go out at night with a flashlight and handpick slugs. (Be brave, they *are* horribly slimy.) Drop into a cupful of salty water. Or, if you're squeamish, mix up a plastic sprayer of water with a teaspoon of ammonia added. Spray directly onto slugs. Make sure the critters die. Squirt twice, if necessary. They can be remarkably tenacious.

✓ Remove the lower leaves of plants, so slugs don't have any damp hiding places. Check regularly underneath pots and in cracks between paving stones.

✓ Be careful of commercial slug baits. Always read labels. The ones containing metaldehyde can cause kidney damage in pets and kids. Varieties containing iron phosphate are less harmful.

Don't

✗ Grow green, leafy plants. Slugs love hostas, nasturtiums, basil, and veggies like Swiss chard and lettuce. They hate hard-leaved plants like rhododendrons. If you must have hostas, look for slug-resistant varieties. Among them are Abiqua Drinking Gourd, Invincible, Serendipity, and Sum and Substance.

✗ Ignore slugs. They're voracious varmints. Even a couple can reduce a pretty plant to shreds in next to no time.

Earwigs

Earwigs are hard-shelled insects, about half an inch (1.25 cm) long, with pincers. Horror stories (mostly exaggerated) abound about them. However, these creepy-looking invaders can actually be beneficial in gardens because they munch on another annoying critter, the aphid.

That said, don't endure earwigs if great mobs of them are chewing and destroying your plants. You can find out if these pincered pests are the problem by checking at night with a flashlight. Plants sometimes crawl with earwigs. Some remedies:

❀ Earwigs like to congregate in damp, dark spaces. Put some old garden hose 6 in./15 cm long around plants that are getting attacked. Every morning, dunk these lengths into a pail of soapy water. The drowned (you hope) denizens should fall out.

❀ Leave scrunched up balls of wet newspapers around plants. Do the same as above.

❀ Get some empty containers with steep sides: tin cans, margarine tubs, yogurt containers. Pour in one tablespoon each of vegetable oil, soy sauce, and molasses. Place containers next to plants where earwigs are munching. Bend a couple of leaves over the cans to stimulate earwiggy interest (but make sure that once the bugs topple in, they can't crawl out). Leave overnight. Check next morning. Some gardeners report huge hauls of dead earwigs with this concoction.

❀ Avoid the chemical antidotes to earwigs that are on the market—they tend to be toxic.

Aphids

The trouble with aphids is that you usually can't see the damn things. They're flying insects, but most are microscopic. That doesn't stop them being big-time nuisances, however. Aphids suck juices from the stems and leaves of all kinds of flowers. If a plant is under attack, it may wilt and appear pale (or even yellow), with curled or stunted leaves and flower heads. Pull up a leaf and look underneath: if it's puckered, aphids are probably to blame. To get rid of them,

❀ Spray with soapy water three times, at three-day intervals. Pay the most attention to the undersides of leaves.

❀ Mix a plastic sprayer full of a semi-environmentally friendly insecticide called pyrethrum (sold pre-mixed at garden centers) with a tablespoon of isopropryl alcohol (from hardware stores). Spray directly on aphids.

- Blast aphids off plants with a garden hose (but be careful of the neighbors.)
- Put up yellow sticky traps next to plants.
- Welcome ladybugs to your balcony. They eat hundreds of aphids a day. (You can buy these Florence Nightingales of the garden by mail order from environmentally friendly pest control companies.)

Dish soap works fine

Commercial insecticidal soaps are expensive. You can get the same results by mixing up a few squirts of a mild dish soap (not detergent) into a plastic sprayer of water. Start treating plants early, the moment you see bugs. Spray everything, including the undersides of leaves. With serious infestations, dunk the entire plant, pot and all, into a bucket of soapy water.

Scale

Scale isn't crud found inside the kettle. It's alive—a horrid insect with a hard, horny casing that sucks sap from stems. If there's a sticky substance dripping underneath your plants and their leaves are yellow and dropping, the problem is probably scale. Many popular plants like euonymus, geraniums, peonies, and canna lilies get attacked by scale. Serious infestations may mean throwing the plant out. To limit scale,

- Scrape the limpet-like casings off stems with the back of a knife, then spray with soapy water.
- Dab insects with a Q-tip dipped in isopropryl alcohol.
- Douse the entire plant in a horticultural spray that contains oil. Before spraying, cut off any stems that are heavily infected.

The matter of mildew

Plant diseases are blessedly few on balconies, provided you buy healthy plants and sterilized growing mix. However, in humid climates, downy mildew can show up. A grayish or white mold may appear on stems, leaves, and flower heads. Eventually, the whole plant gets limp, distorted, and ugly. Once established, mildew is difficult to eradicate. To avoid outbreaks,

Do

✓ Position pots in areas with good air circulation.
✓ Leave plenty of space between plants.
✓ Water early on sunny days.
✓ The moment you detect even a wisp of mildew, fill a plastic sprayer with water, mixed with a tablespoon of baking soda. Douse the plant three times, at three-day intervals.

Don't

✗ Use icy water, straight from the faucet. Let it sit in a watering can for a while.
✗ Wet leaves when watering plants.
✗ Water at night.
✗ Overwater.

> **Hot tip**
>
> "I object to making up complicated concoctions to kill slugs. A simple and effective remedy is to pour hot water over stems of wormwood (*Artemisia absinthium*). Discard stems, let the water cool, then spray or pour on plants."
>
> —*Dominique Leonard, perennials fan*

Those Annoying Garden Gatecrashers

They drop by uninvited. They dig up, eat, maim, and destroy plants. They often leave souvenirs of their visits behind. Here's how to cope with unwelcome interlopers from the animal kingdom.

Pigeons and starlings

Seldom a problem for ground-level gardeners, but people in condos and apartments are often driven crazy by these crappy, persistent high fliers. Deterrents to try:

❀ Stretch narrow mesh black plastic netting (sold at garden centers) over the entire balcony opening. Attach it to side walls, ceiling, and the half-wall facing outside, using strips

of furring and screws. This shut-out approach may sound drastic, but it's worth the effort, according to some pigeon-plagued balcony gardeners. The netting is barely visible and it doesn't block the view, but the birds are stopped in their tracks. Note: this will only work, of course, on an enclosed type of balcony, with solid side walls.

❀ Pull out a kid's wire Slinky toy along the concrete ledge of a balcony. Add some hooks to keep it in place. Or try a length of shiny plastic string attached to the balcony walls and stretched along the ledge. Positioned two or three inches above the ledge, it may deter birds from landing.

❀ Aluminum pie pans, or strips of fluorescent tape flapping about. (These may bother your neighbors more than the pigeons.)

❀ An artificial owl, sitting on the balcony railing, sometimes works. Often doesn't. The best kind have moving heads that bob and turn in air currents. They're scarier to pigeons and starlings. (But if you can entice some real live hawks to make a nest close by, that will work far better.)

Cats

Love 'em or hate 'em, felines find their way into courtyard gardens and, sometimes, onto balconies and rooftops. If you want to stop pussies prowling around,

Do

✓ Try growing an annual called *Coleus canina*. It has a strong smell (particularly when it dries out) that repels cats. You can find it at garden centers, often sold under the name Scardy Cat. Plant several of them among your other plants.

✓ Stick bamboo barbecue skewers, close together, in all your containers. Cats don't take kindly to their sharp, pointed ends.

Don't

✗ Use blood meal or fish emulsion as a fertilizer. Cats are drawn to the smell of both—and will dig up soil in search of a snack.

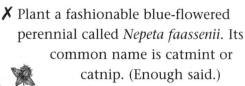

✗ Plant a fashionable blue-flowered perennial called *Nepeta faassenii*. Its common name is catmint or catnip. (Enough said.)

✗ Put up a bird feeder. It will attract feathered friends *and* their predators.

Squirrels

The bushy-tailed brigade come in several colors—gray, red, black. Whatever their uniform, they can all be a colossal nuisance, particularly in ground-level gardens. Tips:

Do

✓ Smooth out areas where you've planted things. Squirrels often dig in disturbed soil in search of edibles such as nuts.

✓ Try the bamboo skewer routine (see under "Cats," on page 129).

✓ Spray plants with a garlic and water solution. Repeat after it rains. But don't use cayenne pepper or mothballs. (Pepper can blind squirrels and cause them incredible pain. Mothballs are toxic to pets and kids. Animal protection societies now frown upon these two deterrents.)

Don't

✗ Grow tulips if your area is infested with squirrels. They will dig up bulbs, break off flower heads, nibble on petals—often right in front of you. Daffodils or other kinds of narcissus are a better bet. (They are poisonous to squirrels.)

✗ Add bone meal to growing mix. It attracts squirrels. Commercial fertilizers high in phosphorus (the middle number on packages, for instance, 10-20-10) are a better bet.

✗ Don't hang up a bird feeder. Squirrels love snacking on all those seedy selections too.

Raccoons, skunks, and foxes

These so-called wild animals are no longer restricted to the wild. They're often found in populated areas, because the pickings are better. (In fact, raccoons are far bigger and healthier in cities nowadays than in the country.) To help deal with them,

Hot tip

"Get a dog. I let mine out on the balcony any time pigeons drop by. That scares them off."
—*Wendy Humphries, balcony gardener*

❀ Store garbage in sealed containers, kept firmly closed with bungee cords.
❀ Don't have a water garden. Raccoons love rummaging around in ponds in search of fish. They will also wash other food they find in pond water—and make a dreadful mess.
❀ Buy a motion-activated sprinkler. It has a highly sensitive infrared sensor that sprays a jet of water when it detects any movement. Many gardeners say this works like a charm at scaring off nocturnal visitors (dogs and cats too).
❀ Leave lights on, or play a radio, all night outside (but check with the neighbors first).

When Winter Comes: Survival Strategies

A balcony or rooftop garden is fine and dandy in summertime, but what about the winter? Probably the biggest drawback to growing things in containers is those dreary, freezing months, in all their guises. Many trees, shrubs, and perennials that do perfectly well planted in the ground can turn temperamental in pots and planters once Jack Frost arrives. Often the severity of the temperature isn't the problem. What affects plants far more is the thermometer going up and down like a yo-yo throughout the winter. This kind of weather is affecting more and more regions of North America; the supposedly cold season has stopped being consistently cold. There's snow one day, then it's rainy and warm the next. When that happens, plants get as confused as humans do. They may start to sprout during the thaw, then their tender buds and burgeoning roots get whomped by winter all over again. No wonder they give up.

Container-grown plants actually survive winter best in areas where heavy snow comes early, then stays on the ground. The white stuff acts as a protective blanket, maintaining plants at much the same temperature for months on end. In areas where that doesn't happen, where there's not enough snow and no constancy to the temperature, even plants that are supposedly hardy in your region may not be able to cope.

Shop wisely

When buying plants for an urban gardener, bear this mind: they'll have a better chance of survival if you pick perennials, shrubs, and trees that are hardy in areas *two zones colder* than yours. For instance, if you garden in Zone 6, select plants that are hardy in Zone 4.

How to protect plants

There are no hard and fast rules to wintering plants over. A lot depends upon the local climate and where your balcony, courtyard, or rooftop is located. Winter winds are often as hazardous as seesaw temperatures. Plants that have to endure icy cold gales, high on an exposed balcony, are obviously going to be far more affected by plummeting temperatures than their cousins ensconced in a ground-floor courtyard, shielded from the elements.

However, experienced balcony gardeners agree that it's worth giving valuable trees, shrubs, and perennials some form of protection once winter comes. One condo green thumb, who lives eight floors up and has never lost a plant during the cold months in her northern city, recommends this routine (which she follows religiously every year):

Do
✓ Start putting your garden to bed early in the fall, because it will take longer than you think.
✓ Tackle houseplants first. If pots aren't too big and cumbersome, remove the plant, scrape soil off their roots, and give the entire plant a "plunge" bath in a plastic basin or bucket. (Use a mild product like Dove, not detergent.) Rinse everything off thoroughly, then leave it to dry outside on a warm day.
✓ If plants are too large for this procedure, slosh a stream of water from a garden hose through them for ten minutes. Or put them in the bathtub and turn the shower on. This laundry routine is an admitted chore, but it does help prevent infestations of bugs like spider mites during the long winter months indoors.
✓ Wash all houseplant containers too, then dry them and refill with fresh growing medium. Repot the plants and bring them inside.

✓ Cut down climbing annuals, like sweet potato vine, morning glories, licorice vine, and runner beans. Empty all annuals into garbage bags. Wash their pots and put them away. Take the bags to a neighborhood composting facility (or find a friend who'll compost the stuff for you).

✓ Trim back potted perennial herbs, such as rosemary and oregano, then bring them indoors to a sunny window ledge. Do this with basil too, but it's an annual and won't last long. When basil stems get woody, throw the plant out.

✓ Keep container-grown perennial vines, upright plants, and shrubs on the balcony *as long as you possibly can*. Water regularly until growth has died down, but don't fertilize. Then hill up earth around anything that's trained up walls.

Try double-potting

Buy some Styrofoam picnic coolers at the end of summer, when they're on sale. Store small potted perennials inside them, nestled in packing peanuts.

✓ Rose bushes: Persuade a friend with a ground-floor garden to winter them over for you. Don't remove roses from containers; simply sink the whole thing into a flowerbed to ground level and cover with a 6 in./15 cm mulch of leaves or cocoa bean hulls. (Canadian shrub roses with the brand names Explorer and Morden are tougher than hybrid tea roses and can often stay on balconies year-round without going through this procedure. But it's a good idea to wrap them. See below.)

✓ Perennials: Don't cut the dead foliage back unless it's very messy. (Wait till spring. It will protect the plants.) Group their containers close together in a sheltered spot, preferably close to a southern wall, where they can pick up warmth from the winter sun. Wrap containers of any perennials that may be frost-sensitive in bubble wrap or plastic sheeting. Then tuck a thick layer of an insulating material—packing peanuts, newspapers, leaves, even pink fiberglass "wool" insulation—between the pot sides and the layer of plastic. Add a 6 in./15 cm "icing" of mulch—leaves, cocoa bean hulls, or composted sheep manure—on top of each container. In windy areas, weigh this layer down with Christmas tree branches, planks, or bricks.

✓ Shrubs and trees: Wrap columnar ones in burlap or plastic netting. Two new products—Arbotec and Bush Jacket—are also good for protecting plants (look for them in garden centres). Group containers closely together for protection, if they aren't too heavy to move. Then follow the same procedure as for perennials. Give everything a good final soak.

✓ Wash off concrete or wood balcony ornaments and store them indoors.

✓ Clean up garden furniture and move them inside if they're made of plastic or resin. (Aluminum, wrought iron, and teak can remain on the balcony.)

✓ Drain fountains and faucets.

✓ Periodically throughout the winter, go out onto the balcony and dump a pail of room temperature water onto the container-grown perennials, shrubs, and trees. Horticulturalists used to advocate leaving dormant plants untouched during the freezing months, but they now say that the drying effects of winter can suck the moisture right out of roots.

✓ In early spring, remove containers' winter wrappings when the soil is starting to thaw. You'll know it's the right time when you can stick a finger into the soil to a depth of about 1 in./3 cm. Water thoroughly and fertilize.

Don't

✗ Try to do everything in one day.

✗ Ignore outdoor plants once winter descends. Check on them periodically. You may need to brush wet snow off branches or adjust wrapping material that has come loose.

Detecting frost damage

Exterior signs are easy to spot in spring. Trees or shrubs may have brown leaves and/or dried-out branches and twigs. Brown, falling needles on conifers are another dead giveaway. What's harder to discern is root damage. If a tree or shrub that was healthy the previous year fails to send out new buds in spring (or the buds are few and far between), it's probably been zapped by the frost.

Many container-planted specimens won't recover from winter's icy grip—but don't be in too much of a hurry to throw them out. Some can be remarkably resilient. Trim all the dead branches and twigs off, water well, and wait. You may be surprised by new shoots later on in the season.

Your own live Christmas tree

It *is* possible to cultivate one on a balcony, with a bit of effort. Here's how:

❁ Buy an evergreen already planted in a papier-mâché pot (it looks like rough brown cardboard) a few weeks before the big day. Best bets are a dwarf Alberta spruce (*Picea glauca conica*) or a Scots pine (*Pinus sylvestris*). (Avoid cedars and firs. They won't take kindly to being brought indoors.)

❁ Leave the tree out on the balcony for a couple of weeks. Water every few days with a big bucket. Then bring your Christmas showpiece into the living room for a maximum of seven to ten days. While it's inside, stand the tree on a big plastic tray, water daily, and pick a spot that's as cool as possible. Use miniature Christmas lights. (They generate less heat than big ones.)

❁ With the turkey and eggnog over, put the tree (still in its papier-mâché pot) inside a larger pot. Add some kind of insulation, evenly distributed between the layers of the two pots (see above). Store next to a wall of your building, not in an exposed area.

❁ In spring, remove winter wrappings and pot up in a bigger container. Fertilize with a water-soluble fertilizer in a formula like 20-20-20. Trim off any dead bits. Watch it grow throughout the summer. Then, if you're lucky, bring it indoors again the following holiday season. Some conifers will last for years given this treatment.

Making poinsettias last

Summer and fall have faded away. The outdoor garden is put to bed. How to import a bit of color indoors?

Many condo and apartment dwellers plump for poinsettias. These popular plants, originally from Mexico, have become indelibly associated in the minds of North Americans with the Christmas season—and we buy millions of them.

Here's how to make a poinsettia last past December:

❀ Don't leave it sitting in the car while you go Christmas shopping. Tropical poinsettias can take a maximum of twenty minutes outside in winter conditions. Even carrying them out to the parking lot is hazardous. Always make sure they are wrapped in a protective sleeve and a layer of paper.

❀ Put it in bright light, but not direct sunshine.

> **Hot tip**
>
> "In fall, don't throw out perennials that are borderline hardy, because they can surprise you. Fountain grass has survived on my balcony in mild winters."
> —Sue Martin, northern rooftop gardener

❀ Keep it away from cold windows, drafts, and heating vents. The ideal room temperature is 55 to 70°F/12 to 20°C.

❀ Don't let it dry out. A good deep watering every few days is best.

❀ If the pot is wrapped in foil, pierce a few holes in the bottom. Put a tray under the pot. Don't leave water sitting underneath.

❀ Keep the plant away from kids and pets. It's not poisonous, but if nibbled on, it may upset tummies.

❀ When the vivid scarlet starts to fade (as it inevitably will), forget trying to bring the color back. For most gardeners, the procedure is too complicated. Experts do it in greenhouses equipped with blackout curtains, but we're better off buying new plants every holiday season.

Where to Go for More Information

Surf the Web

Use a search engine like Google, and simply type in the words "container gardening." You'll be promptly deluged with dozens of places to look for more information.

Some of this information is useful. A lot isn't. Many gardening Web sites are simply promoting products. Along with all the hype, they sometimes offer good gardening tips, but these are often badly written and hard to read. Tracking down genuinely useful material is difficult and time-consuming. However, try:

www.windowbox.com: This site carries down-to-earth gardening tips, geared especially for container gardeners. Their advice guru is called Dr. Botnic, and he delivers his messages in a short, punchy style. Well worth checking out.

www.icangarden.com: An award-winning Web site with solid gardening information. Much of it is aimed at people with bigger gardens, but there are sometimes tips on container gardening.

Ask a Master Gardener

Master Gardeners are trained volunteers who take courses in horticulture. They spend much of their spare time educating the public about gardening, simply because they love it so much.

You'll find Master Gardeners in information booths at flower shows and agricultural shows. In many cities, they also run gardening information phone lines, which provide free answers to gardening questions.

To find out if there's a Master Gardener group operating in your area, ask your local horticultural society or garden center.

Get to know other gardeners

If you live in a condominium or apartment building, get a gardening group going. Swap ideas, plants, and tips. Local green thumbs are by far the best sources of practical information about gardening in your area. Another good bet is to join a local horticultural society. Garden centers usually know how to get in touch with them.

Acknowledgments

Gardeners have to be the most generous people on earth. I've had the good fortune to meet dozens of them in the course of writing a column on condo gardening for a major North American newspaper. In every instance, these individuals were delighted to share with me their knowledge, creative ideas, and, often, their plants. I have headed home clutching seeds, cuttings, and green garbage bags stuffed full of stems and roots (hastily dug up for my benefit), with the gardener's classic admonition, "You simply *must* try this plant!" ringing in my ears.

Without the enthusiastic advice of so many open-hearted souls, I could not have written this book. In particular, I am grateful to Sue Martin, whose jewel of a garden, on a condo balcony, provided much inspiration. Thanks are also due to a long list of contributors. They include: Steve Aikenhead, Mara Arndt, Kenneth Brown, Dugald Cameron, Christopher Cantlon, Cathie Cox, Ann Dobec, Susan Dyer, Denis Flanagan, Tony Fleishmann, Gwen Farrow, Mark Hartley, Wendy Humphries, Martin Knirr, Nona Koivula, Anne Kotyk, Debbie Kucheran, Anna Leggatt, Dominique Leonard, Jack Lieber, Ross McKean, Mary-Fran McQuade, George Makrygiannis, Shirley Martin, Bev Mitchell, Ellen Moorhouse, Vera Muth, Ben Ng, Catherine Pitt, Kim Price, Jennifer Reynolds, Conrad Richter, Larry Sherk, Athina Smardenka, Yoga Thiyagarajah, Mary Lu Toms, Pauline Walsh, Ida Weippert, Dave Wilson, Karen York, and Elsa Young.

I also wish to thank Barrie Murdock for his expertise in scanning (and vastly improving) my photographs, and editor Sue Sumeraj for her suggestions on improving the text.

Index

The
Urban
Gardener
Indoors

Contents

Introduction

A bit of greenery. That's what many of us in the city crave. While the urban lifestyle has its advantages, one drawback is that we tend to have no connection with nature, especially during the winter months. A woman I know who lives in a downtown condo loves being close to her office. She walks to work and doesn't own a car. But she often wails that she's tired of technology and of "being surrounded by concrete" all day—and that it would be wonderful to have something green to look at once she gets home.

This book explains how to fulfill that need. It contains down-to-earth ideas on bringing a touch of the great green world indoors—whether you live in a condo or apartment in the sky, or a house on a city street. You'll learn about all kinds of great plants that are easy to grow, and which ones you'd be wise to avoid. There's practical advice on how to keep plants healthy and happy in less than ideal conditions, such as low light and too-dry central heating. For those who get a kick out of gardening, there are step-by-step instructions on growing plants from seeds or cuttings (it's surprisingly simple, if you pick the right ones) and forcing a few spring bulbs. If you don't have much time to spare, there are some suggestions on green things that will perk up the living room, but not take over your life. And for the budget-minded, many chapters contain a money-saving idea or two.

Finally, you'll find plenty of nitty-gritty tips from real people who grow things indoors in the city. These folks have learned, mostly by trial and error, what it takes to have healthy herbs, or huge, leafy houseplants, or spectacular blooms of amaryllis, or flourishing geranium cuttings on the window ledge. A few work in the gardening business. Most, however, are enthusiastic amateurs who have forged a link with nature simply because they love it.

"There's no better way to relieve the stresses of urban living," one of them, Richard Tawton, told me recently. "I derive incredible satisfaction from my houseplants. I wouldn't be without them."

After dipping into these pages, perhaps you will feel the same way.

Houseplants Don't Have To Be a Hassle

Growing things indoors isn't as popular as it used to be. The Victorians loved houseplants. So did most of us during the 1970s. Back then, you saw greenery everywhere—festooning homes, restaurants, and offices. Just about every window had a trailing plant in it, usually supported by a harness made of macramé—and people didn't throw their avocado pits out. Instead, it was trendy to root the pits in water and let them develop into spindly indoor trees. We also planted orange and grapefruit pips, and were filled with pride when these grew too.

Nowadays, however, outdoor gardening is what's fashionable. It seems that only dedicated green thumbs bother with leafy plants indoors (and the fad for weaving string and wool into those ghastly macramé hangers has vanished, thank heavens). "Houseplants? No way," shudders one condo dweller who loves growing all kinds of flowers on her balcony in summertime, but refuses to maintain even a smidgen of something green indoors. She limits herself to a few artificial silk flowers, arranged in a vase on her dining room table—an attitude echoed by many modern gardeners.

What has caused this change of heart? Different tastes in decor are partly responsible (sleek minimalism doesn't lend itself to lots of greenery), but in addition, the criticism often voiced about leafy green houseplants is that they "make a mess everywhere." They take up valuable space in our homes (which are smaller than they used to be), they're a pain in the neck to look after, and they often become infested with bugs and diseases, thanks to central heating. However, what's overlooked by the new breed of houseplant haters is that there can be real therapeutic benefits to having a touch of Mother Nature indoors (see page 134). And they don't have to be a hassle.

Stick to these easy ones

The trick, if you want a bit of green, is to steer clear of the troublemakers and go for specimens that aren't too picky about their surroundings. The following is a list of houseplants for beginners to try. Hardly any of them produce flowers worth a damn, but their foliage can be truly heart-warming on a gray winter's day.

Chinese evergreens

If you admit to being horticulturally challenged, here's one plant that will probably survive your neglect. Chinese evergreens (*Aglaonema*) are often called "starter plants" by the pros because virtually anyone can manage to keep them going. They produce big, beautiful, tropical-looking leaves in shiny green, often with white or yellow stripes, blotches, or spots. (They have no connection with evergreens, such as cedars and spruces, that we see outdoors in North America.)

The biggest draw of Chinese evergreens is that they tolerate low light. So you can put them in a dark corner of a living room and not worry. Their preferred location, however, is in medium light. They'll produce more leaves under those conditions, and you'll also see more of the attractive markings on their leaves. Never place their pots in direct sunshine (it will scorch the foliage). High humidity helps too (see page 100).

The variety that's on sale virtually everywhere is *Aglaonema commutatum*, which has pointy leaves about 8 inches (20 cm) long. Another variety, called *A. crispum* (which has the rather sinister nickname of "painted drop-tongue"), has bigger, leathery leaves in gray-green.

This houseplant is grown mostly for its leaves. But it belongs to a family of plants called aroids—and like its outdoor cousin, Jack in the Pulpit, it will sometimes send up a whitish stalk that unfurls, flag-like, followed by pretty bright red fruit that resembles holly berries. If that happens, congratulations. It's a sign your Chinese evergreen is healthy and happy.

As the plant ages, fat, rough-looking stems will develop, with leaves clustered on top, like a headdress. Eventually, you may get lots of stem and very little foliage. That's when it's time to give your Chinese evergreen the chop and make a new one. Cut the top section of the stem off and re-root it (see page 78).

Croton

Croton's leathery leaves are so colorful the plant has the nickname "Joseph's coat." The leaves come in lurid combinations of yellow and green, red and green, and even yellow and orange. In the tropics, crotons (*Codiaeum variegatum pictum*) are cultivated as big, bushy garden shrubs. They're great indoors because their bold hues will brighten any room—and they act as a nice "anchor" to a grouping of green leafy plants. They need lots of light (but preferably not direct sunshine) and, most important, high humidity. Without the latter, spider mites can completely cripple crotons in the space of a few weeks.

Devil's ivy

A trailing plant seen everywhere, devil's ivy goes under three Latin names nowadays—*Pothos, Scindapsus,* or *Epipremnum*. No matter. It's virtually foolproof. The variety sold most often is *S. aureus*, which churns out bright green leaves blotched with yellow or white bits. It tolerates most temperatures, doesn't mind low light, and keeps on growing. If it gets overwhelming, chop the trailing stems off, preferably in spring.

Dieffenbachia

Fussy types won't have this plant around because of its much-vaunted ability to strike dumb any warm-blooded creature that dines on it. (Its nickname is "dumbcane." See page 132.) If you have kitties that nibble everything they can lay their troublesome little paws on, it's probably best to avoid dieffenbachia. But in pet-free households, this is a delightful plant that's easy to grow. It develops fat stems carrying very decorative large leaves, in green mottled with white.

Give dieffenbachia high humidity, warmth, and bright light (but not direct sunshine), and they'll usually thrive, sometimes growing tall. But one drawback as this plant ages is that lower leaves may dry up and fall off. Then you're stuck with an uninspiring stick of a stem carrying only the odd bit of greenery. When that happens, decapitate the plant, cut a center section of stem off, and root it sideways (see page 83).

Be sure to wear gloves, or wash your hands after picking off dead leaves or taking cuttings from dieffenbachia. The poisonous sap can irritate skin.

Dracaena

One variety of dracaena, *D. marginata*, should be called the "office plant." Sad-looking specimens of it sit in corners of corporate offices everywhere—ignored and neglected. It has clusters of spiky, grass-like leaves with sharp edges (so sharp they can actually inflict a cut, as paper sometimes does) bunched on top of wobbly stems that look a bit like snakes. *D. marginata* survives virtually everywhere because it's one of the toughest plants on the planet. It will cling on even if the light is dreadful and you forget to water it for months. However, if treated kindly, this type of dracaena can soar into an attractive-looking tree up to 10 feet (3 m) high. Magnificent specimens of *D. marginata* sometimes grace the glassed-in areas of shopping malls.

There are many other kinds of dracaena too—some difficult, some durable. They all do best in bright, filtered light—but not direct sunshine. Position them behind a thin curtain or blind if you face south or west. When they're churning out leaves, keep the soil mix moist but not waterlogged. Ease back on watering during their winter resting period. Two of the easier varieties are:

❀ *D. fragrans:* Quite unlike *D. marginata*, this one produces big glossy green leaves that arch attractively out of pots. It's called *D. fragrans* because its flowers are scented—but they seldom appear indoors. The stripy-leafed varieties, such as *D.f.* 'Lindenii' and *D.f.* 'Massangeana' are the most eye-catching. After a few years, these plants will start shedding their lower leaves, so you wind up with a stem, topped by a leafy clump (not to worry, it looks rather chic).

Avoid going overboard when buying houseplants for the first time. It's easy to spend too much on exotic-looking purchases and to come home with too many plants. But don't necessarily buy "small." One big houseplant can really liven up a dull room—and it's a lot cheaper than redecorating or getting a new sofa.

❀ ***D. surculosa* (or *D. godseffiana*):** Commonly called the gold-dust or spotted-leaf dracaena. Its leaves are very striking—big, luscious, and spotted with cream—and in the right conditions, it will produce them profusely.

Goldfish plant

Florists often recommend this cheerful plant to beginners because it doesn't mind being neglected. A native of Costa Rica, and a member of the huge gesneriad family, "Goldie" trails nicely out of pots, producing shiny, dark green leaves and (if you supply enough light and fertilizer) orange flowers that resemble goldfish or red flowers with orange borders. Don't overwater this plant, though (it hates wet feet), and leave it alone (repotting isn't appreciated). Given the right conditions, it will last for years, blooming frequently. Goldfish plant is also sometimes known in horticultural circles by the hideous mouthful of a name *Hypocrita radicans*—or *Nematanthus gregarius*—but most people (fortunately) use its nickname only.

Hibiscus

This is one houseplant that does produce gorgeous flowers. Although the foliage is nothing special, the blooms—in peach, pink, white, and red—are to die for, especially when they appear in the middle of the winter. They usually last only a day before shriveling up.

Although it's a fave houseplant, hibiscus (*Malvaceae*) can actually be quite a handful indoors. Down south, in the Caribbean and Mexico, it grows into a bushy shrub—way too large to fit in most North American living rooms. As a result, growers usually treat the potted specimens we buy with a growth retardant to keep them a manageable size. That's fine. It works. But eventually, the effect of this retardant can wear off—and you may suddenly find branches of your hibiscus exploding in all directions. To stop this happening (the plant will develop an ugly shape if you let it continue), don't be afraid to get the pruners out. Shape your hibiscus every spring—and if you can, put the pot outside for the summer. It loves a taste of fresh air and will often do spectacularly well in a sunny setting. But be sure to bring it in before frost hits.

Indoors, hibiscus is prone to attacks by spider mites. To avoid outbreaks, give it lots of humidity.

Jade plant

Lazy gardeners should jump for joy over the jade plant (*Crassula argentea*). It requires virtually no maintenance and will occupy the same pot for years without complaint. (In fact, it should really be called the "tortoise tree" because of its ability to keep plodding on and on.) You often see monstrous jade plants sitting in windows of Chinese restaurants. Ignored and rarely watered, they just keep on quietly growing bigger, eventually spreading all over the glass. Neglected in this fashion, jade plants wind up looking rather strange. They develop fat trunks and stubby branches, ornamented by only a few sparse leaves clinging to the ends. Both branches and leaves may periodically break off and fall to the floor. (But it's easy to turn them into new plants. See page 82.) However, when it's well cared for, jade plant is remarkably handsome. Its fleshy leaves do somewhat resemble pieces of green jade, and it will branch nicely into a small tree. Keep it in bright light and put it outside for the summer if you can, in a spot that's protected from the wind and not too sunny. It will thank you by sending out lots of fresh new growth.

Norfolk Island pine

Also called Christmas tree plant or Australian pine, this is an "absolutely foolproof" choice for beginners, according to one condo houseplant addict. It produces branches with bright

green needles that darken as the plant ages—and it does indeed look a bit like a Christmas tree.

Outdoors, in tropical and subtropical climates, Norfolk Island pine (*Araucaria heterophylla*) can be a skyscraper, soaring up to 200 feet (60 m) high. Indoors, however, it's another tortoise. Expect only a few inches of growth a year. Even at maturity, it rarely reaches 6 feet (2 m). It prefers medium light, but don't put this pretty little pine too far from the window or its needles will start to drop.

Peace lily

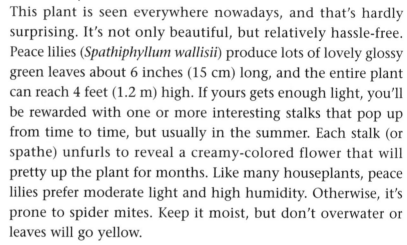

This plant is seen everywhere nowadays, and that's hardly surprising. It's not only beautiful, but relatively hassle-free. Peace lilies (*Spathiphyllum wallisii*) produce lots of lovely glossy green leaves about 6 inches (15 cm) long, and the entire plant can reach 4 feet (1.2 m) high. If yours gets enough light, you'll be rewarded with one or more interesting stalks that pop up from time to time, but usually in the summer. Each stalk (or spathe) unfurls to reveal a creamy-colored flower that will pretty up the plant for months. Like many houseplants, peace lilies prefer moderate light and high humidity. Otherwise, it's prone to spider mites. Keep it moist, but don't overwater or leaves will go yellow.

If you put your peace lily outside in summertime, pick a shady spot, out of direct sunshine (it's very prone to sunburn), and always wait till the weather warms up. You often see frizzled-up spathiphyllums sitting on balconies—the consequence of being hauled outside and exposed to the elements too soon.

> ### Hot tip
> "Size matters. Do not buy a plant so small you will forget about it. One day you'll spot the shriveled stalk in the corner and feel terrible."
> —*David Eddy, houseplant lover*

Philodendrons

This is a big family of leafy plants that can grow huge (up to 8 feet/2.5 m tall), but thankfully, in the artificial environment of our homes, most are well-behaved. They need bright light (but not direct sunshine) to thrive. If it's too dark, the biggies will droop downward and look lousy. Philodendrons also like it warm—never expose them to temperatures below 60°F (15°C)—and need lots of humidity (see page 100).

There are, amazingly, over 225 varieties of philodendrons. One drawback to the climbing kinds is that, as they develop, they need to grab on to a rough surface. New roots keep appearing above the surface of the soil; in their natural habitat (the tropical jungles of South America), these cling to the bark of trees. Indoors, the best bet is to wrap a flat piece of wood, a few inches wide, with wire netting or sphagnum moss. Then push this plank into the plant's pot. Look for the "sheet" moss used to line hanging baskets. (Don't buy peat moss, which is sold compressed in bags.) Also, try to keep the plank damp. Wet it now and then, or mist it regularly. Don't try to prop a philodendron up with bamboo stakes. They aren't strong enough.

Some varieties to try:

❀ **P. bipennifolium:** Commonly known by a host of names (panda plant, fiddle-leaf or horsehead philodendron), this can be a biggie. Don't try it in a small condo or apartment, but it's a great impact plant if you have lots of space. It can rapidly reach a height of 6 feet (2 m), with heart-shaped leaves with pointed tips. Curiously, the leaves change their appearance as the plant ages, and they wind up shaped like violins. A climber, it definitely needs a stake for support.

❀ **P. bipinnatifidum:** Don't try this in a small space, either. Its jagged leaves can measure 18 inches (45 cm) across, it keeps spreading, and it may grow to 4 feet (1.2 m) under the right conditions. One advantage of *P. bipinnatifidum*, however, is you don't have to provide anything for it to climb up. Unlike other "phillies," it sends out foliage from a squat, self-supporting trunk. Another variety, *P. selloum*, looks similar, but has smaller leaves.

❀ **P. melanochrysum** (also called *P. andreanum*): Nicknamed the "black-gold" philodendron, this one— unlike many of its buddies—grows at a snail's space. It may eventually reach a height of 6 feet (2 m), but you'll probably be collecting your pension before it gets there. Its blackish green leaves with paler green veins are very striking. Shaped like big hearts when young, they lose their curves as the plant gets older. This one needs a stake.

Hot tip

"Don't be afraid to whack back houseplants that get too straggly. They'll thank you."
—Mary-Fran McQuade,
long-time indoor gardener

❀ *P. scandens*: A "classic" houseplant that used to be seen everywhere, suspended in those tiresome macramé hangers. It has small, heart-shaped leaves of dark green and either trails or climbs. *P. scandens* soared in popularity because it's one of the easiest plant on the planet to grow. In fact, this one is hard to kill—and it may become too much of a good thing, extending its nosy tentacles everywhere. When that happens, pinch off the long trailing bits or the plant will have a skimpy look.

Ponytail palm

This peculiar plant is fun to have around (people always comment on it), but it's not for neatniks. What fascinates everybody is the base, which swells into a giant "onion," topped by a bunch of untidy, trailing leaves. The drawback is that these leaves inevitably get dried out at the ends, they flop everywhere, and they eventually fall off as the "onion" sends up a stem. You wind up with a squat tree that looks downright weird: a fat trunk, topped by a ponytail of foliage, anchored to the pot by this strange bulbous object sitting on top of the soil. But ponytail palm (*Beaucarnea recurvata*) is a real conversation piece—and it's easy to grow. It prefers bright light (but will tolerate less than ideal conditions), and it won't sulk if you forget to water it (because, like a camel, it stores water in that "onion"). Give it a good soak once in a while and be careful of the leaves. They're so sharp, you can cut yourself on them. Originally from Mexico, ponytail palm is not really a palm tree at all; it's often sold at garden centers under its true name, Nolina.

Prayer plant

So named because its leaves tend to fold up at night (as if in prayer), this is a smallish plant with interesting leaf markings. You'll find many varieties on sale nowadays, but they're all recognizable by the contrasting stripes that run through the center and the veins. Particularly pretty is *Maranta erythoneura*, which combines olive green with bright red stripes and is purple on the underside of the leaf. Don't grow them in strong sunlight (it fades the colors, and leaf edges will go dry), and keep the soil moist. They are fun to watch as it gets dark, when the leaves close.

Rubber plant

If you want something that's really "in," buy this throwback to the 1950s. Like the fridges, stoves, and furniture of that era, retro rubber plants (*Ficus elastica*) are hot again with trendies. And one advantage of this kind of ficus is that it's virtually indestructible. A rubber plant won't usually throw hissy fits (unlike its bratty cousin, *F. benjamina*, see page 25) and drop leaves all over the floor if you neglect it.

Rubber plants have big, shiny, leathery leaves on sturdy central stems—and they are aptly named. Cut a leaf off, and a latex-like sap will leak out. One way to staunch this flow of sap is with a bit of cigarette ash applied to the wound—so they were highly appropriate plants for the 1950s, when everybody smoked. Back then, the only variety of rubber plant available was *F.e.* 'Decora.' It had dark green leaves that emerged from a bright red sheath (that eventually dropped off), and it stood straight and tall, like a soldier. Nowadays, however, you can find interesting alternatives. Look for *F.e.* 'Black Prince,' which has impressive greenish-black leaves and makes a super accent plant. There are also variegated varieties. *F.e.* 'Tricolor' produces decidedly jazzy leaves in a mix of green, pink, and cream. *F.e.* 'Schrijvereana' sports squarish cream and pale green patches.

All rubber plants prefer medium light or a spot where they'll get some sun. However, they will survive remarkably well in low light (the reason they wound up on every coffee table in the sixties) and cope well with central heating.

> ## Hot tip
> "Retro rubber plants are back in fashion. Get one for your coffee table. It's really easy to grow."
> —Sara Katz, Master Gardener

Sansevieria

This used to be known by the nickname "mother-in-law's tongue," but in our politically correct times, that's a no-no. Another common name is good luck plant, because in some

parts of the tropics, voodoo is associated with sansevierias. Whatever its title, this plant with the striking, sword-like leaves is virtually indestructible. (In fact, in the Bahamas, it's regarded as a nuisance weed because of its ability to multiply anywhere.) If you forget to water it, sansevieria won't curl up and die. The hard, tough leaves last for years and don't change their size or appearance much, as it's slow-growing. The most common variety is *S. trifasciata* 'Laurentii,' which grows up to 18 inches (45 cm) high and has dark green marbled leaves with golden yellow edges. But there are other kinds, with white edging and gray-green leaves.

Sansevieria look good mixed with rounder, leafier plants such as philodendrons. But for a hip contemporary look, try a trio of sansevieria plants in a row, in identical aluminum containers. And pick a sunny spot. This is one houseplant that doesn't mind a front-and-center location in direct sunlight. Don't overwater it.

Schefflera

This has a charming nickname—"Queensland umbrella tree"—but it's rarely used. Everyone simply calls this leafy plant schefflera. It produces big, tough, shiny leaves that radiate outwards, like spokes in an umbrella. Give it a large container, and it may grow up to 6 feet (2 m) tall. It prefers medium light and is fussy about dust. Sponge the leaves off every couple of weeks if you want your schefflera to do well.

Spider plant

Around for years, poor old spider plant (*Chlorophytum comosum*) gets snubbed as "too boring" by many people nowadays. And that's too bad, because it has several pluses: it's a snap to grow, it produces pretty pointed leaves in creamy white and green that look great poking their way among other big-leafed houseplants, and it's one of the plants NASA says is terrific for removing toxins from the air (see page 134). Also, if you take care of your spider plant, it will keep having babies. It's fun to watch the little white flowers emerge on long stems, then turn into new plantlets arranged in a "skirt" around the momma plant. (These plantlets are very easy to propagate. See page 82.)

One drawback to spider plant is that it grows rapidly and thus gets pot-bound easily. A telltale sign is the leaves turning brown at the tips. If that's happening, tip it out of its pot, tease out the roots, and divide it. Also, although it's high on the hassle-free list, don't put this popular plant in the sun or its foliage will get scorched. It prefers bright indirect light. Spider plant is seldom bothered by bugs.

Swiss cheese plant

The leaves of this delish plant start out looking unremarkable, but later on, they get huge and holey, and are somewhat reminiscent of Swiss cheese. That's how *Monstera deliciosa* got its nickname. Sometimes sold as a split-leaf philodendron (*P. pertusum*), it actually belongs to the aroid family (which includes another popular plant, the schefflera). Whatever its lineage, most people love having this not-so-cheesy novelty around. The cut-out leaves are the main attraction, but in the wild, they're not there for aesthetic reasons. They serve a practical purpose, letting high winds waft through without flattening the whole plant. (On some islands of the Caribbean, where Swiss cheese plants clamber up trunks of massive trees, they're called hurricane plants.)

If you have space for only one biggie, make it an *M. deliciosa*. It's relatively easy to grow but must be kept moist and watered frequently. It does best in medium filtered light. Be warned, though: this eye-catching tropical treat can get huge—over 10 feet (3 m) tall and 6 feet (2 m) wide (although in most cases, it won't get that big indoors). It will need a stake for support. Prune if it gets too pushy.

> ### Hot tip
> "Get a Swiss cheese plant. It has real attitude. Everyone who visits my place asks, 'What's *that?*'"
> —*Richard Tawton,*
> *condo houseplant fan*

Tapeworm plant

Don't be put off by the noxious name. This curious plant is fun to have around and will prompt "What's *that?*" comments from your friends. It grows like a tapeworm, sending out a procession of flat, green, segmented stems with no leaves. During its blooming period (usually in winter), little whitish-green flowers appear on the edges of each segment, then red fruits follow. A native of the Solomon Islands, tapeworm plant *(Homalocladium platycladum)* develops into big bushes in California, but indoors, it seldom grows bigger than 3 or 4 feet (1 or 1.2 m). It likes a growing mix that contains plenty of peat moss, and should be kept moist. Fertilize it once a month in the summer months. If tips of segments turn brown—a common problem during winter—it means this not-so-well-known house-plant is begging for more humidity in the air.

Tradescantia

Another houseplant whose popular name (wandering Jew) is now considered politically incorrect. There are many varieties of tradescantias, and they're all trailing plants. Very easy to grow (some would call them indestructible), they look good on their own in hanging baskets or combined in pots with upright plants. They're related to zebrinas, which look very similar. One tradescantia variety, *T. fluminensis* 'Quicksilver,' grows like gangbusters, producing stripy green and white leaves, and is a good bet if you want fast results. You can also find pretty purple varieties. Give them all bright light, with some direct sun if you can—or they'll often lose their pretty leaf coloring. They also like to be well watered. Pinch back the trailing bits if they get too long.

Grow your own coffee

Well, not really. But there is a type of coffee tree that makes a surprisingly good houseplant. If you're patient, it will also cough up enough beans to make at least one cup of caffeine fuel. It's called *Coffea arabica* and, although not well known as an indoor plant, it's very decorative, with big, oval leaves in bright, shiny green. This little tree may reach about 4 feet (1.2 m) high. After at least four years (but often much longer) sweet-scented white flowers will appear, usually in midsummer or early fall. Then comes the surprising part: red "cherries." Open these up, and you'll find a pulpy substance inside, surrounding two seeds that look like peanuts. These are the coffee beans. Let the beans dry off naturally (don't be tempted to push the process by using a microwave), then brush off the papery flakes surrounding them and roast them in a popcorn popper.

To get *C. arabica* to thrive, give it medium light, close to— but not sitting in—a window, and warmth (leaves will drop if the temperature goes below 55°F/13°C). Black or brown leaf tips are a sign that there's not enough humidity. Even if you don't get blessed with coffee beans, this plant is a real conversation piece.

Some houseplants to avoid (unless you're experienced)

English ivy

It's sold everywhere—and gardening books often claim that it's trouble-free. But the truth is, English ivy (*Hedera helix*) can be a huge hassle indoors. The problem isn't growing it—it's bugs. Kept in your average centrally heated, warm room, this kind of ivy often gets inundated by spider mites (see page 120). They can quickly reduce a nicely trailing plant to a shriveled mess—and then the mites will probably move on to your other plants.

If you insist on ivy, keep the humidity high. Mist the leaves every week, and put the entire plant under the kitchen tap (or shower) every month, to dislodge any mite eggs lurking in the soil. And if you keep the plant in a cooler room (it prefers the temperature to be around 50°F/10°C), it's less likely to be bothered by buggy invaders.

> ## Hot tip
> "Don't panic if your tropical houseplants drop a few yellow leaves in the fall. It's normal. So long as their new young leaves are healthy, the plants are probably okay."
> —*Charlie Dobbin, tropical plant expert*

Ficus

The weeping fig tree, or *Ficus benjamina,* is a hugely popular houseplant, with good reason. Indoors, it grows into a graceful tree, over 6 feet (2 m) tall, with lots of bright green shiny leaves that harmonize nicely with any decor, contemporary or classical. However, ficus can be problematic.

One of the mostly commonly asked questions on gardening hotline shows in North America is: "Why did the leaves of my ficus fall off?" The answer is: it depends. Ficus comes from

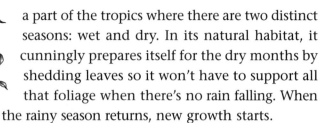

a part of the tropics where there are two distinct seasons: wet and dry. In its natural habitat, it cunningly prepares itself for the dry months by shedding leaves so it won't have to support all that foliage when there's no rain falling. When the rainy season returns, new growth starts.

Indoors, however, leaf-shedding is usually a sign that something in the tree's environment has changed, and—since ficus are creatures of habit—it's become unhappy. Did you move the plant to a different location? Forget to water it? Administer too much fertilizer? Subject it to insufficient light or to temperatures below 60°F (16°C)? Expose it to a sudden draft? These will all cause leaf drop.

If the leaves are also turning yellow, the problem could be overwatering. If they're pale (with tiny yellow spots), spider mites may be the culprit. If there's a sticky substance dripping on the floor, it could be aphids. (See page 121 for solutions to these nasty nuisances.)

Tea plant

Camellia sinensis, the source of the black tea loved around the world, is hot as a houseplant. You will often see potted versions for sale in garden centers. It's certainly attractive (like other camellias, *C. sinensis* produces sweetly scented white flowers and shiny, dark green foliage), but it tends to sulk in central heating. This little shrub prefers a cool location and may be quite happy on a north-facing window ledge. But in the kind of hot, dry air that's prevalent in our homes, it's very prone to attacks by aphids and other insects.

Other plants that are difficult to grow inside include:

- 🏵 **Begonias:** Prone to mildew indoors, better outside.
- 🏵 **Bougainvillea:** Seldom flowers indoors.
- 🏵 **Fittonias:** Finicky about light and humidity.
- 🏵 **Fuchsias:** White flies love them.
- 🏵 **Gloxinias:** Need indoor lights to do well.
- 🏵 **Roses:** Best grown outdoors.

Ideas for houseplant haters

The comedian Jerry Seinfeld once joked that "when house-plants see me coming, they commit suicide." A lot of people feel the same way. They're hopeless at looking after any kind of greenery, and more to the point, they simply don't want the hassle of leafy stuff getting in the way of their busy lives.

If you hate the idea of "conventional" houseplants, but want something green and low maintenance around, try these.

Cat grass

This is usually perennial rye grass or oat grass, and its true domain is the countryside, in farmers' fields. But ever since someone discovered that cooped-up kitties liked nibbling on the thick, raspy blades of these grasses, they've been treated as indoor plants. Cat grass is now sold everywhere from city greengrocers to gift boutiques. The leaves are bright green, and the plants are attractive indoors, even if you don't own a frustrated feline. Try a row of three little aluminum pots of cat grass for a hip, contemporary look. Toss the grass out when it gets straggly. You can also try trimming it with nail scissors.

Forced branches

Coaxing barren-looking branches into bloom is a morale booster in February and March, when winter is getting tedious. It's also easy. Virtually any flowering tree can be forced, but the best bets are early bloomers, such as forsythia, quince, and witch hazel (whose flowers hang in neat little yellow curls), and pussy willows. You can also use flowering fruit trees such as crabapple and cherry.

Wait till buds have formed, then cut branches using sharp pruners (he-man-sized loppers make for a cleaner cut). Look for buds that appear a bit "wrinkly"—the smoother buds are the leaves. For best results, make your cuts on a day when there's a bit of a thaw and the temperature has risen a few degrees. If you don't have a supply of branches in your own garden, you can find them—ready for forcing—at city florists.

Indoors, soften the branch ends by bashing them with a hammer on a durable surface. This will help them absorb water faster. Then immediately plunge them into a vase containing lukewarm water. Big branches look great in any large jug—florists' buckets or recycled sap buckets are all the rage. Daintier branches are best arranged in something smaller.

Top up the water every couple of days, but don't bother to tip it out and change it. If you keep the branches in a cool room, they'll last longer. It can take anywhere from three days to a couple of weeks for the buds to open up—and the suspense is fun. Kids especially love forcing branches indoors.

Lucky bamboo

Mostly imported from Taiwan (where it is considered a good-luck symbol) bamboo has become a hot home decor item. Its chief advantage is that it's hassle-free. You just stick the bamboo stalks in a vase, add some pebbles to prop them up, pour in water (preferably bottled, purified water, the experts say) then watch nice, leafy green growth develop on the sides of the stalks. Add a few drops of fertilizer to the water, and the thick stems will grow taller. (Then you can chop them in half and give pieces to friends as good-luck charms.)

For best effect, display bamboo in an Oriental-style vase. And shop around. Because it's trendy, you may be unlucky enough to get charged far too much for this "lucky" import from the East.

Baby pineapple

Miniature pineapples are becoming the hottest indoor plants on the planet. You can even find them for sale in supermarkets. They make fascinating centerpieces for a dining table—and you can even eat them, although each pineapple won't supply more than a few mouthfuls because they are so tiny. Wait till the fruit is really ripe before cutting it off the stem. The attraction of these "minis" is that they grow very slowly and require little water and virtually nothing else in the way of care. Just enjoy watching the curious way the pineapple gradually gets bigger, on top of its "perch," then toss the plant out when the fruit rots (which will take a few months, under most conditions).

And don't attempt to make a regular kind of pineapple

grow, by cutting off its crown of leaves and standing it in water. This was a fashionable pastime a couple of decades ago (along with rooting avocado pits), but it usually doesn't work. Unless you're willing to keep changing the water, the sawn-off bit of pineapple just rots and turns stinky.

Colorful capsicums

These are sassy little versions of the green and red peppers we buy at the supermarket. Buy them as started plants in the fall or winter, with their fruit already formed. The variety that's sold everywhere is a species of *C. annuum* and is also known as Christmas pepper. The peppers may be white, scarlet, orange, bright yellow, purple or a mix of purple and white. (Try harmonizing them with your decor.) Capsicums like bright light for at least three hours a day, and they don't mind sitting in direct sunshine. The fruit will last anywhere from two to three months, depending upon how warm your room is (they prefer it on the cool side, from 55 to 60°F/13 to 15°C). When the peppers have wrinkled and dropped off, toss the plants out without feeling guilty. Only pros know how to get them to fruit again, so they aren't worth saving.

One perfect orchid

The stark shape of many orchids is ideal for anyone into the minimalist style of home decor. In fact, one perfect orchid (preferably white) sitting on a glass or stainless steel coffee table is a breathtaking sight.

Orchids used to be the private domain of mad collectors. They were expensive, required complex lighting systems, and were extremely difficult to grow. But now you can find orchids for sale everywhere, and some of the newly developed hybrids are said to thrive on neglect. Pick a *Phalaenopsis* variety. Its blooms are gorgeous and will often last for weeks. Orchids require bright, filtered light, a warm room where the temperature doesn't drop below 68°F (20°C), and *lots* of humidity. If you really get into orchids, you'll need to buy a humidifier (see pages 100–101) and some indoor lights (see page 69).

Growing Herbs Indoors

Decorating magazines tout the pleasures of keeping a few fresh herbs on hand to use in cooking. They often feature photographs of well-known favorites—such as basil, chives, and parsley—planted in cute pots and strategically positioned on the window ledges of gleaming kitchens. Accompanying the photos there's usually some purple prose exclaiming how glorious—and easy—it is to grow herbs in this way. "Then you just snip Mother Nature's gifts into salads and soups," the writers gush.

This is an appealing idea, especially when there's lots of snow and a howling gale outside. However, the decorating divas are deluding us. Big time. Growing herbs indoors is not as easy as it sounds, particularly during the winter months in northern climates. That's because most culinary herbs originate in the Mediterranean (or farther south, in Africa and across the ocean in Mexico).They are not like leafy houseplants, which often tolerate poor lighting conditions because they come from tropical jungles, where there's a mix of shade and sun. Herbs are used to growing on open hills, mountainsides, valleys, and coastal areas. They require *lots* of sunshine—and in most houses, condos, and apartments, there simply isn't enough for them to thrive.

How to have healthy herbs

Do

✓ Check which way your windows face. You should have a southern aspect—and be able to position herbs where they will receive at least six hours of direct sunshine a day. (A western aspect may work, provided there's nothing outside to block the flow of light.)

✓ Use grow lights if you can't provide sufficient natural light (see page 69).

✓ Use a lightweight container growing mix (not garden soil). Mix a scoop of gritty sand into it, if you can (see page 106). Most herbs seem to love a bit of sand.

✓ Trim herbs regularly. Avoid letting their stems get spindly and weak. You can keep whacking herbs back, and they will respond by sending out new growth.

> ## Hot tip
> "Herbs need lots of light. If you have herbs of different heights under indoor lights, raise the smaller ones up on upturned flowerpots or bricks. They should all be the same distance from the lights."
> —Mary-Fran McQuade, herb expert

Don't

✗ Overwater herbs. Most of them prefer to be kept on the dry side. Let the top get crusty-looking before you water.

✗ Fertilize. Generally speaking, most herbs don't need to be boosted with plant food—and they do better without it.

✗ Grow several different herbs together in one container. Garden centers often sell these ready-made "herb gardens." While they look nice at the outset, they will wind up looking messy indoors, because the herbs have different growing schedules. It's a particularly bad idea to mix perennials (such as oregano) with annuals (such as marjoram or basil).

Basil can't be beat

The Greek name for basil is *basileus*, meaning "king," and many people consider this herb tops in the flavor department. Basil is also, conveniently, one of the best herbs to grow in pots; planted in the garden, it tends to get attacked by bugs (particularly aphids). Another plus is that, indoors, basil is a snap to start from seed (see page 66). However, if you want quick results, started basil plants are sold everywhere in spring. Replant these in bigger pots. You can also group several basil plants together in one container.

There's a bewildering variety of basils available nowadays—more than thirty-five at last count—and they're fun to experiment with. Some have that traditional "licorice" flavor, others are quite spicy and don't even taste like basil. A few, like East Indian basil (*Ocimum gratissimum*) grow into large-leafed houseplants. Mammoth basil (*O. basilicum*) produces leaves the size of your hand that are surprisingly tasty. The purple varieties, such as *O. basilicum* 'Purple Delight' or 'Purple Ruffles,' are good choices if you want decorative herbs—they look particularly pretty mixed with annuals on a balcony in summertime. If you're a beginner, stick to plain old sweet basil (*O. basilicum*), which is still hard to beat for flavor. If you want to save it and dry it, get the bush type (*O. basilicum minimum*), as its tiny leaves are easy to strip off the stems.

Basil is an annual, so it won't usually last long indoors. Don't be afraid to keep cutting off the leaves and stems; otherwise, it will get too long and leggy. Nip off the flower heads, too (they'll keep trying to form), or the plant will produce few leaves. If you're bringing basil in from outside, carry on snipping until the stem gets woody-looking and tough. That's the time to throw the plant out. It's not worth trying to keep an old basil plant going over the winter. Buy a new one instead.

Caution: basil is highly susceptible to fusarium wilt (a fungus carried in the soil). If your plant suddenly goes droopy and dies, it has contracted this nasty disease. When that happens, throw the plant out immediately, wrapped in a plastic bag. Don't leave it sitting around to contaminate other plants. Throw the soil out, too, and scrub out the pot with bleach and water (see page 104).

Fusarium wilt has become such a huge problem, it's estimated that over half the world's supply of basil seeds has become infected. Look for a new basil variety called 'Green Gate,' which is resistant to fusarium wilt, but unfortunately not yet widely available.

Chives are cheering

Ah, the pleasure of snipping fresh chives into soups! This can actually be accomplished, just as the decorating divas claim, because chives are virtually indestructible, even indoors. The only problem with them is that their roots quickly become too

If you have chives in your garden, here's an easy, cheap way to import the taste indoors during the winter. In the fall, cut an established chive plant back to its nubbins. Then dig it up, hack a section of the roots off, pot this lump up, and bring it in. It will soon send up lots of nice new shoots. Cooks in Germany make a ritual of doing this with their chive plants every fall.

tightly packed in a container. When that happens, the plant stops producing leaves and looks awful.

To avoid messy-looking chive plants, try growing garlic chives (*Allium tuberosum*). These produce flat, wide leaves that are not as prolific as those of regular chives—but just as tasty—and they won't resemble a haystack as they age.

Or look for a variety called Grolau chives (*A. schoenoprasum* 'Grolau'). It was developed in Switzerland especially for pot culture indoors.

Don't parch your parsley

Probably the world's most popular herb, parsley (*Petroselinum crispum*) can work indoors, provided it receives plenty of water. Keep the soil moist. If it's allowed to dry out, those crinkly leaves get bitter-tasting. Although this herb is a biennial (and sometimes a perennial in warmer climates), it's best to buy new started plants every spring. Older plants are tough, will produce less leaves, and have too strong a flavor. If you're bringing a parsley plant in from the garden in fall, snip all the leaves off before you pot it up.

There are two kinds of parsley: curly and plainleaf. The curly kind is seen everywhere and is great for garnishing food. Look for a new variety called 'Afrodite'; its finely curled, moss-like leaves are very decorative. The plainleaf kind (also called flat-leaf or Italian parsley) is preferred by cooks because it's supposed to have more flavor—although that's debatable.

Don't try growing parsley from seed. It is very difficult to germinate.

Moving rosemary is risky

Although it grows wild on islands in Greece, rosemary (*Rosmarinus officinalis*) will cope well indoors, provided it stays in the same spot. In fact, some experts say it's best to keep this particular herb inside year-round and not move it outdoors for the summer. Rosemary is very sensitive to being moved. Horticultural honchos call it an "inefficient high-light plant," which means it doesn't absorb light well and reacts badly to changes in lighting conditions. If you suddenly shift rosemary from a sunny spot outdoors to a window ledge indoors, it will likely throw a hissy fit— even if the window ledge gets lots of sun.

Gardening hotlines are deluged every fall with calls about thriving rosemary bushes that have given up the ghost after being moved inside at the end of summer. Puzzled owners complain that the plant's leaves are shedding (usually from the bottom up), or it's getting mildew, or it's drying up, or "it's doing fine one day, then dead the next." The problem can usually be traced to insufficient light or a sudden change in light.

If you're bringing rosemary indoors, make the adjustment process gradual. Prune it back, early in fall. Then put it in a spot where it gets less sun than in its accustomed position. Move it again, to a shadier spot, a few weeks later. Finally, take it indoors before the frost hits. Obviously it's easier to do this if you stick to growing rosemary in a container rather than planting it in the garden.

If you grow rosemary indoors all year, make sure it gets the sunniest spot you can find—and stays there. Period.

Be savvy with sage

Sage is a so-so plant indoors. The regular variety, garden sage (*Salvia officinalis*), tends to grow too big in containers. Its stems get woody, and once it becomes pot-bound, the plant will stop producing lots of leaves.

Try the dwarf variety, *S. officinalis* 'Dwarf', which was developed for use in rock gardens. It often adapts well to containers. Purple sage (*S. officinalis* 'Purpurea') and tricolor sage (*S. officinalis* 'Tricolor') also work, and both have very decorative leaves.

If you can get your hands on hard-to-find Bergarrten sage (*S. officinalis* 'Bergarrten'), it may be the best bet. Developed in Germany, it produces big, gray-blue silvery leaves. But this one doesn't grow too tall—and it's a very pretty plant.

Grow sweet marjoram from seed

This herb is an annual relative of oregano and has a similar taste. It works better indoors than oregano (see below) and produces nice little leaves that are great for snipping off in the kitchen. It won't become root-bound in a container. However, started marjoram plants can be hard to find, particularly in fall, because oregano habitually hogs the limelight. If you want some marjoram indoors, try starting it from seed in a container (see page 73). Look for a variety called *Origanum majorana* 'Kitchen Wonder,' which was developed especially for pot culture.

Tarragon can be touchy

Some cooks wouldn't be without tarragon because of its highly distinctive taste. (Others hate it, but that's another story.) This herb can do well indoors, but likes to be subjected to a period of cool temperatures. If you want to haul a potted tarragon plant in from outside, wait till *after* the frost has hit. Let the

Aloes are indispensable

No kitchen is complete without an Aloe vera (*Aloe barbadensis*). This well-known succulent, originally from South Africa, is a famous—and very effective—antidote to burns. If you get burned while cooking, slice off a piece of aloe, cut it open length-wise, and place the jelly-like interior on the burn. It instantly takes the pain away. (Be careful of a yellow juice between the skin and the jelly. See page 130.) There are also several varieties of aloes in the crassula family of fleshy plants. They're all easy to grow in bright light. One kind produces bunches of smallish spiky leaves that keep multiplying in rosettes. Look for the bigger version, which sends up a single stalk and big, pointed leaves with jagged edges that look prickly (but aren't). It's more attractive and won't crowd itself out of a container the way the bunching variety does. If your aloe plant is old enough, it may send up a stalk topped by a dense cluster of blossoms in red, yellow, or white—a nice bonus, especially in winter.

pot freeze a bit on the surface (don't wait till it's frozen solid, however), then cut off the foliage and bring the pot indoors. This will trick the plant into thinking it has gone through winter, and it should start sending out new shoots.

Tarragon can't be started from seed. The only variety worth growing is called French tarragon (*Artemisia dracunculus sativa*), and it's all grown from cuttings. Buy a started plant. Don't even think of buying its Russian relative (*A. dracunculus dracunculoides*) to use in the kitchen. It's coarse-leafed, grows tall, and tastes lousy.

Herbs that can be a hassle indoors

❀ **Dill *(Anethum graveolens):*** Produces pretty, lacy foliage, but grows too tall and spindly. Pull the plants out when they reach 6 inches (15 cm) high.

❀ **Lovage *(Levisticum officinale):*** A trendy herb. Tastes great in soups and stews, but grows far too big for containers.

❀ **Mint *(Mentha):*** There's an amazing variety of mints on the market nowadays. You can find everything from French banana mint (which really does smell of bananas) to Hillary's sweet lemon mint (named after former First Lady Hillary Clinton). The problem with virtually all mints is that they're spreaders, with roots that keep crawling everywhere. Grown in a garden, they have room to expand, but indoors, in containers, they quickly get root-bound and then stop producing leaves. If you want mint, buy a new, small plant—and be prepared to dig it up and divide it when it gets too big for its britches.

❀ **Oregano *(Origanum):*** Related to mint. The same drawbacks apply.

❀ **Thyme *(Thymus):*** Thyme is a spreader, too, although not as problematic as mint. Indoors, try a pint-sized version of true English thyme, *T. vulgaris* 'Compactus.' It has the same wonderful fragrance and flavor as its garden variety relative. Avoid lemon thyme (*T.* x *citriodorus*). It's a lovely plant that's great to use in cooking, but it spreads like crazy. In a container indoors, its roots will soon get too cramped.

Novelty herbs to try

🌸 **Broadleaf thyme (Coleus amboinicus):** Not really a thyme, but a relative of a popular container plant with striking foliage. Produces large, pretty, greenish-gray leaves edged with white. It looks great in a container, and you can eat it. It's treated as thyme in Jamaica.

🌸 **Cuban oregano (Plectranthus sp.):** Not really an oregano, and not edible. But it makes a pretty houseplant, and if you brush up against it, a pleasant fragrance is released. It produces little fleshy leaves that are rounded, with toothy markings on the edges.

🌸 **Eucalyptus (Eucalyptus globulus):** Grows into enormous trees in Australia. Eucalyptus deserves to be better known as a houseplant because it's decorative and a wonderful room deodorizer. If you boil some dried eucalyptus leaves in water on the stove, they will get rid of an unpleasant smell quickly. The leaves of lemon eucalyptus (*E. citriodora*) have a nose-tickling fragrance and are the "secret" ingredient in botanical non-DEET insect repellents.

🌸 **Mexican oregano (Lippia graveolens):** Visit Mexico, and you'll see this sold in bunches as "oregano" in markets. It has a distinctive taste but isn't really oregano. Indoors, it will grow into a pretty little tree, provided it's pruned.

🌸 **Vietnamese coriander (Polygonum odoratum):** Regular coriander (*C. sativum*) is a hassle to grow because it goes to seed quickly. But this herb, which is related to a common weed that grows in North America, gives the same zip to Mexican and Oriental dishes. It also makes a good potted plant. Snip off a few leaves at a time (its flavor is strong) to use in cooking.

Hot tip

"Try tea tree *(Melaleuca alternifolia)*. It comes from Australia and is easy to grow. I love mine because it looks pretty but is also a powerful antiseptic. If you cut yourself and lay a leaf of tea tree on the wound, it will heal right away."
—*Sandra Henry, herb expert*

Amaryllis: The World's Best Winter Pick-Me-Up

Some people cope with the long, cold months by jumping on planes to Florida. Others go skiing. If you're disinclined to do either (or you can't afford it), pot up an amaryllis bulb and watch it grow. This tropical flower is the best—and cheapest—antidote to the winter blahs that city folk can buy.

Amaryllis bulbs are sold everywhere nowadays—in supermarkets, big box stores, neighborhood greengrocers, as well as establishments that cater to gardeners. As a result, some people huff that these remarkable plants have become too "ordinary" to bother with. Ignore the hoity horts. It's certainly true that there's no novelty factor to growing amaryllis anymore (unlike back in the 18th century, when the bulbs were highly prized by Empress Josephine, wife of Napoleon Bonaparte, and third U.S. President Thomas Jefferson), but they still have six stupendous points in their favor:

❀ They are perhaps the easiest flowering plant to grow indoors.
❀ They produce some of the biggest and most spectacular blooms you'll ever see, and their blooms last longer than those of many other tropical plants.
❀ Their strappy green leaves look decorative when flowers have finished blooming.
❀ You can now find dozens of amaryllis varieties, in many shapes, sizes, and colors.
❀ Amaryllis bulbs will last for years—and with a bit of extra effort, you can coax them into blooming again.
❀ They are seldom affected by bugs and diseases.

Where do amaryllis come from?

Amaryllis have their origins (like many tropical indoor plants) in South America, and their correct botanical name is the rather weird-sounding *Hippeastrum*. They wound up being called "amaryllis" because of a blooper that began with Linnaeus, the Swedish horticultural honcho who devised a system for naming plants in the 18th century. (Linnaeus made a similar goof with geraniums, which should correctly be called "pelargoniums.") No matter. Few people call these plants by their proper name. You'll see them labeled as "amaryllis" everywhere.

Amaryllis still grow wild in some parts of South America, and if you take a winter holiday in Mexico, you can sometimes spot their glorious, trumpet-shaped blooms flourishing in people's gardens. However, the amaryllis we buy in North America (packed in boxes or simply sold as big, bare bulbs, with labels around their necks and a mess of roots sticking out the bottom) come mostly from Holland. South Africa is also an increasing supplier of amaryllis bulbs. This plant is now so widely known and admired around the world, new varieties are constantly being developed by plant hybridizers in countries as diverse as Australia, Israel, and India.

Commercial growers in the Netherlands cultivate amaryllis in huge heated greenhouses. They plant offsets (baby bulbs that sprout from the sides of a main bulb) from October to March. Then they harvest them by hand—a time-consuming process, with tight deadlines—during the summer months. The bulbs are quickly dried, cured, and sorted, ready to be shipped abroad in time for early fall—the time of year when we northern gardeners snap them up so they can cheer us during the dog days of winter.

Buying amaryllis bulbs

No more boring red blooms

Amaryllis used to come in just one color: red. It was certainly an exciting shade of scarlet, and the trumpet-shaped blooms were as big and loud as a jazz band. But, oh dear, the uniformity. That was one reason many people started to turn up their noses at this plant.

The predictability of amaryllis has been banished by growers in recent years, however. There's now a huge array available in many sizes, shapes, and colors. You can still find enormous, classic red blooms, four to a stalk, if you're so inclined, but there are many other types of blossoms. Some petals have a pointier appearance. Other flowers are double, with such elaborate layers of petals that one stalk is enough to make a bouquet. 'Amputo' resembles a frilly-petaled Easter lily, and *H. papilio*, or butterfly, is as intriguing as an orchid. A few amaryllis make a more modest impact, sending up clusters of small blooms rather than a huge stalk with a dazzling topknot.

Colors have changed for the better too. There are still many shades of red—from crimson to fire engine—but amaryllis now come in brilliant orange, shocking pink, salmon, peach, apricot, white, and striped or blotchy combinations of those colors. Growers are trying hard to produce a purple amaryllis, but so far these specimens, despite names like 'Lilac Wonder,' tend to be on the pinkish side.

Amaryllis is a show-off plant, and size counts. Big bulbs cost more (expect to pay up to $18 apiece for some varieties), but they're worth it. The King Kong types produce whacking great blooms that will take your breath away in the middle of winter.

Monster bulbs are the size of a tennis ball, or larger. Look for them as soon as amaryllis go on sale in September. Aficionados snap up the best picks early.

If you want to get adventurous with amaryllis, investigate the offerings of a bulb specialist. Supermarkets and other mass market stores usually stock only the plain-Jane versions. And check the labels; they should tell you how big to expect the blooms to grow.

Size matters

- ❀ "Giant," "Jumbo," and "Superbulb" are big, older bulbs, about 13 to 14 inches (34 to 36 cm) in diameter. They will produce whopper blooms on multiple flower stalks, and will probably have a long blooming period. These are usually the most expensive.
- ❀ "Standard" bulbs are smaller, usually 10 to 11 inches (26 to 28 cm) in diameter. Amaryllis sold in gift boxes are usually standards.
- ❀ "Miniature" bulbs produce multiple small blooms on several stems. They are charming, and very fashionable, but don't buy them if you want in-your-face blooms.

Appearances can be deceptive

Don't take too much notice of the photos of amaryllis that appear on plant labels and in catalogs. Often, the colors shown aren't anything like the real McCoy. Blooms may look scarlet in the illustration, but may prove to be an entirely different red once the plant flowers. Or the fat pink stripes you anticipated may turn out to be tangerine-colored instead.

This happens because it's notoriously difficult to capture the extraordinary hues of amaryllis in photographs (if you try it, use a very slow film—ISO 100). Also, no two bulbs will produce flowers that are identical. But who cares? Winding up with amaryllis that don't look exactly as expected is all part of the fun.

Some amaryllis varieties to try

- ❀ **'Apple Blossom':** A perennial favorite. Grows 15 to 18 inches (38 to 46 cm) tall and has huge, somewhat transparent white flowers, with delicate stripes of pale pink. It's a fast mover, and will strut its stuff within six weeks of planting.

- **'Dancing Queen':** Like the Abba song of the same name, this one's a crowd pleaser. Blooms aren't huge (they usually reach about 6 inches/15 cm) but they sure are sassy. You get masses of double petals striped in orangey-red and white. 'Dancing Queen' is tall, reaching about 24 inches (60 cm), and takes at least six weeks to come into bloom.

- **'Green Goddess':** If you find big, in-your-face red blooms overpowering, try this variety. The flowers are pristine white with lime green in the center, and it's not a "toppler" because stems grow only about 15 inches (38 cm) high, with blooms measuring about 6 inches (15 cm). Be warned, though: the goddess takes her sweet time, and you can wait up to four months for flowers.

- **'Lady Jane':** This showy but not too tarty variety grows 12 to 14 inches (30 to 36 cm) tall. Its big, double flowers in salmon pink, with stripes of vermilion and white, bloom in about eight weeks.

- **'Las Vegas':** A flashy showgirl. Fairly leggy, reaching about 16 inches (40 cm), with shocking pink flowers striped in white. Wonderful in the window on a grim January day. After it blooms, leaves sprout energetically, often extending to 3 feet (1 m). Takes only six weeks to bloom.

- **'Lemon Lime':** This variety produces lots of smallish blooms, no bigger than 5 inches (13 cm), that are pale yellowy-green streaked with brighter green. Grows up to 20 inches (50 cm) tall, and takes up to eight weeks to flower.

- **'Pamela':** Miniature, modest and ladylike, 'Pamela' produces lots of small bright red flowers no more than 5 inches (13 cm) across. Grows about 12 inches (30 cm) tall. Miss Pammy takes up to twelve weeks to make her debut, but she's a charming change from her brasher cousins.

- ***H. papilio*, or butterfly:** This extraordinary amaryllis looks rather like an orchid or, yes, a butterfly. It produces prolific, average-sized flowers, on stems 12 to 14 inches (30 to 36 cm) tall. Petals are striped in reddish-maroon and pale green, turning to vivid lime in the center. It blooms in about eight weeks. Caution: some people find this one difficult to grow.

❀ **'Picotee':** A fave of many gardeners, its name is taken from the French word *picoté*, which means "marked with tiny points." Its heart-stoppingly beautiful white single flowers are large and elegantly contoured and have lime green centers. But what really makes 'Picotee' a knockout is that every petal is rimmed in salmon pink. One of the tallest varieties at 24 inches (60 cm), it takes about seven weeks to bloom.

How to grow amaryllis successfully

Do

✓ Buy big bulbs. Generally speaking, the bigger the bulb, the bigger the flowers.

✓ Examine bulbs carefully before buying. Make sure there aren't any reddish-brown blotches on their sides. (This may indicate disease.)

✓ Open up boxed bulbs quickly. Often there's an anemic-looking flower spike poking up inside—or pushing its way out of the box. *Don't cut this spike off*, even if it's spindly or a bit damaged. Once you plant it, the spike will turn green and recover remarkably quickly.

✓ Lay bulbs in a dish and spread out the roots gently (after cutting off any dried-up bits). Then cover roots (but not the bulbs) with an inch or so of lukewarm water. Leave for a few hours, or overnight. Experienced gardeners do this to "jump-start" the bulbs.

✓ Plant bulbs in clay flowerpots, not light plastic ones. Amaryllis plants can get huge, and you need a heavy pot to hold them. Clay will also wick moisture away from the bulbs, which don't like getting waterlogged. For a change, try rectangular containers rather than the classic circular kind. Square is trendy right now.

✓ Buy a mix that contains peat moss and vermiculite (Pro-Mix works well). If you can add a handful of coarse sand (get it at a builder's yard), your amaryllis will thank you, and will probably last longer, because sand improves drainage.

✓ Put a mound of mix in the bottom of the pot, spread out the roots, and position the bulb on top, trying not to damage the roots.

✓ Tuck more mix firmly in around the bulb and roots with your fingers. Fill to within half an inch (1.2 cm) of the pot's rim.

✓ Make sure the top third of the bulb is poking above the surface of the soil. If it's too low or too high, tip it out of the pot and start again.

✓ Add decorative gravel or moss on top if you want, but it's not strictly necessary.

✓ Give the pot a really good drink with tepid water. Pour the water around the bulb, not onto it.

✓ Put the pot in a brightly lit room that's about 75°F (24°C) in the day and 65°F (18°C) at night. If you can't provide these temperatures, don't worry. Amaryllis are very adaptable. Water occasionally, but don't soak.

✓ Watch—and be amazed—as a big bud noses its way out from the center of the bulb, followed by a long green flower stalk.

✓ When this stem has reached its full height, and the flowers start unfurling, move the pot to a cooler spot out of direct sunshine. The blooms will last longer.

✓ To stop the plant from leaning like the Tower of Pisa, turn it toward the light every day or so.

✓ Water sparingly, but don't fertilize.

Don't

✗ Be disappointed if you can't find big bulbs. Smaller varieties of amaryllis are all the rage now—and virtually every amaryllis bulb, whatever its size, will produce respectable-looking blooms.

✗ Worry if the bulbs' papery skin is peeling off. This is normal and won't affect their ability to grow.

✗ Select any amaryllis bulb that feels soft and squashy. They should be firm.

✗ Buy amaryllis that come in boxes with small plastic pots as part of the package. These pots are invariably too light and flimsy to cope with the weight of burgeoning amaryllis stems. The plants will topple over and become a hassle.

✗ Use big pots. Amaryllis prefer cramped quarters. Hold bulbs upright inside their intended pots before you plant. Check that there's no more than an inch or so of space between the bulb's outer perimeter and the pot sides.

✗ Use shallow pots. The kind of bulb pans used for tulips and narcissus are a no-no. Amaryllis need more room than spring bulbs because they are evergreen tropical plants and develop much longer roots. (Tip an amaryllis out of its pot at the end of the summer and take a peek at its tightly packed roots. They are often amazingly long, twirling round and round the sides of the pot.)

✗ Fertilize during the blooming period.

> **Hot tip**
> "Try growing several amaryllis together, in one container. People usually plant them in individual pots. But several flower spikes coming up at once are fascinating to watch in winter."
> —*Carol Cowan, condo amaryllis fan*

From bulb to bloom: How long?

Be patient with your amaryllis. They can take up to three months after you've planted them to produce flowers. But most strut their stuff far earlier than that. In the typical house, condo, or apartment, you can expect to see blooms within six to eight weeks. And if they are sitting in a room where the central heating is cranked up, they'll often send up their long green hollow stems, topped by a big bulbous bud, at amazing speed.

Watching amaryllis develop is magical. The stems may grow as much as an inch a day; some people even swear they can see this growth happening. However, a cool room, where the plant can develop at a slower speed, is preferable. Blooms will last longer too. Blooming times—and the length of bloom—vary depending upon the variety of amaryllis you plant and the temperature. Some will have longer growing cycles and blooming periods than others. But once they open, most of the spectacular, trumpet-shaped blooms will last at least a week and often two. They usually bloom sequentially— that is, one bloom will unfurl, then another.

Busty beauties need support

The drawback to those biggie amaryllis bulbs is that they produce such huge flower heads the whole plant can topple over. If this looks imminent, prop stems up with either

- ❀ a bamboo stake and a length of raffia, wrapped gently in a figure-eight fashion around the stem; or
- ❀ dogwood or corkscrew hazel branches (sold at florists). Pink, crimson, and white amaryllis flowers look particularly delightful offset by dogwood stems, which are purplish-red.

Whatever you use as a stake, pick something unobtrusive that's not going to compete with the flowers, and poke it gently into the pot without scraping scales off the edge of the bulb or disturbing roots.

After amaryllis finish blooming

Some bulbs, particularly the jumbo ones, will send up two—and, on rare occasions, three—flower stalks. Be thankful, not puzzled, when this happens. When all the flowers on these stalks are completely finished, cut the stalks off 2 inches (5 cm) above the top of the bulb.

Long, strappy green leaves should have started pushing up out of the bulb by this time. This foliage sometimes puts in an appearance before flower stalks, but it's usually the other way around. If the greenery grows first, don't fret. If no flower stalk appears at all, however, you've got problems. It means this particular bulb did not build up sufficient energy in its interior to send up a flower stalk (see the following section). If it's a newly bought amaryllis bulb that you just potted up, you have a right to contact the store and ask for your money back.

Let leaves develop all summer. They look as decorative as any other houseplant, and some will grow more than 2 feet (60 cm) long. Put the pots outside in a shady area if you can (but they are also fine kept indoors). Fertilize every couple of weeks with a plant food in a formula like 20-20-20. Try not to let the pots dry out. When they are planted in small pots, they get thirsty remarkably quickly.

Getting bulbs to bloom again

Heated arguments are waged in gardening magazines about the right way to do this. Some experts insist that, like spring bulbs, amaryllis need a period without any light to go dormant before gearing themselves up for the arduous task of sending out flower stalks again. They bring their amaryllis bulbs indoors in fall, stop watering, and let the foliage wither and shrivel in a completely dark, cool spot for up to three months. Then they bring them out into the light, cut off the dried-up leaves, add fresh growing mix on top of the pot, and wait for new blooms.

> ## Hot tip
> "A lot of people claim you have to put amaryllis in the dark in the autumn to get it to bloom again. That's absolute nonsense. I just put mine in a cooler part of my house and leave the window open."
> —*Veronica Read,*
> *British amaryllis expert*

Other experts pooh-pooh this procedure and argue that it actually damages the plants because amaryllis are tropical and, in their natural habitat, they carry on growing all year round, unlike spring bulbs such as tulips, which originate in the mountains of Asia. (Their roots die off every year, then are replaced by new ones the next.) These experts simply place pots in a cool, north-facing room or basement to "rest," and keep the temperature at about 50°F (10°C). They continue to water (but not fertilize) the plants as usual. After ten to twelve weeks, they bring them out into a warmer location.

The choice is yours. Amaryllis are remarkably tough plants and seem to cope well with whatever we do to them. Some gardeners even advocate doing nothing at all. "Just leave them as is, in pots, carry on watering, and let the leafy growth develop," they suggest. "The plants will bloom again unaided, at unexpected times, like later in the summer."

Well, yes, that *can* happen. However, gardening gurus do seem to agree that a period of "chilling out" (when the plant has an opportunity to take a breather in a cooler location) is required to coax bulbs to produce those spectacular blooms again the following winter. If that's your goal, follow the experts' recommendations.

And if you don't want to be bothered with any of this rigmarole, just throw the plants out in the fall, clean their pots, and buy new bulbs.

Making amaryllis multiply

Some amaryllis bulbs will last and last. Keep treating yours to the three-step formula—bloom; leafy growth, boosted with fertilizer (essential to bring energy back into the bulb); then a cool rest period—and they may carry on flourishing for years in the same pot. Some gardeners report owning amaryllis that are nine years old and still produce beautiful blooms every winter. Eventually, these "mother" bulbs, if they are comfortable in their surroundings, will probably start giving birth.

Small bulblets may develop on their sides, usually after at least three years. Pry these offsets or "daughters" off carefully and pot them up in their own containers. They'll grow into big bulbs in a few more seasons.

Momma bulbs, however, will ultimately become exhausted by the business of reproducing—or just plain tired of living. When they stop sending out blooms and start shrinking (the bulbs will also usually feel soft and squashy, with exterior layers that turn brown and flaky), it's time to pitch them out.

> ## Hot tip
> "Try growing amaryllis in water. Use the kind of vase that some people grow hyacinths in. It has a special basin at the top that holds the bulb. Amaryllis grow more slowly in water, but it's fun to watch the roots developing."
> —*Anne Travis, condo gardener*

What ails amaryllis?

Not much, thankfully. One great plus of these plants is that they are seldom attacked by bugs and diseases. Even so, it's important to grow them in an area that's well ventilated and not too hot and dry. In centrally heated homes, they can attract the usual plethora of pesky nuisances such as mealy bugs and fungus gnats (see page 119). But amaryllis are certainly not as prone to these pests as many other houseplants.

One affliction to watch out for, however, is a horror called *Stagonospora curtisii*, commonly known by a host of names: red blotch, fire spot, red leaf spot, or leaf scorch. This disease is, unfortunately, fairly common in amaryllis. If you notice flowers and/or stalks developing red patches, red stripes, or raised cankers, your amaryllis has been infected. Leaves can sometimes look quite attractive with red blotch—they may become outlined in scarlet (with bumpy bits in the red part) or start twisting sideways in bizarre shapes. But there's nothing attractive about this disease. It tends to develop during hot, humid summers when amaryllis sit outside, and it's a killer. Eventually, the bulb will shrivel and give up the ghost.

Throw out affected plants (and their soil) and scrub the containers thoroughly (see page 104). Act quickly once you notice red blotch. If left to its own devices, it will spread and start to disfigure your other amaryllis too. Make sure not to crowd pots too close together.

Buying cut amaryllis flowers from florists

Cut amaryllis flowers are a hot trend. They're pricey (expect to pay up to $25 for each flower stem), but more and more florists are importing cut amaryllis from Dutch, South African, and Israeli growers because they look so fantastic in floral arrangements.

Pick amaryllis stems with buds, not open flowers. Limit your bouquet to one variety: amaryllis in too many different colors and shapes will compete with one another. Buds may look a bit pinched because they are shipped and stored in very cool conditions. To get them to perk up, fill their huge hollow stems with tepid water as soon as you get home. Otherwise, your pricey purchases will wither and fade far too quickly. To do this:

- Cut about an inch (2.5 cm) off the bottom of each stem, on a 45-degree angle, using a sharp knife or florist's scissors.
- Upend the stems and pour water into them, using a watering can with a small spout or a plastic kitchen funnel.
- Plug the stems with a piece of cotton, or put your finger over the ends, then turn them right side up and plunk them into a vase already filled with water.
- Display in a cool location, if possible. Blooms should last a week or more if you take the trouble to do this.

Get Clued In to Clivias

Once you become accustomed to growing user-friendly amaryllis (see page 38), they may start to seem a bit ho-hum. That's when it's time to move on to a new challenge: cultivating clivias. These are bulbous tropical plants that belong to the amaryllis family. But because clivias are stingier with their blooms than their workhorse cousins—and cost much more—they have great snob appeal.

Some folks value clivias as highly as rare orchids. If you tell other gardeners you have a clivia at home, they will probably raise their eyebrows and be instantly impressed. Then, in their next breath, they will ask you, "Has it bloomed?" This question comes up in conversation about clivias because they are definitely the divas of the amaryllis family. Although gardening books often say that clivias are easy to bring into flower, they can be prone to inexplicable sulks. Some may sit in their pots for years and refuse to bloom, while others will send forth flowers with no problem. Nurseries often get calls from anxious owners of non-performing clivias. That's hardly surprising when you consider that an established specimen of this striking plant with stupendous blooms can set you back a hefty $50 (or even a few thousand bucks, if you hanker after a really rare variety).

Is that CLIH-vee-a or CLY-vee-a?

In North America we pronounce "clivia" to rhyme with "trivia," but that's actually wrong. Clivias were discovered in South Africa back in 1823 and named after Lady Charlotte Florentina Clive, Duchess of Northumberland, who was the

PRETTY TOGETHER: Grouping indoor plants conserves moisture. Urn plant, Aechmea fasciata *(left), needs humidity and warmth to flower. The leaves of crotons (center) are colorful, but watch for spider mites!*

*KITTY CANDY: Cats love nibbling on spider plants (*Chlorophytum comosum*). Let them—it doesn't really hurt the plant, or the cat.*

EYE-CATCHING: A pineapple plant is easy and fun.

COOK'S DELIGHT *(above): Chive plants* (Allium) *tend to get straggly indoors, but they're still great for snipping into soups. Dig up a chunk of chives from the garden in fall and pot it up on a sunny window ledge for the winter.*

TINY PERFECT GEMS: *It's hard to grow tomatoes indoors. Buy a started plant, with fruit already formed. They'll ripen nicely in a sunny, warm spot. Cherry tomatoes work best, and they look terrific cascading from a container.*

COLOR CASCADE
(above): Amaryllis
'Las Vegas' (top left)
produces spectacular
flowers. So do forced
double tulips 'Angelique'
and (below 'Las Vegas')
amaryllis 'Papilio
Butterfly,' which resem-
bles an orchid. All
amaryllis are a snap to
grow. When flowers
have finished, cut the
long stalk off 2 inches
(5 cm) from the base.

NOT FOR BEGINNERS:
The flower heads of
Clivia miniata, *a relative*
of amaryllis, are a
gorgeous mix of tangerine,
salmon, and orange. But
it's a huffy plant that
often refuses to bloom.

WORTH TRYING: Not all African violets (Saintpaulia) are that boring purple. This one, 'Chicago Flair,' produces big flowers and unusual, frilly leaves in dark green and white.

PRISTINE BEAUTY: Buy Easter lilies (Lilium longiflorum) with lots of buds. Plant them in the garden afterwards if you have space. They may bloom again in late summer.

SIMPLE SEEDING: Get a plastic seed tray with a see-through lid. It makes starting plants easy. Tip seeds slowly out of packets. A plastic dibber is useful for making holes.

CUTTINGS: Taking cuttings from your existing plants is a cheap way to get more plants. Coleus cuttings are very easy to start in old film canisters.

ALWAYS WEAR GLOVES: Hyacinths (front) are easier to force than tulips (rear) but touching their bulbs can cause a nasty rash.

WINTER GLOW: Nothing beats amaryllis 'Picotee' (left), dainty daffodils, and hyacinth 'Blue Jacket' when there's lots of white stuff outside.

NARCISSUS ARE NIFTY: Narcissus force well indoors, but pick smaller varieties such as 'Jack Snipe.' NETHERLANDS FLOWER BULB INFORMATION CENTRE

PRETTY PAPERWHITES: Easy to grow in water, but beware: their strong fragrance can cause headaches! NETHERLANDS FLOWER BULB INFORMATION CENTRE

HEAVENLY HYACINTHS:
They're the best spring
bulbs for beginners to
force. This shocking pink
variety is called 'Jan
Bos,' but they come in
many shades of pink,
blue, purple, and white.
NETHERLANDS FLOWER BULB
INFORMATION CENTRE

TIME FOR TULIPS:
Tulips are terrific, but
can be difficult to force.
Pick varieties with short,
sturdy stems, such as
'Pinocchio,' and don't
leave them in the dark
too long. NETHERLANDS FLOWER
BULB INFORMATION CENTRE

EASY DOES IT: Overwatering kills more houseplants than anything else. Check for dryness by touching the top of the soil. If it feels dry, water. If it's damp, don't. A humidifier is helpful too.

BYE-BYE, BUGS: Always give houseplants a bath before bringing them indoors in the fall. Dip the entire pot in a pail of soapy water, then rinse under the tap. This kills critters and their eggs.

first person to coax them into bloom in Britain. So it's definitely CLY-vee-a. But no one bothers to use that pronunciation on this side of the Atlantic (and if you do, people will secretly think you're a snotty pseudo-Brit).

Whichever way you say it, clivias have always been highly prized. The Victorians, who were mad for indoor gardening, clamored to get their hands on this curiosity the moment it hit their shores, because the clivia's sophisticated appearance and huge size fit into their glass conservatories so perfectly. However, as with most new fads, only the wealthy were fortunate enough to get clued in to clivias: in the 19th century they were even more expensive than they are today.

Why all the fuss about this undeniably classy but sometimes cantankerous plant? Several reasons:

❀ They have majestic tropical blooms that appear in huge, bouquet-like clusters on top of typical amaryllis stems. When one of these blooms appears, it's extremely exciting.
❀ Arranged in stacks from the base of the plant, the novelty braid-like growth of clivia leaves is more attractive than the leaves of regular amaryllis. In fact, it's fascinating to watch new leaves weaving themselves into this braid. The foliage also forms a beautiful, graceful arc over the pot.
❀ There are only a few varieties of clivia available in the world—and some are extremely rare.

Varieties you may see include:

❀ *C. miniata:* Sold in some garden centers, this is virtually the only kind available to people who don't have deep pockets. It has gorgeous tangerine blossoms with hints of salmon and vivid orange, and golden yellow stamens.
❀ *C. miniata* **'Aurea'** (also sometimes called 'Citrina' or 'Flava'): This variety has lemon yellow blossoms that, truthfully, aren't as striking as the tangerine variety. Even so, this is the Cadillac of clivias. Collectors fork over hundreds of dollars for a single specimen because they are so hard to get. Most are grown in Belgium and South Africa. You won't see it for sale in your average garden center.

There's no economical way to acquire a clivia. Buy from a nursery that sells lots of tropical plants, is familiar with their quirks, and gives them the growing conditions they prefer. Pick a specimen that has healthy-looking leaves, not brown or shriveled at the edges. Expect to pay up to $50 for a Clivia miniata *(the only variety likely to be on offer), depending upon the size.*

✽ ***C. nobilis:*** The original version that the Victorians went nuts over. Not a patch on its cultivated cousins, its blooms are comparatively dull and buff-colored, with green on their tips. But it usually does flower reliably.

How to grow clivias

Buy a ready-planted clivia. (Raising them from seed is strictly for collectors. It takes years.) But transfer it to a bigger clay container because, at maturity, these plants reach 2 to 3 feet (60 to 90 cm) tall. Garden center flowerpots made of cheap plastic are rarely big or heavy enough. Growing mix and fertilizer requirements are the same as for other amaryllis (see pages 43 and 46).

To prepare the plants for winter bloom,

Do
✓ Water very little once fall arrives. Stop fertilizing too.
✓ Keep the pot in a cool spot; a north-facing window ledge, close to the glass, is fine. Ideally, the temperature should dip to 45 to 55°F (7 to 13°C) at night. Clivias cope quite well with low light conditions in such locations and like to have their foliage shaded from harsh sunlight.
✓ In late November, start watering and feeding once every three or four weeks until sets of buds appear. Then stop fertilizing.

Don't

✗ Let leaves shrivel or go brown during the resting phase in early fall. The plant should still look in tiptop shape, unlike other amaryllis, whose foliage can be allowed to dry out before a new flower stalk appears.

✗ Worry about older plants getting too big for their britches. Although they grow huge, clivias like being pot-bound.

✗ Be too disappointed if your clivia fails to bloom. They are very fussy about temperature and humidity. When summer comes, put the pot in a shady spot outside. You might get luckier the following year.

After clivias flower, fruits will form. These take an inordinately long time (usually a year) to ripen. You can grow new plants from the seeds inside these capsules, but it will be at least four years before the new plants gets big enough to produce flowers.

Although they don't mind cramped quarters, clivia clumps will eventually need dividing, but it's a tricky task because the interwoven brittle roots can snap easily. Do it only if you're brave —and very careful. Klutzes may end up ruining the entire plant.

All things considered, clivias are classy, and they're worth adding to your indoor garden if you like the challenge of something different —and difficult. Owning one will certainly engender admiring glances from other gardeners and give you a reputation as a plant connoisseur.

But if you live in a small space, have problems controlling the heat and humidity in your condo, apartment, or house, and don't want disappointments, stick to clivia's down-scale relative, the amaryllis. These reward us with blooms that are as every bit as stupendous as those of the huffy clivia—and in the long, dreary winter that's what matters.

> ### Hot tip
> "My clivia often refuses to bloom in the winter. But when I stick the pot outside in summer-time—and completely ignore it—the darn plant always blooms. That's clivias for you."
> —Paul Zammit,
> container gardening expert

African Violets: Dainty and Underestimated

African violets have been around for years, and are sometimes dismissed as "old ladyish," probably because we've all seen too many of the boring purple-flowered kinds. But take a close look at these taken-for-granted houseplants—you might be pleasantly surprised. There are dozens of varieties to choose from, in many shapes, sizes, and colors. You can grow African violets that resemble shimmering deep blue jewels, or frilly pink petticoats, or tiny Victorian posies. Some African violets have striking flowers, as big as a pansy. Others are so dainty the whole plant would fit nicely into a teacup. And their rosettes of leaves—which come in various shades of green, gray and white—often look as fetching as the flowers.

African violets originated in Tanganyika (now Tanzania) and were introduced to the west in the 19th century by a German gent called Baron von Saint Paul—hence their botanical name, *Saintpaulia*. These violets (which are distantly related to the garden violets grown in North America) are not difficult to grow, once you know how. Many varieties will produce flowers prolifically, and unlike other houseplants, they don't hog too much space. Even if your condo, apartment, or house is small, you can usually find room to squeeze in an African violet or two. In the middle of a gray January, their delightful little blooms with the characteristic "dot" in the center can be a real morale booster, brightening any room.

Is the light right?

The most common complaint voiced about African violets is that they won't flower. The problem can usually be traced to a single source: not enough light, or the wrong kind of light. African violets that get plunked in locations where it's too dark stop flowering. Their leaves may also become leggy or turn yellow. Indeed, aficionados of this plant consider light so crucial they nurture theirs under fluorescent lights twelve hours a day. Beginners don't need to go that far. Even so, get the light level right and you're halfway there. Other crucial factors are:

- ❀ watering;
- ❀ growing mix;
- ❀ the size of the pot;
- ❀ the right fertilizer; and
- ❀ temperature.

Success with Saintpaulias

Do

✓ Use a *small* container. These plants are perfectly suited to urban living because they actually thrive in cramped quarters. Pick pots no more than 4 inches (10 cm) deep and one third the size of the plant's leaf span. For example, if your African violet's leaves spread about 12 inches (30 cm) wide, you'll need to gently push the roots into a pot only 4 inches (10 cm) wide. (Yes, really.)

✓ Park the pot in a spot where it receives bright light (preferably near a window), but no direct sunshine. If the sun does stream in, hang up some sheer curtains to diffuse its rays.

✓ Use only water that is *room temperature*. Don't mix water from the cold and hot taps. Just fill your jug or watering can with cold water and leave it to sit overnight.

✓ Place the African violet on a saucer. Pour water into the saucer, not on top of the leaves. Let it soak in for fifteen minutes. Then tip out any excess water promptly. African violets hate being overwatered or having wet leaves.

> **Hot tip**
>
> "If your African violets produce beautiful leaves but no blooms, gently thump the pot on a table top or squeeze its sides. This will often trigger a 'panic response' and make the violet start setting flowers. Sounds silly, but it's actually good science."
> —*Sandy Morgan*, Saintpaulia *expert*

Buy soil mixes especially formulated for African violets. These often cost more than plain potting soil, but it's worth spending the extra bucks because Saintpaulias *are very fussy about drainage. They need a loose and airy mix that contains at least 30% vermiculite or perlite. Feel the bag of mix. It should be loose and fluffy, like a pillow.*

✓ Keep the plants warm—but don't overdo it. Generally speaking, if you feel comfortable with the temperature, African violets will too. They prefer an environment in the range of 60 to 80°F (15 to 27°C). Like many tropical houseplants, they also take kindly to a constant flow of moisture in the air. A humidifier is worth the investment.

✓ Feed regularly and you'll get more flowers. Mix a water-soluble fertilizer with a formula like 20-20-20 into your watering can. Many African violet addicts recommend doing this every time you water, but at a quarter of the strength indicated on the fertilizer package or bottle.

Don't

✗ Use potting soil. It's too heavy for African violets.

✗ Put these plants in containers more than half the diameter of their roots. They like being pot-bound. African violet addicts say that once the roots collide with the walls of the pot the plants often start flowering like crazy.

✗ Let plants become so dry that leaves wilt. On the other hand, don't overwater. Try to keep the soil evenly moist. Poke your finger in every day to check.

✗ Get water on the leaves. They'll turn brown. Always water from the bottom.

✗ Use soft water. It's too salty.

✗ Allow more than one "crown" to reside in each pot. Crowns are the central bit, where the flower buds appear. If you see new crowns (four new leaves without a bud) developing elsewhere on the plant, give them the chop. Otherwise your African queen may get haughty with the competition and decide to stop producing flowers.

Groom for bloom

We function better when we look good. So do African violets. A regular grooming routine helps the plant (and is a great stress reliever for the plant's owner too). Nip off flower heads as soon as they've finished blooming.

Because the leaves are covered in tiny hairs that may get damaged, don't clean them with a piece of cloth. Use an artist's soft bristle brush or a makeup brush instead. Brush gently to remove dust, dirt, and potting soil that may have accumulated on the leaves. Reserve the brush strictly for this purpose; you don't want to be spreading bacteria to the violet from somewhere else.

African violets can be bothered by the usual bugs and diseases that afflict other houseplants. See page 121 for tips on how to deal with these pests.

> ## Hot tip
> "I confess that I'm forgetful—and I often let my African violets dry out. When that happens, I put each pot in a big bowl, half-filled with lukewarm water, for a few hours. They usually recover."
> —Irene Day, African violet lover

Leafing your way to more plants

One of the delights of African violets is that they're easy to propagate. Beg a leaf of a favorite specimen from a friend, bring it home, and start a new plant. To do this successfully,

- ❀ With a sharp knife, re-cut the stem diagonally, about an inch (2.5 cm) from the bottom of the front side of the leaf.
- ❀ Prop the stem up in a tiny plastic pot (no more than 2 inches/5 cm in diameter). You can also use Styrofoam cups with holes punched in the bottom.
- ❀ Mix up equal parts of moistened vermiculite, perlite, and peat moss. Then fill the container carefully, gradually building the mix up around the stem with your fingers.
- ❀ Put the container in a Ziploc bag and seal it. Water regularly. Don't let it dry out.
- ❀ Be patient. Wait six weeks—or even longer—for new cuttings to "take." Repot as the plant grows bigger.
- ❀ Don't keep a cut leaf waiting for its new home. They dry out quickly.

What To Do with Holiday Plants

Most of the plants we bring into our homes become permanent fixtures, prettying up the coffee table or the window ledges or the toilet tank in the bathroom year-round. But a few have developed special significance during certain seasons of the year. We invite these in (or coax them into bloom) for only a few brief weeks—and during that festive time, we want them to look their glorious best. Here are some tips on getting holiday plants to perform perfectly—and on how to recycle them when the festivities are finished.

Making Easter lilies last

We buy millions of them as pot plants just before Easter. And that's fitting. Divinely scented, with pure white, virginal-looking petals, this lily has become commonplace in North America, probably because it's so perfect for the Easter season. But the *Lilium longiflorum* isn't native to this part of the world. Once rare and highly prized, it's originally from Japan, where it still grows wild on the shores of some islands. It came to us via Britain and Bermuda over a century ago.

Most of us keep Easter lilies indoors for a couple of weeks, gracing the living room, then we toss them out when they've finished blooming. However, if you have the space, *L. longiflorum* can be grown in the garden afterwards. Just take it out of the pot, plant it in a sunny location with good soil, and cut the foliage down to the ground. Often it will send up nothing but stems and leaves, but if you're lucky, new lily blooms will appear very late in the summer. Some gardeners who can't bear to throw Easter lilies away wind up planting them every year in their flowerbeds. But this is very hit and miss in northern climates. Some produce gorgeous blooms the following summer; others fail to flower at all. Don't do it unless you have plenty of space.

Some tips for making the most of Easter lilies indoors:

Do

✓ Look for plants with at least eight buds on each stem. Cheap Easter lilies don't have many buds. The bloom count is what matters.

✓ Put your lily in a bright area, but not in direct sunlight.

✓ Keep it moist, but not soggy.

✓ Do the fingertip test to determine if you're watering enough. A surface that feels crusty dry means your lily is thirsty. A wet feeling is a signal that you're overdoing things.

Don't

✗ Leave lilies sitting in water. Place the pot in a saucer, water well, then remove the pot after a couple of minutes.

✗ Try to keep Easter lilies going indoors. Once their blooms are finished, they're uninteresting-looking plants.

Poinsettia pointers

Some people so despise this popular plant, they refer to it as "nothing more than Christmas wrapping paper"—and that's too bad. Poinsettias (*Euphorbia pulcherrima*) are certainly far too prevalent in December, but they're colorful plants with an entertaining history.

The name "poinsettia" sounds vaguely French or Italian but it's neither. This plant is actually named after an autocratic American gent called Joel Poinsett, and it comes from Mexico, where it grows into big straggly shrubs. Poinsett was ambassador to Mexico in 1825, saw the plant growing there, became captivated and brought it back home. Horticultural honchos in the U.S. promptly dubbed it the "poinsettia," but no one really knows why it has become so indelibly associated with Christmas.

Perhaps it was the plant's red leaves, called "bracts." They are what grabbed Poinsett's attention in the first place. This plant is part of the euphorbia family, and like all euphorbias, it produces interesting leaves, but inconspicuous flowers. (On the poinsettia, they're little yellow nubbles, barely noticeable, in the center of the plant.) Nowadays, you can find no less than 150 variations on the original Mexican poinsettia that enchanted Poinsett. Their bracts come in a constellation of colors—cream, all kinds of rosy pinks, peach, pale green, gold, mottled—and they may be plain, or curly-edged, or downright peculiar-looking. One hot new variety, 'Plum Pudding,' is a rather strange shade of purple. However, most of us still plump for a traditional poinsettia— i.e., scarlet—and there's now an amazing variety of such reds to choose from.

Some tips on caring for poinsettias:

Do

✓ Look for plants with healthy bracts that aren't dropping off. (That's a sign they've been exposed to cold.)

✓ Put your poinsettia in bright light, but not direct sunshine.

✓ Keep it away from cold windows, drafts, and heating vents. The ideal room temperature is 55 to 70°F (13 to 21°C).

✓ Pierce a few holes in the bottom of the foil wrapped around the pot. Better still, take this wrap off. It looks tacky, it's not waterproof, and it detracts from the plant.

✓ Put a saucer under the pot and water well every few days with lukewarm water. Drain after twenty minutes.

Don't

✗ Expose plants to cold air when leaving a garden center. They are *very* sensitive and should always be wrapped, preferably in plant sleeves, with more paper wrap on top. If salespeople offer them to you unwrapped, don't buy them.

✗ Give poinsettias teacups of water. They like a good soak.

✗ Place pots on top of VCRs, TVs, or any other heat source.

✗ Pretty up poinsettias with Christmas bows. These plants look best on their own, in plain, dark green pots.

✗ Try to get the red leaves to come back after they start turning green (which will usually happen a few weeks after Christmas). Growers coax poinsettias to parade their glorious colors by subjecting them to black-out curtains and complex temperature schedules—but the procedure is too complicated for most amateur indoor gardeners. It's simpler to buy new plants every Christmas.

A live Christmas tree

If it bothers you that millions of cut trees are thrown out every January, try something environmentally friendly: a Christmas tree planted in a pot. Once the holiday's over, you can put the pot in the garden, or on the balcony.

However, keeping the tree going so you can reuse it the following year does require a bit of effort. First, it's important to choose the right kind of conifer (the collective name given to evergreens). The best kinds are dwarf upright varieties, preferably spruce. White spruce (*Picea glauca*), especially dwarf Alberta spruce (*P. glauca* 'Conica') or blue spruce (*Picea pungens*), are good. The latter come in varieties called 'Hoopsi,' 'Koster,' and 'Moerheim.' Pick a specimen that has a good conical shape and is a minimum of 24 inches (60 cm) tall. Expect to pay a lot for them.

Another option is a Scots pine (*Pinus sylvestris*) or a tough variety from New Hampshire called 'White Mountain' (*Pinus strobus*), which tends to be very expensive. Don't pick the Austrian pine (*Pinus nigra*), as its branches look too open and spindly in pots.

Don't buy cedars, either, as they need too much moisture indoors. Firs are temperamental too, but a dwarf balsam variety like *Abies balsamea* 'Nana' may work. Other options are an upright Japanese yew (*Taxus cuspidata*) or a container-grown holly bush, *Ilex meserveae* 'Blue Princess,' whose red berries look very Christmassy.

These evergreens are usually sold in fiber pots. Whatever you choose, TLC is crucial if you want them to survive. After buying one,

Do

✓ Leave it in a cool spot, in its original fiber pot, for a few days. An unheated garage or a sheltered balcony is good.

✓ Stand it on a big plastic tray indoors and water it daily.

✓ Pick a spot that's as cool as possible, away from heating vents.

✓ Keep the tree indoors for no more than seven to ten days over the holiday.

✓ After Christmas, plant the tree in the garden as soon as possible. If the ground is frozen, or you garden on a balcony, put the tree (still in its fiber pot) inside a larger container, filled with some kind of insulation. Use Styrofoam packing peanuts, leaves, old newspapers, or even pink fiberglass wool, but make sure this stuff completely surrounds the pot. Then put another layer of leaves on top. Water well, whether you've planted the tree in the ground or put the pot inside a larger container.

✓ If you left it in a container, go outside occasionally during the winter and throw a pail of lukewarm water over it. Don't worry if the container is frozen solid (as it's bound to be, in a northern climate). Doing this is a good idea because it helps to prevent the tree from getting completely dried out.

✓ In the spring, take the pot out of its protective container when it starts to thaw. If you can peel back the mulch of leaves and stick your finger about half an inch (1.25 cm) into the soil, it's time.

✓ Trim off any dead bits and fertilize with a water-soluble plant food with a formula like 20-20-20. (Do the same if the tree has been planted in the garden.)

Don't

✗ Bring a potted tree into a warm room right after buying it. It needs to adjust in a cool area for a few days.

✗ Use big Christmas lights on the tree. They generate more heat than miniature ones and may fry its branches.

✗ Leave potted Christmas trees in a windy location over the winter. If you're up high, nestle them close to the side of the building—but if the tree can get covered in snow, so much the better (it's a terrific insulator).

Getting Christmas cactus to bloom

It *can* be bang on the mark. But sometimes this tropical plant with the pretty flowers will strut its stuff in October or November—or it may keep us in suspense until the New Year. Sometimes, for inexplicable reasons, it refuses to flower at all. That's vexing to some people, because the so-called Christmas cactus has become a symbol of the holiday season in the same way that the poinsettia has. Its striking pendulous blooms in flame red or shocking pink are a wonderful sight in the gloomy days of December. However, the timing of these flowers is never a sure thing—and that's hardly surprising, when you consider where Christmas cacti come from.

With a true name of *Schlumbergera buckleyi* (or *bridgesii*), this is a fleshy succulent plant from the tropical forests of South America. Over a century ago, intrepid plant collectors found it growing there in the leaf debris that gathers in the clefts of tree branches. *S. buckleyi* caught on as a houseplant here partly because it's remarkably good-natured about being forced to grow in northern living rooms. But it's also unpredictable. Many gardeners leave Christmas cactus to set its own schedule. "I just let it bloom when it wants," says one laid-back indoor gardener. "If I get flowers at Christmas, that's fine. But other times are fine too."

If you do want to get this plant to light up your living room during the eggnog and turkey festivities, here's a method that usually works:

Do

✓ Starting in October, shut it in a closet at night. You aren't punishing the plant. It actually craves total darkness from 8 p.m. until 8 a.m. for at least six weeks to two months to form buds.

✓ If your closet's too crammed with other stuff, a chilling-out period in the basement (or a cool room) will do instead. But the temperature should be around 50 to 55°F (10 to 13°C). Start this in early November.

✓ When buds begin to form, bring the pot out to a brightly lit area. You'll get more blooms in intense light (but it shouldn't be direct sunshine).

✓ Water when the top feels dry.

✓ After it's finished blooming, prune the plant with a sharp knife or break off sections with your fingers. This will encourage it to branch out. Plant these cuttings and they'll grow easily (see page 81).

✓ Put the plant outdoors in the summer in a shady spot. Never let it fry in direct sun or the branches will actually get sunburned.

> ## Hot tip
> "Potted up sections of Christmas cactus make great gifts for friends in the holiday season. People are always thrilled when I tell them the name of this cactus.
> —*Irene Day, condo gardener*

Don't

✗ Let your Christmas cactus completely dry out. It's a succulent plant, and needs more water than most cacti. If flower buds drop off, it's not getting enough water.

✗ Expose the plant to drafts or sudden changes in temperature. This can also make flowers fall off.

✗ Keep it in a very hot room. Blooms will last longer where it's cooler.

✗ Fertilize during the blooming period. At other times you can use a regular houseplant food with a formula like 20-20-20, but it's not strictly necessary.

✗ Use a potting mix that retains water. Above all, Christmas cacti like good drainage. A good formula is one part plain potting soil, one part sand (see page 106), and one part vermiculite.

Christmas cactus is one of the easiest plants in the world to propagate. Just break off a section and stick it in a pot. For detailed instructions, see page 81.

Try Growing Something from Seed

It's not as difficult as it looks. Many gardeners, even highly experienced ones, shy away from starting plants themselves, for a number of reasons. They presume that it's too difficult, that they won't be able to provide sufficient light, or that it's going to mean buying complicated (and costly) equipment.

None of the above needs to be true. Some seeds germinate and grow into strong, healthy plants with very little assistance from us. You also don't have to spend a lot of money to make it happen. The trick is to try easy seeds first (there are lots) and get simple equipment. Whatever you use, the payback can be incredible. In the middle of winter, when we are stuck indoors, turning tiny seeds into new life seems like a miracle. You will be awestruck. Even old hands at the ritual of seed-starting admit that they still get a rush when they discover a new batch of seedlings popping up.

Some seeds will germinate quickly in warm surroundings. It may take hours, days, or weeks. Other tricky specimens will keep us in suspense for months—or even years. But whatever the incubation period, the end result is usually uplifting and satisfying. It reminds us that, while everything may look dead outside, the spring will eventually return and turn everything green again.

Raising plants from seed also has a practical advantage: it's cheap. With gardening becoming the number one pastime in North America, everything is getting expensive. Why pay huge prices for plants you can grow yourself? Savvy gardeners eventually turn to starting their own plants from seed, simply because it pays. You can grow dozens of plants for less than the price garden centers charge for a single specimen.

The marvel of seeds

Once you get into growing plants from scratch rather than buying ready-planted ones at the garden center, it's easy to become utterly fascinated by their humble beginnings. Look closely at seeds. They come in all shapes, sizes, and colors. Some seeds are the size of a pinhead and a few are even tinier (you can't examine them properly without a magnifying glass). Others resemble grains of rice, or graceful little urns, or throat lozenges. They may be tufty, rock hard, or black and shiny like a patent leather shoe. Several seeds have a positively sinister feel and appearance—the castor bean (*Ricinus communis*) is one—and they can be deadly if used in the wrong way. (Terrorists have turned the active ingredient (ricin) in *Ricinus* into a poison so powerful it could wipe out entire cities if mixed into the water supply.)

Seeds, in short, vary drastically, and so do their growing requirements. Some like it hot; others prefer it on the chilly side. While many will germinate easily, a few may take an astounding amount of time to get going. Try growing a common garden plant, Solomon's seal (*Polygonatum*), from seed and you'll wait up to eighteen months before a seedling pops up in your tray. Never presume that you can treat all seeds in the same way.

If you're a beginner, start the seeds of annual plants first. They are generally easier to cope with than those of perennial plants—and you'll usually see results faster.

And if you don't want to fiddle and fuss, steer clear of two important words beginning with S: "stratification" and "scarification." The former means a period of cold and darkness and is necessary for some stubborn seeds, to kick-start them into germinating. The latter means nicking or chipping seed coats to release the embryo inside. Some armor-plated types must be subjected to this treatment. Plants that have to be started from "fresh seed" are also best avoided by beginners.

Easy seeds to try

Herbs

❀ **Annual pot marjoram**

❀ **Basil:** Most varieties of basil are a joy to grow from seed.

❀ **Dill:** Great, but watch it. Seedlings grow very tall. Pull them out before they hit the grow lights.

Don't bother with:

❀ **Rosemary:** Very tricky from seed indoors.

❀ **Perennial oregano:** Too slow.

❀ **Mint:** Planting a piece of root is preferable.

❀ **Parsley:** Seed is extremely slow to germinate.

Flowers and foliage plants

❀ Black-eyed Susans (*Rudbeckia*)

❀ Coleus

❀ Coreopsis

❀ Cosmos

❀ Flowering tobacco (*Nicotiana sylvestris*)

❀ Hollyhocks (*Althaea*)

❀ Licorice vine (*Helichrysum petiolare*)

❀ Mallow (*Malva*)

❀ Pot marigolds (*Calendula*)

❀ Snapdragons (*Antirrhinums*)

❀ Sunflowers (*Helianthus*)

Seeds need bright light

The most crucial factor in getting plants to grow from seed is light. Lots of it. Most plants need at least fourteen hours of light a day to thrive. That's a tall order for most urban gardeners. There are really only two ways to provide plants with the lighting conditions they crave:

A superbly sunny window

In a house, condo, or apartment that faces south, you may have a spot that fills the bill. But the operative word is "may." Bear in mind that the sun doesn't rise particularly high in the sky in northern climates during the winter, and it sets much more quickly in the evening. Even if the view from your window is smack south, and you're not shaded by other buildings during the day (a common drawback in densely populated cities), there still may not be enough sunlight for seedlings to grow properly.

Another point to remember: seeds need to be positioned right next to the window, not on a coffee table or bookcase a few feet away from it. That means you'll require a wide window ledge (a rare commodity in most modern condos and houses) on which to stand them.

Seeds started on windowsills also have to be watched constantly. The moment you see them straining sideways, towards the light, it's time to turn their containers so plants will straighten up again.

Many seeds get off to a promising start on windowsills, thrilling their owners. But then their stems get leggy and weak. If yours wind up looking like bits of pale thread and start toppling over, they simply aren't getting enough light.

Artificial lights

People often resist getting artificial lights because they assume they'll be expensive, use a whacking amount of electricity, and be a hassle to install. That certainly is the case with high-intensity grow lighting systems that have metal halide (MH) or high-pressure sodium (HPS) tubes. There is a bewildering array of these systems on the market now, they cost a bundle, and you need to be a rocket scientist to understand the catalogues sent out by the manufacturers.

Don't let the bewildering jargon about "blasters" and "ballasts" put you off, though. The high-tech lighting stuff is designed for pros who want to raise tomatoes from seed indoors, or cosset ultra-finicky things such as rare orchids. The truth is, only a basic lighting system is necessary to grow most plants. A couple of standard fluorescent tubes will do the job nicely. Here's how to set up a satisfactory system:

- Buy a ready-made unit that takes two fluorescent tubes from a hardware store or home renovation center. They don't cost much and come in various lengths.
- Longer tubes are a better bet if you have space. The cost of electrical power for long tubes versus short ones is virtually the same—and you'll soon find that containers of seeds take up a quite a lot of room. Also, light is weaker at the ends of tubes, so for best results your seedlings need to be clustered together under the tubes' midsection.
- Buy one cool tube and one daylight (or warm) tube for the unit. Opinions are divided on the merits of "cool" versus "warm" tubes, but many experienced seed-starters say it's best to have one of each.
- Suspend the unit from the ceiling, using strong hooks and plugs. Attach chains (or ropes) and add pulleys so you can move the lights up and down. Being able to adjust the height of the unit is a plus because, to grow properly, most seedlings should be no more than 4 inches (10 cm) from the light source; you can raise the lights as the plants develop.
- In a small space, attach a fluorescent tube unit to the underside of a shelf. If the shelf beneath the unit is too far from the lights, elevate your seed tray—using a pile of books, perhaps.
- If you're feeling flush, buy a made-for-the-job plant stand equipped with lights, trays, and shelves that slide up and down. These are terrific. They accommodate dozens of plants, but they're pricey. Try starting a few seeds with a basic, inexpensive system first, to see if you enjoy it. And watch ads in horticultural society newsletters if you start hankering after a plant stand. Secondhand ones are often advertised for sale.

Old milk cartons? Nope, a seed tray is simpler

A plastic seed-starting tray with a see-through lid is a boon. These are sold at garden centers and hardware stores in late winter and they're dirt cheap (a few dollars apiece). Trays are usually oblong or square, and they come with a collection of plastic cell paks, which fit neatly inside the tray. Each pak is then divided into little compartments (usually four or six compartments to a pak).

Trays are what many experienced gardeners use. They're terrific because they make seed-starting simple and straightforward. Gardening books often advocate recycling containers— old milk cartons, coffee cans, and so on—and using them will help the environment and make you feel virtuous. But if you're a beginner, say to heck with what's right for once. Go for the "guilt" of a bought plastic tray, because it's much easier.

Containers such as milk cartons are adequate for starting seeds, but they're a hassle. You have to cut the cartons down to a manageable size, wash them thoroughly, punch holes in the bottom, and place plastic wrap on top of the incubating seeds. Then you must keep peeling this wrap back to check if the growing medium is still moist (taking care not to bunch the wrap up lest it stick together in a wad and become unusable). Finding saucers that fit well underneath square containers is also a chore.

> **Hot tip**
> "Plant at least three seeds in every section of a cell pak. One may not germinate. Another may not grow well. But with three, you're safe."
> —Cathie Cox, seed-starting expert

By contrast, seed trays are designed for the job. These marvelous inventions catch the drips when you're watering (no more ruined coffee tables). But their most useful aspect is their see-through lids. You can watch your seeds' progress through these lids, then simply lift the lids off to mist the seeds or water seedlings. It's also a snap to start a few seeds—or many different ones—in one tray.

If you feel guilty about buying a plastic tray, remember that you can reuse it next winter. Just wash it out first (see page 104).

Cleanliness helps

When starting seeds, keep everything as squeaky clean as a hospital operating room. The first step in this direction can be summed up in three words: sterile, soil-less mix. A growing medium that's absolutely free of potential nasties in the disease or bug department is a must. Don't be tempted to use up old potting mix you have lying around, or to recycle the stuff your dead dieffenbachia is sitting in. And definitely don't dig up soil from the garden. Instead, go out buy a bag of mix that's specially formulated for the job.

Seed-starting mixes are usually labeled as such at garden centers. They contain mostly peat moss, with some vermiculite or perlite. Sometimes fertilizer is thrown in too. Whatever the contents, they've all been exposed to high temperatures to kill bacteria.

Avoid mixes that contain fertilizers. These can have weird side effects because the additives are often too strong. If they're nitrogen-heavy, your seed tray may develop a distressing green fuzz all over the top. Tender seedlings can also be stunted or completely fried by an overdose of fertilizer.

It's best to add fertilizer yourself, because you can control how much the plants get. An ordinary plant food in a 20-20-20 formula (such as Miracle-Gro) works fine. If you want to go organic, fish emulsion fertilizers do the job well, too. But don't mix fertilizers in your watering jug at the strength indicated on the bottle. This stuff needs to be diluted for seeds—a lot. See page 75.

Other equipment to buy

🌸 Something to water plants with. If you use a watering can, get one with a long spout, not a wide nozzle (it will make a mess everywhere). A tall plastic jug is good, as it's easy to mix fertilizer into it.

🌸 A plastic spray bottle for misting plants. There are some very fancy misters on the market now, but a cheap hardware store version works fine.

🌸 A timer for the lights. Ask a sales clerk to explain how this gizmo works before buying it. (The instructions are often a pain to figure out.)

🌸 A heavy-duty extension cord that will accommodate several three-prong plugs. The cords on lights and timers are never long enough to reach wall plugs, and you'll need several sockets anyway.

🌸 A seed-starting spoon. They're made of plastic and cost pennies. Spoons are great for doling out seeds, because you don't wind up using too many. Get them at garden centers or from mail-order seed suppliers.

❀ A small fan. This will circulate the air around your plants and help prevent the big bugaboo of starting seeds: damping-off disease (see page 77).

Old narrow Venetian blinds, in metal or plastic, make a terrific substitute for plant labels bought from garden centers or mail-order seed companies. Cut these blinds up into pieces about 6 inches (15 cm) long and write the names of seeds on one end, using a 2B lead pencil or permanent marker. (Avoid ball point and felt-tip pens that aren't marked "permanent." The ink will wash off.)

Stick the labels, upright, in your cell paks. Every cell pak in your seed tray should contain a label; otherwise, you'll never remember what you planted there.

How to make seeds grow

Getting seeds to sprout is the easy part. The hard part is deciding which ones will then be nurtured into new plants. Seed-starting requires ruthlessness, because all your new seedlings can't be allowed to survive. Like it or not, you have to systematically weed out the weaker ones. The process of culling sometimes feels like "throwing out all your children," sighs one maternal type, who hates doing it. Most beginners voice similar sentiments. In fact, the biggest mistake that neophyte seed-starters make is to leave too many sprouted seeds in their containers. Crammed together, the seedlings compete for space and light. The end result is that none of them grow properly, and they're more prone to disease.

You'll find it gets easier to play Lord High Executioner the more you start plants from seed. Here are some tips:

Do
✓ Read what's printed on seed packets. Vital information— how deep to plant, germination time, days to bloom or

harvest, special requirements—is usually provided. (Keep reading glasses handy. Often, everything is in infuriatingly tiny type.)

✓ Tear a strip off the bottom of seed packets, not the top. Usually, the names of plants appear at the top. If this torn-off bit gets thrown away, you'll forget what's inside the packet—a nuisance if you want to save some of the seeds to use later on.

✓ Soak your planting mix. Open up the package; if it feels damp, no problem. But if it's dry and flaky, pour a jug of warm water in and let it sit overnight.

✓ Dig out a bit of dry mix before you do this and reserve it in a yogurt container.

✓ Fill plastic cell paks with the damp mix to within a quarter inch (0.6 cm) of the rim.

✓ Tip seeds out of packets *very* cautiously. Tiny ones often come out in a whomp. To prevent this happening, pour seeds into a piece of stiff white paper, folded in half. Then tap this strip so the seeds come out one by one. Or try using a seed spoon.

✓ Push seeds gently into the damp mix with fingers or the end of a pencil.

✓ Leave half an inch (1.25 cm) of space between each seed, if you can. This is easier said than done. Beginners usually wind up with too many seeds packed closely together. If that's your problem, and you're all fingers and thumbs trying to separate them, don't worry. You can pull out unwanted seedlings later on.

✓ Sprinkle the reserved dry mix *thinly* over the seeds (or use a sieve). Generally speaking, you need a layer of mix that's three times the size of the seed itself. Tiny, pinhead-size seeds should be left uncovered.

✓ Mist thoroughly, so the top feels damp.

✓ Put the seed tray lid on and place it in a warm, dark place. (Some seeds require light to germinate, but most will pop up quicker if they're kept in the dark.) A cupboard above a fridge is good. So is a furnace room.

✓ Check the tray every day, without fail. Keep misting if the top looks dry. Seeds must never be deprived of moisture.

✓ Once—hallelujah!—the seeds sprout (some will germinate astonishingly quickly), remove the lid immediately and put the tray under your lighting unit.

✓ Set your timer to deliver fourteen hours of light a day.

✓ Watch for cotyledons. These are little oval leaves—and they're the first ones to appear on all seedlings. After the cotyledons' brief burst of glory, you should start seeing regular leaves develop. That's when to start fertilizing.

✓ Mix fertilizer into your watering container at only a *quarter the strength* that it says on the bottle or package. (Too much will burn seedlings.) This usually works out to about half a teaspoonful (2.5 mL) in a gallon (4.5 L) of water. Let this concoction sit for a few hours, then carefully pour it on to each little compartment of the cell paks. Or water from the bottom by pouring your watering can's contents into the tray. (You'll have to remove one of the cell paks to do this.)

✓ Add this diluted fertilizer into your jug every time you water. But let it sit for a few hours before use.

✓ As seedlings grow, thin out the weakies with your fingers (trying not to uproot the toughies), or even better, snip them off with nail scissors. Be ruthless. You should wind up with only one seedling in each section of the cell pak. It's tempting to leave two or three of these plant babies, especially if they're flourishing. But keep only the best one.

✓ Transplant seedlings that make it to the finish line into bigger pots, 4 inches (10 cm) in diameter, when they're several inches high. Continue giving them mild dollops of fertilizer when you water. (*Note:* Don't bother with this transplanting step if you intend to plant the seedlings outdoors in a garden. Just leave them as they are, in their cell paks. Put the paks in a shady spot outside to acclimatize for a couple of weeks before planting, but keep them well watered. And pay attention to how quickly these seedlings develop. If they start busting out of their cell paks before you can get them into the ground, move them into bigger individual pots, let them grow a bit longer, then transplant into the garden. However, it's a lot less hassle if you can let them stay in their cell paks.)

✓ Store seeds you don't use in a film canister in the refrigerator. Label them with the name and date, but don't keep these leftovers for long. It's easy to squirrel away all kinds of seeds you'll never use.

Don't

✗ Presume all seeds are planted in the same way. Their requirements differ drastically.

✗ Plant different kinds of seeds in one cell pak. Germination times vary widely. Snapdragon seeds, which sprout in a few days, won't take kindly to sitting in a cell pak, in the dark, with other cellmates that take much longer to germinate. Also, plants grow at different rates. Tall seedlings shouldn't be mixed with smaller ones— they'll overpower them. Experienced gardeners put only one plant variety in each cell pak.

> ### Hot tip
> "Store seeds in old teabag envelopes. I label these bags and shut them with tape. Then I put the envelopes back in the teabag box. The small boxes of individually wrapped herbal teas are the perfect size for this."
> —*Truc Nguyen, gardener*

✗ Use little pots made of peat moss to start seeds unless you can keep an eagle eye on them. Peat is biodegradable and certainly more environmentally friendly than plastic cell paks, but it tends to dry out at the drop of a hat.

✗ Cover tiny seeds, such as basil, or presoak them. Just press them into the mix.

✗ Slosh a lot of water over newly planted seed trays. This will wash the seeds out of their cell paks.

✗ Forget seed trays that you put in the dark to germinate. If seeds have sprouted into a leggy mess of hair-like threads pushing up under the tray lid, they've been kept in darkness too long.

✗ Position your seed-starting setup close to where you relax, eat meals, or sleep. Seeds respond well to fluorescent tubes, but humans generally don't. This is cold, unfriendly lighting, best reserved for a spare room or basement, rather than a living room or bedroom. Also, some grow light units make a humming noise that can drive you nuts after a while.

Don't be a cheapskate and use old seeds. It's worth buying new ones. A packet usually costs no more than a couple of dollars. Beginners often make the mistake of hauling out seeds that somebody gave them donkey's years ago. Then they wonder why they won't germinate.

Smart folk stroke

Humans respond to a bit of loving. So do plants. Gently brush the palm of your hand back and forth over seedlings every few days, and they'll grow sturdier and stronger. This isn't New Age claptrap. Scientific experiments at an agricultural college in Tonbridge, England, have proven that it pays to stroke plants when they're growing under lights. You'll wind up with bigger, healthier specimens. The technique is called—yikes!—thigmomorphogenesis.

Dratted damping-off disease

Damping-off disease is the number one plant problem to watch out for. You'll know your seedlings have been zapped by this infuriating fungus if their stems suddenly start getting thin at the bottom or turning black. Or the poor tiny plantlet may suddenly collapse. Throw out affected victims immediately. Never give this dratted disease the chance to leapfrog to other seedlings. To prevent damping-off,

❀ Leave plenty of air space between the cell paks of planted seeds.

❀ As seedlings grow and get bushy, avoid cramming them too closely together. Start juggling the cell paks around in your seed tray to create gaps between the plantlets.

❀ Aim a small fan at your seed-starting setup. Position it about 3 feet (1 m) away, and run it constantly to help circulate the air.

❀ Always use sterile, soil-less mix. Don't add anything to it.

> **Hot tip**
>
> "You can check if old seeds are still viable by wrapping a few of them in some damp paper towel. Put the towel in a warm place, such as the top of a fridge, and keep checking. If these seeds don't sprout in a few days, throw the rest of the batch out."
>
> —*Barrie Murdock, seed collector*

Cultivate a Cutting Attitude

Buying plants is certainly easy, but it can get expensive. One way to avoid big bills at the garden center is grow a few things from seed. However, it's quicker, and often simpler, to take cuttings from the plants you currently have and nurture those. Watching a tiny offshoot gradually develop into a big new plant gives most indoor gardeners a great sense of accomplishment. Cuttings of favorite plants, potted up and ready to go, also make great gifts for friends.

Propagating from cuttings isn't as difficult as it may appear. As with seed-starting, the trick is to stick to user-friendly plants. If you're a beginner, don't try propagating any plant that needs to be subjected to air layering (a complicated procedure best left to experienced gardeners). Instead, choose plants that can be easily rooted in water or a container of soil-less mix.

How to take cuttings

Do

✓ Wait till there's lots of fresh new growth on the plant. When you're growing plants indoors, this might be any season of the year, but spring is often the best time.

✓ Pick a stem that's shot up quickly and is undamaged. It's probably green (or greenish) and definitely youthful-looking. Generally speaking, don't select hard or wizened stems.

✓ Use a sharp pair of pruners, not some old blunt scissors you have lying around.

✓ Cut the stem cleanly, in one go. Don't saw away at it.

✓ Make sure you cut a long piece of stem—at least 6 inches (15 cm). It should be twice the length of the cutting you want.

✓ Cut right under a leaf or node. The latter is a swelling where a new leaf or offshoot is going to appear or has already started to come out. Examine plant stems carefully and make sure you understand what a node looks like before you start.

✓ Take at least two cuttings of a plant you want to propagate (one may die).

✓ Wrap the cuttings in damp paper towel and put them inside a plastic baggie until you're ready to plant. Plastic sandwich bags with zip-up seals are great for this.

✓ Before potting them up, remove cuttings from the bag with care, one at a time. It's easy to damage them. Lay the cuttings flat on a clean chopping board or table top.

✓ Cut off the bottom section of each cutting below a leaf joint, using a knife (not scissors). Then remove any leaves and the top section of the cutting, so that you wind up with a midsection that's about 4 inches (10 cm) long.

✓ To get the cutting off to a good start, dip the end in a hormone rooting medium. These are sold in little plastic containers at garden centers (as powders or liquids). If the rooting powder won't stick to the stem (and it often doesn't), dip the cutting in water first. (Note: rooting hormone isn't necessary with some really easy plants such as coleus and tradescantia.)

✓ Fill a flowerpot that's at least 4 inches (10 cm) wide with fresh, damp seed-starting mix, not recycled stuff. The mix should contain peat moss and vermiculite or perlite.

✓ Make a hole in the mix with a pencil or a plastic made-for-the-job gadget called a dibber. Slide the cutting into the hole gently. Don't squeeze the cutting.

✓ If you want to plant several cuttings of one plant, use a bigger pot and poke a circle of holes in the mix.

✓ Label the cutting, water it thoroughly, and enclose the whole kit and caboodle in a see-through plastic bag. Put an elastic around the pot to seal the bag. Don't leave it flapping open.

Recycled film canisters are the perfect size for rooting cuttings in water. Use one canister (the kind that holds 35 mm film) per cutting. Just fill the canisters with water and stand the cuttings in them. Change the water every few days. Miniature bottles (airline liquor bottles or food coloring bottles) also work well. But make sure there's no residue left in them. A clean mascara wand is good for poking into bottle necks to clean them.

✓ If you're rooting cuttings in water, use a clean container and lukewarm water. Change the water every few days. When hair-like roots have developed, carefully transfer the cuttings to flowerpots and pot up.

✓ Put flowerpots containing cuttings in a warm, well-lit place. Under an indoor fluorescent unit is best—they need a lot of light to stimulate growth. But a windowsill is fine.

✓ When leaves start to appear, take the bag off.

✓ Wait till a couple of leaves develop. Then start fertilizing with plant food, at a quarter the recommended strength (see page 75).

Don't

✗ Use dirty equipment. Propagation of plants is surgery. You need a clean operating theater, or your patients may fall victim to germs. Make sure scissors, knives, chopping boards, and flowerpots are clean before you start. It's a good idea to sterilize them. Work on a clean, dry surface, not a potting-up table that has soil scattered on it.

✗ Take too many cuttings at once. If you want to propagate from several different plants, it's best to tackle one plant at a time.

✗ Leave cuttings exposed to the air. They may dry out or acquire an infection. Put them in plastic bags as soon as they've been cut. Remove the cuttings one at a time when you're planting them.

✗ Mix up cuttings of different plants in the same plastic bag. The rule is one bag per type of plant—and be sure to label the bags.

✗ Shove new cuttings roughly into planting holes. They are as delicate as newborn babies.

✗ Be disappointed if cuttings fail to "take." Depending upon the plant, propagation can be a chancy business. But you can always try again.

Hot tip

"Upend a jam jar over cuttings when you're rooting them in water. The humidity helps."

—Alison Hunberstone, home gardener

Plants you can propagate easily

❀ **African violets (*Saintpaulia*):** See page 57.

❀ **Aloes:** Most aloes produce "babies"—that is, little rosettes attached to the base of the momma plant. Simply remove these rosettes and push them into a pot of growing mix. Wait till the babies have started sending out new spiky leaves; otherwise, they are difficult to root. And don't overwater. The top should stay crushy dry.

❀ **Christmas cactus (*Schlumbergera buckleyi*):** Easy. Just cut off a section of the stem, including several jointed segments, allow it to dry for a few hours, then push it gently into some growing mix. The piece should be planted just deep enough to support itself. Christmas cactus don't have big root systems, so you can use a small pot.

❀ **Coleus (*Solenostemon scutellarioides*):** Easy and fun, because there are many colorful varieties to experiment with. Toward the end of summer, try propagating a coleus that's in a container on your balcony or deck. Simply snip off a healthy section of stem, remove the big leaves, and stand the cutting in water. Pot up when there's a mess of hairy roots twirling around inside the container (it won't take long). Keep baby coleus indoors and watch it develop over the winter. The best site is under lights or on a sunny window ledge. These tropical plants prefer semi-shade outdoors, but they get pale, leggy, and knock-kneed when there's insufficient light inside.

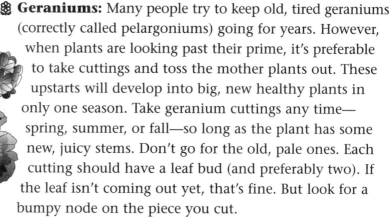

Geraniums: Many people try to keep old, tired geraniums (correctly called pelargoniums) going for years. However, when plants are looking past their prime, it's preferable to take cuttings and toss the mother plants out. These upstarts will develop into big, new healthy plants in only one season. Take geranium cuttings any time—spring, summer, or fall—so long as the plant has some new, juicy stems. Don't go for the old, pale ones. Each cutting should have a leaf bud (and preferably two). If the leaf isn't coming out yet, that's fine. But look for a bumpy node on the piece you cut.

Jade plant (*Crassula argentea*): Easy as pie. Simply take an individual leaf, or cut off a little stem and stick it in a pot. Side shoots of old jade plants sometimes fall off the main stems all by themselves, especially if you've forgotten to water for a while. Pick up these castoffs and pot them; they'll usually grow. Sand in the planting mix helps.

Pothos (*Scindapsus* or *Epipremnum*): These often trail all over the place (perhaps that's why their nickname is "Devil's ivy"). If yours are getting too big for their boots, cut sections off and follow the preceeding instructions. Several cuttings rooted in one pot will develop into a nice bushy plant.

Spider plant (*Chlorophytum comosum*): This one's a snap too. Just cut off the baby spider plants that sprout on the plant's long, thin stems. Stand them in water till they develop roots an inch (2.5 cm) long. Then pot.

Tradescantia: Another trailer that often becomes too much of a good thing. Cuttings will root easily in water, but don't put the container in direct sunlight. And avoid leaving it too long—these roots rot quickly. Pot up when roots are 1 to 2 inches (2.5 to 5 cm) long.

Dieffenbachias do it sideways

One popular houseplant, the dieffenbachia, tends to lose its looks as it ages. You wind up with a long stem topped by a few half-hearted leaves. When this happens, there's a neat way to make a new plant. First, chop the top right off. Then cut off a 3- to 4-inch (7.5 to 10 cm) section of the remaining stem. It should contain at least one growth bud (a ridgy bit on the side of the stem). Lay this piece of stem *sideways* on top of a pot of moistened growing mix. Roots will go downwards into the mix from the stem and, after a few weeks, you should see a new shoot appear. Just leave this shoot as is, and it will develop into a new dieffenbachia.

Don't throw the old momma plant in the garbage. Repot it in some fresh mix, and the remaining stem will probably sprout some fresh new leaves.

Picky plants to avoid

If you haven't taken cuttings before, stick to the ones above. The following are more difficult to propagate:

- Chinese evergreens (*Aglaonema*)
- Coffee plant (*Coffea arabica*)
- Dracaena
- Most ferns
- Ficus. The familiar *F. benjamina* (weeping fig tree) and *F. elastica* (rubber plant) are best avoided by amateurs. However, two trailing varieties, *F. pumila* and *F. sagittata*, will grow easily from cuttings.
- Norfolk Island pine (*Araucaria heterophylla*)
- Palm trees

Forcing Spring Bulbs Indoors: Tricky but Fun

Smart urban gardeners indulge in a bit of enforcement once autumn arrives. But there's nothing kinky or illegal about it. "Forcing" is the term used to describe the practice of making plants bloom artificially, before their normal flowering period. While the word itself may sound a tad unpleasant (plant "persuading" would surely be better), this kind of gardening is great fun—and the payoff can be terrific in the winter months.

If you dread the prospect of those dreary gray days when there's nothing green growing outside (and who doesn't?), pot up a few spring bulbs in fall and try forcing them. Come January or February, the thrill will be indescribable. It's very satisfying to see gorgeous flowers you planted yourself burst into bloom on a window ledge or dining table. They're guaranteed to make your heart soar.

What's not guaranteed, however, is success. Forcing is a tricky process that doesn't always work—no matter what gardening books may tell you. Some bulbs get huffy when asked to perform before their time. They refuse to sprout. Or they go moldy. Or, darn them, they send up a mess of leggy greenery, but no flowers. Horticulturists force as a matter of course (usually in specially darkened greenhouses kept at exactly the right temperature), but for amateurs this practice can be fraught with disappointments.

The secret is to stick to easy bulbs (forget the finicky ones) and try to duplicate the outdoor growing conditions spring bulbs like. No easy feat, but it can be done.

Let's hear it for hyacinths!

Ah, heavenly hyacinths. If you've never forced bulbs before, try these first. Hyacinths seem to adapt far better to the rigors of forcing than any other spring bulbs. Narcissus and tulips can be touchy, but hyacinths—so good-tempered and dependable—almost always come up trumps. Their frilly plumes of flowers are delightful (especially when you can look at them close-up), and most varieties are fragrant. Mother Nature undoubtedly intended hyacinths to be indoor plants, cheering up northern gardeners in the dog days of winter, for they don't look or smell half as good planted in a spring garden as they do lighting up a living room when there's a mess of slush outside. (In a small room, though, some people find the scent of hyacinths overpowering. Don't plant them if you hate strong fragrances.)

Hyacinths are biggish bulbs that resemble purple-skinned onions. They come in several shades of blue, as well as pinks, purples, and white. A single hyacinth looks striking on its own in a pot. Half a dozen of them potted up together are even better, but bear in mind that they may not all bloom in unison.

Some varieties to try:

🌸 **'Blue Jacket':** A fave everywhere because of its classic deep purply-blue flowers and strong fragrance.
🌸 **'Carnegie':** White with a fresh perfume. If you like the minimalist look in decor, go for white hyacinths.
🌸 **'Hollyhock':** Shocking pink. This striking plant is great for banishing the winter blahs.
🌸 **'Splendid Cornelia':** Neat name, unusual-looking hyacinth. Pale violet, mixed with a deeper, purply-blue. Not for traditionalists. The fragrance isn't strong.

There are special glass vases in which you can grow hyacinths with their roots dangling in water. But you'll get better results if you plant them in a pot (see page 89).

Hyacinth itch hurts!

Handle hyacinth bulbs with caution. They give some people a rash similar to poison ivy. But don't presume (as many gardeners do) that pesticides sprayed on the bulbs are to blame. Dutch bulb bigwigs say the culprit is actually the hyacinth's outer skin. When this onion-like casing peels off or tears, it breaks down into minute, needle-shaped crystals of calcium oxylate. These get into our pores, making us feel itchy. So we scratch, push the crystals deeper in, and wind up with a painful pink rash.

"Hyacinth itch is not a new problem," says a report from the Dutch Bulb Research Centre in Lisse, Holland. "It has been with us ever since the bulbs were traded." The report adds that the itch "has never been found to be detrimental to a person's health." Even so, it's a good idea to wear rubber gloves when planting hyacinths. And when picking them out of cardboard boxes at garden centers, handle the bulbs as little as possible.

Narcissus: Nitpicker about light

Commonly called daffodils, many narcissus varieties don't force well because they require very bright conditions to bloom. After being brought out of the dark, they often sulk, as lighting is too muted in our homes, even on sunny windowsills. Miniature or dwarf varieties are the best bet. Try:

❀ **'Erlicheer':** A double variety that needs only four weeks of darkness. Has ivory-and-gold blooms and grows about 12 inches (30 cm) high.

❀ **'Jack Snipe':** Has white petals with a yellow cup. Grows about 12 inches (30 cm) high.

❀ **'Jetfire':** A dwarf variety that combines yellow petals with orange cups. Somewhat fragrant. Grows 8 inches (20 cm) tall. Often sold as a potted bulb in winter-time because it produces lots of blooms.

❀ **'Tête à Tête':** A cute little "traditional" daffodil in cheery yellow. Also seen a lot in florist shops. Grows 8 inches (20 cm) tall.

Paperwhites: Unlike their narcissistic cousins, these don't need a period of darkness at all. Just place the bulbs in a shallow bowl containing water and pea gravel (which you can get a garden center or tropical fish store). Add a bit of charcoal to stop the water from getting smelly, and watch the bulbs grow. They often get too tall and flop about, but their dainty white flowers are delightful. The drawback of paperwhites is that some people positively hate their fragrance (and some sensitive souls are allergic to it). In a small room, this scent can be overpowering, particularly when the flowers reach maturity.

Tulips: Terrific, but temperamental

Some bulb experts say that, to force tulips, it's best to stick to early-blooming varieties that have short, sturdy stems. But other experts say that's hogwash. "Tulips are picky about conditions," says one. "But if you get the temperature and the cooling period right, you can force all kinds of tulips. Doesn't matter how early or late they bloom."

Experts in Holland also offer this tip: if forced tulips get too leggy, you have kept them in the dark too long. If they're too short, their chilling-out period wasn't long enough.

Some hybrid tulip varieties that seem to adapt well to forcing are:

'Abba': These tulips have several great things going for them: they have double petals in a wonderful tomato red, they're fragrant, and they may produce blooms earlier than some other varieties. They grow about 12 inches (30 cm) tall. Unfortunately, they are very hard to find.

'Angelique': This unusual double tulip has layers of frilly double blooms in pink and white that look like petticoats. Very feminine. Ideal in pots indoors, rather than growing in the garden, because you can see the layered petals up close. Smells faintly of roses (which is heaven indoors in the wintertime). Tends to get leggy and sprawl. Grows at least 14 inches (35 cm) high.

✿ **'Apricot Beauty':** You'll wait ages for shoots to pop up, but it's worth the suspense. Tangerine-colored blooms are streaked with pink—and it's another of the few fragrant tulips. Grows about 14 inches (35 cm) high.

✿ **'Christmas Marvel':** Pot this one up in early October, and it may bloom in time for the big holiday. Pretty cherry pink blooms. About 14 inches (35 cm) high.

✿ **'Flair':** Buttercup yellow, with red "feathers" on the petals. Grows 14 inches (35 cm) high.

✿ **'Monsella':** A fragrant early double with canary yellow blooms feathered in red. Grows about 12 inches (30 cm) high.

✿ **'Monte Carlo':** Another fragrant double tulip that some bulb fanciers say is easy to force. The blooms are a bright yellow. Great on a window ledge when everything's covered in snow outside. Grows about 12 inches (30 cm) tall and may bloom early.

Species tulips to force

These are the closest cousins to the original tulips found growing in the wild. Some forcing enthusiasts have better luck forcing them than the hybrid varieties. Try:

✿ **Any *greigii* variety:** Very different-looking tulips, these are popping up more and more in flower shops nowadays—either potted or as cut flowers. They are real "toughies" in the tulip world, with leaves that are surprisingly large and wide, and mottled or striped in rust red. This leaf patterning is controversial. People either love it or hate it. Varieties include 'Red Riding Hood,' whose flowers are a brilliant scarlet; 'Yellow Dawn,' which is rose pink with a wide yellow band; popular 'Cape Cod,'

> ## Hot tip
>
> "Forced bulbs can be unpredictable. They often produce flowers much quicker, or slower, than the experts say. I've had tulips that are supposedly late-flowering sprout and send up buds in only a few weeks! The temperature at which they are stored is certainly a factor. The colder it is, the slower they'll start to sprout."
> —*Stewart Hamilton, forced bulb fancier*

which is apricot edged with yellow; and 'Toronto,' which is red with pointy petals.

🏵 **'White Emperor':** a *fosteriana* class of tulip, with thick tough stems and big squarish blooms. Very striking.

A forcing formula that works

Do

✓ Buy big bulbs. Generally speaking, the bigger the bulb, the bigger the flowers. (You'll also get more of them.)

✓ Examine bulb labels carefully. Some helpful growers now indicate when their offerings are "suitable for forcing."

✓ If you can't plant right away, store bulbs in the refrigerator or a cool room.

✓ Use any kind of pot—plastic, clay, or glazed pottery—so long as it has a drainage hole. Shallow pots tend to show off spring bulbs better.

✓ Buy potting soil or a mix that contains compost and peat moss. If you can, add a bit of coarse builder's sand. (Bulbs love it.)

✓ Plant bulbs so that they are close together, but not touching. They don't mind being crammed together in one container. They also look better in a mass.

✓ Make sure bulbs are securely positioned in the mix, with only their snouts sticking out of the soil. Potted bulbs are inclined to heave up as they grow. If you haven't surrounded them with enough soil, they may wind up sitting too high in the pot—and they will topple over when leaves and stems develop.

✓ Take a good, hard look at tulip bulbs before planting them. Make sure they are planted with their *flat* side facing outwards. Tulips throw out their first and biggest leaves on that side, and if those leaves face into the container, they'll crowd (and mask) the blooms.

✓ Water well, then put the pot in a cool place *in complete darkness* (see page 91).

✓ Leave the pots alone for ten to twelve weeks. Check periodically. If the tops look dry, give them a bit of water.

✓ Little shoots (they'll be white or yellowish) will eventually appear. Wait till they're about an inch (2.5 cm) tall, then bring them out into a room with subdued lighting.

✓ After a week or two, when the tops have turned green, move again to a well-lit spot. (If it gets direct sun, that's fine.) Blooms should follow in a few more weeks.

✓ Keep all spring bulbs in a cool room if you can. The flowers will last longer, and leaves and stems won't get as leggy.

✓ Prop blooms up with dogwood or corkscrew hazel stems if they get too leggy.

Don't

✗ Buy spring bulbs packaged in sealed plastic bags. The bulbs may be moldy. The bags should have holes punched in their sides.

✗ Leave bulbs sitting around for weeks in a warm room before you plant them.

✗ Add bulb fertilizer to the pot. It's not necessary.

✗ Worry if a bit of mold develops on top of the soil during the chilling-out period. It is harmless, and you can easily brush it off once you bring the bulbs into the light.

✗ Shut potted bulbs up in a closet without any ventilation if you want to prevent mold from growing on the surface.

✗ Fertilize forced bulbs when they're blooming. All they require is the occasional bit of plain water.

✗ Plant forced bulbs in the garden after their burst of glory is over. Experts say they will bloom again, but they often don't—and why devote space to iffy plants that are going to take up tons of space? Your best bet is to buy new bulbs for the garden the following fall. In the meantime, dump their forced fellows on the compost heap.

> ## Hot tip
> "Winter heat in homes is too dry and warm for many flowers. If you mist forced bulbs several times a week, or use a humidifier, you can extend their blooming period."
> —Becky Heath, bulb expert

Cool it, man

If forced bulbs could talk, that's what they'd probably tell us. To bloom, spring bulbs must be subjected to a period of cold—and preferably complete darkness—beforehand. Finding a suitable site, particularly if you live in a condo or apartment, can be tricky. In fact, for amateur gardeners, it's the most difficult aspect of forcing. The temperature should be between 41 and 50°F (5 and 10°C), but it mustn't freeze. You also can't place the bulbs' containers in a spot that's exposed to bright daylight—or where somebody will keep turning a light on. So where? Here are some suggestions:

- a dark corner on an unheated porch;
- a garage attached to a house (where the temperature is unlikely to drop below freezing);
- an underground garage in a condo (if there's a lot of artificial light in the garage, place a cardboard box, with holes punched in it for ventilation, over the pots); or
- a pit dug in the garden with straw or leaves on top, weighted down with a board.

Skip forcing these

Some bulbs hate being pushed to perform before their time. The troublesome ones may produce leaves but no flowers, or their buds may fail to open and fall off, or their blooms may be few and far between, or their stems may get too tall and flop over. Experts at the Netherlands Flower Bulb Information Center recommend that you don't bother to try forcing these:

- **Narcissi:** 'Little Beauty'; 'Little Gem'; 'Small Talk'; *N. canaliculatus*; *N. bulbocodium*; 'Golden Bells.'
- **Tulips:** 'Happy Family'; 'Purple Prince'; 'Mickey Mouse.'

Too busy to force your own bulbs?

Ready-potted spring bulbs are now sold everywhere—in supermarkets, city greengrocers, florists, and convenience stores. In fact, you can find a surprising variety, particularly of tulips and narcissus. If you go for these (and they are certainly cheap),

🏵 Check that plants have healthy-looking buds, not yet fully open. If flowers are already in bloom, they may look glorious, but they won't last long. Don't buy plants that have lots of foliage but no buds visible.

🏵 Skip crocus and snowdrops. Their blooming period is so short they aren't worth hauling home.

🏵 As soon as you get home, remove the plant sleeve (a funnel made of paper or see-through plastic wrapped around plants to protect them). It stops air from circulating around plants.

🏵 Take off any foil wrap around the pot too. It looks tacky, detracts from the flowers, and contrary to popular opinion, won't stop water from dripping onto the tabletop.

It's worth buying pricier bulbs. Order them by mail from a bulb specialist or visit an established garden center. At the latter, choose the ones sold in open cardboard boxes (they're usually nestled in wood shavings, and you simply pick out what you want) rather than prepackaged net bags. Bagged bulbs are cheaper, but can end up costing more in the long run as moldy, broken, or otherwise unusable specimens are sometimes mixed in with the good bulbs.

If the papery skin has come off the bulbs, don't worry. That won't affect their ability to grow. In fact, it sometimes enhances it. But don't buy bulbs that are squashy, dried up, wrinkled, or split. A bulb that's broken in half or missing a chunk of its fleshy layers won't grow and isn't worth planting.

Watch for bargains late in the season. Garden centers often sell off the last of their stock at half-price before Christmas. But make sure you can see what you're getting. Avoid boxed bulbs.

- Stand pots on a saucer and give them a good drink if they look dried out. But after that, water sparingly. Bulbs don't need much sustenance during their blooming period. And don't mix fertilizer into the water.
- Display in groups if you've bought several pots. Spring bulbs look nice mixed together.
- If flower stems start flopping everywhere, prop them up with branches (see page 89). Potted forced bulbs sold at florists and garden centers are particularly prone to flop because they've been goosed with lots of fertilizer.

The Importance of Light

We often ignore one of the most crucial aspects of getting greenery to grow well indoors: light. All of us are guilty of spotting an appealing plant on sale, buying it on impulse, and then plunking it anywhere we can find space in the living room. Then, when our new purchase promptly bites the dust, we get mad. But usually the plant isn't to blame (nor is the store where we so rashly bought it). The problem is probably light. Indoors, the amount of light plants receive—and what kind of light—is far more crucial than outside in a garden. In fact, it's worth spending a few minutes to figure out exactly how much light you have inside your house, apartment, or condo before buying anything.

Check these factors

🏵 which way the windows face;
🏵 how big the windows are;
🏵 the obstructions that block the light coming in; and
🏵 how far north you live.

If your room faces south, and it isn't shadowed by trees or other buildings, in most locations you can expect to receive at least several hours of sunlight a day (that is, when the sun shines!). Facing east or west, you'll get a lot less sunshine. Bear in mind that afternoon sun (western exposure) is much stronger and hotter than morning sun (eastern exposure). If you face north, your room may not get any direct sunshine at all, although that also depends upon your location. In northern lati-

tudes, the sun swings surprisingly far north in summertime and
a north-facing window can pick up direct sunlight in the mornings or afternoons, particularly between June and September.

Five types of light

The type of light indoor plants require is generally divided into five basic categories:

Hot tip
"I like to turn my houseplants
180 degrees every week.
Then they grow in a balanced
manner."
—Charlie Dobbin,
houseplant expert

❀ **Direct sun:** South-facing windows with
unobstructed sunshine for much of the day.
If a plant carries a label that says "requires
sun" or "sun-loving," it needs this kind of
location. Bear in mind that many indoor houseplants hate
this kind of light. Sun beaming through the glass can fry
them, particularly in the summer.

❀ **Bright filtered light:** Also direct sun, but filtered
through blinds or thin curtains. Many houseplants adapt
well to this kind of light.

- 🏵 **Bright indirect light:** An area of the room that receives lots of light, but isn't hit directly by the sun. This works well for many houseplants.
- 🏵 **Medium light:** A north-facing window, where no sun streams in, usually has this kind of light. So do the shaded areas of sunny rooms. Some houseplants do fine in this environment.
- 🏵 **Low light:** Corners of rooms that are a long way from a light source fall into this category. Only a few toughies can tolerate this kind of lighting.

Ways to lighten things up

Do

✓ Paint walls white or a pale color.

✓ Position plants against a pale background or in a spot where they can pick up light that's bounced off another surface.

✓ Plant everything in white pots. (This will also create a feeling of unity in a small space.)

✓ Buy some indoor lights. They don't have to be expensive or complicated (see page 69).

✓ Turn plants when you see them straining towards the light. If a plant keeps doing this, it needs a brighter location.

Don't

✗ Leave reading lamps or overhead lights on, hoping they'll help houseplants grow. The amount of light spread from such sources is minimal.

✗ Shift plants abruptly from a brightly lit area to a dim one—or vice versa. Move them gradually, increasing their exposure to the new light source over a period of two weeks.

✗ Presume you can't grow anything. A few plants adapt amazingly well to low light conditions.

✗ Turn a plant with a bud-ready bloom into direct sunshine. The sudden change may prompt the bud to fall off.

> ## Hot tip
> "Don't put houseplants too close to indoor grow lights or they'll get crisped. Six inches (15 cm) is a good distance."
> —*Mary Fran McQuade, urban gardener*

Get Hip to the Two H's

To cultivate anything successfully indoors, pay attention to two important factors: heat and humidity. You must be able to provide the right temperature for your plants, but what's equally important, and often overlooked, is the amount of moisture in the air.

Unfortunately, in modern homes, it can be difficult to fulfill both these requirements. The problem is central heating. This kind of heat maintains a steady temperature twenty-four hours a day—and it is usually very dry. That's tolerable for people, but not for plants. Many so-called houseplants grow naturally in the tropical rainforests and coastal areas of Africa, Asia, and South America. In such locations, the sun bakes down during the day, but the temperature often dips sharply at night—and it's very humid. Obviously, it's hard to duplicate that kind of environment in the average North American condo, apartment, or house.

First, the heat ...

Do

✓ Take the trouble to check what temperature houseplants prefer when buying them. This information is usually marked on their labels. Most plants can cope with an environment that's 5°F (3°C) warmer or cooler than their desired range. But if the temperature in your home is consistently higher or lower than what's indicated on the label, the plant probably won't last long.

✓ Go for plants that prefer a range of 65 to 75°F (18 to 24°C). They are the easiest choices for most North American homes.

✓ Turn down the heat at night if you can. Most houseplants like a dip of between 5 and 10°F (3 to 6°C). But don't overdo it. Fluctuations of more than 20°F (12°C) over a twenty-four-hour period are not a good idea.

✓ Stick to really easy houseplants if you live in a condo or apartment where it's not possible to adjust the thermostat at night (see page 13).

✓ Be careful about placing plants on shelves over radiators or heating vents. It's usually too hot and dry.

Don't

✗ Buy indoor flowering plants such as cyclamens if your place is very warm during the winter. Most flowering houseplants prefer it cool. Blooms won't last long if the central heating is cranked up.

✗ Put plants in drafty locations. Check if there's a draft by putting a lighted candle in a saucer and watching the flame. If it blows sideways (or worse, gets extinguished), that's definitely not a good spot! You often get drafts from front and back entrances or doors leading out to balconies or patios.

✗ Place anything near a refrigerator. Plants don't take kindly to the blasts of cold air that come out when you open the door.

Watch for the "drape droops"

This happens when plants are shut between a heavy curtain and a window on a cold night—and it's very common. The poor plant, banished suddenly from the cozy warmth in the room, goes into shock. It gets droopy, its leaves may go brown or black at the tips—and it often won't recover.

If you have drapes at your windows, always tuck them behind plants during the winter months (ditto if you use blinds). Better still, keep tropical plants away from window ledges if you live in an area that's cursed with long, cold winters.

... And then the humidity

Humidity is crucial for houseplants, but the word is often misunderstood. Many beginners assume that if their plants are watered long enough—and regularly enough—their plants will get enough humidity. Unfortunately, that's not the case. The term "humidity" means the relative amount of water vapor contained in the air. It has nothing to do how wet you keep your plant's containers.

Why plants need that moisture

The leaves of all plants are covered in stomata (tiny pores) that open to receive gases in the atmosphere. When the stomata open, the leaves lose moisture, in a process called transpiration. If there isn't sufficient water vapor in the air to accommodate for this loss, the leaves get parched. They may shrivel. The buds (and/or flowers) may fall off. The whole plant will fade. This can happen remarkably quickly in buildings that are centrally heated.

Scientists measure the amount of moisture in the air through what's called the "relative humidity factor." A factor of 100% equals fog—you can actually see the droplets of moisture under those conditions. Most houseplants don't need to spend their lives drenched in this kind of foggy mist. A humidity factor of around 40% will keep them happily churning out juicy green leaves. (Some specimens that come from steamy tropical jungles do prefer the air to be practically dripping with moisture, but they're the kind of plants you see growing in greenhouses.)

Generally speaking, houseplants with thick, leathery leaves are better able to withstand the winter dryness in our homes because they lose less moisture to transpiration. But all plants prefer some humidity. To ensure there's enough water vapor in the air to keep your plants healthy and happy,

Do

✓ Buy a humidifier. It's the best way to make sure houseplants stay fresh and green. Small table-top models that vaporize water (such as Pure Mist) are terrific if you live in

Spraying a fine mist of water over plants helps keep humidity high—and costs peanuts. Pick up a cheap plastic misting bottle at a hardware store (you can find fancier models at garden decor boutiques, but the cheapies work just as well). Spray daily, directly onto the foliage and flowers. Make sure the water's clean. Don't let it go stagnant in the bottle.

a small space. Drum humidifiers are a good choice in large homes because they circulate moisture to a wider area.

✓ Ask to see a demonstration of the humidifier before buying it. Some models are much noisier than others.

✓ Run the humidifier for a few hours every day of the year if you live in a contained environment that's heated in winter and air-conditioned in summer.

✓ Put it in the same room as the majority of your houseplants.

✓ Make sure the unit is in an accessible spot and can be filled easily. (You don't want to be slopping water all over the floor.)

✓ Put saucers under your plants, filled with half an inch (1.25 cm) of water.

✓ Raise the plants up in the saucers, on a layer of pebbles.

✓ Put several plants together on a tray, with pebbles underneath them. Grouping the leaves together helps the plants retain humidity.

Don't

✗ Forget to fill the humidifier. They run out of water awfully quickly!

✗ Leave water to get stagnant in plant saucers. It should be changed regularly.

✗ Buy tropical plants that have thin, papery leaves, such as caladiums, if the humidity in your home is low. Generally speaking, these need more moisture than the kinds with thick, strappy greenery.

> ## Hot tip
> "Put your humidifier in an unobtrusive spot, like behind the sofa, and run it every night. I turn mine on at 8:30 p.m., then turn it off when I get up. My plants love it."
> —Richard Tawton,
> *condo houseplant fan*

Potting and Fertilizing

Most indoor plants have one big advantage over plants bought for the outdoor garden: they don't have to be planted. Not initially, anyway. Whether you bring home a strapping ficus tree or a tiny cactus, it usually comes potted up in its own container. Eventually, however, most houseplants need to be repotted into bigger pots as their roots take up more and more space. The growing mix also gets tired and starts to disappear (yes, really. It actually does turn into dust).

How to tell when a plant is pot-bound

A plant that's pot-bound is like a kid wearing shoes that are too small. Its "toes" get pinched, and eventually the whole plant may become permanently deformed or stunted. This is a very common occurrence. People often call up gardening hot lines to complain that there's "something wrong" with their indoor plants; on investigation, it turns out to be not insects or a viral infection (as the callers expect), but simply a case of the plants getting too big for their boots. A plant may be pot-bound if

- ❀ it's wilting—and doesn't perk up when you water it;
- ❀ leaf tips are turning brown;
- ❀ leaves are constantly turning yellow and dropping off (though this might also be caused by other factors, such as inconsistent watering (see page 112), or moving the plant);

- ❀ the leaves seem to be shrinking;
- ❀ water doesn't soak into the soil but runs over the top and down the sides of the container;
- ❀ roots are poking out the drainage holes at the bottom.

Repotting the wise way

Do

✓ Water the pot-bound plant about an hour before you plan to give it a new home; the roots will be less inclined to be brittle—and break.

✓ Lay newspaper on the floor for easy cleanup.

✓ Turn the pot upside down and, cradling the plant in your hand, knock the pot against the side of a table. This should loosen the root ball. (It may take a few raps.)

✓ With big pots, run a knife blade around the soil ball to loosen it, then enlist the help of a friend to tip the plant out. If the plant won't come loose, you may be forced to break the container open (let's hope it's a cheap plastic one).

✓ Lift out the root ball and inspect it.

✓ If roots are entangled in crockery at the bottom of the pot, loosen them gently.

✓ Check for bugs (particularly mealy bugs) and cut off diseased or mushy-looking bits. If the plant is full of creepy-crawlies, throw it out.

✓ Choose the same kind of pot as before for the plant's new home. Plants are like people: they don't like drastic change foisted upon them. If the plant was growing in a plastic pot, don't switch to clay—and vice versa.

✓ Put crockery, stones, or a coffee filter in the bottom of the new container.

✓ Add some growing mix or potting soil, pushing it up the pot sides a bit. Then position the root ball on top. Aim to have at least half an inch (1.25 cm) of space between the top of the soil and the rim of the pot so soil won't run over the sides of the pot when you water.

✓ Pack more soil around the root ball with your fingers. Push it in firmly.

✓ Thump the pot on the table as you're doing this. It helps the soil settle in the pot.

✓ Have lots more soil on hand than you think you'll need. Running out halfway through the job is annoying (and often happens).

✓ Water the plant thoroughly as soon as you have finished repotting.

Don't

✗ Yank plants out of pots by their leaves and stems.

✗ Use a pot that's too big. It's tempting to repot a plant in a huge container to save the task of doing it again down the road. But most plants prefer to "move up" slowly. Generally speaking, there should be about an inch (2.5 cm) of air space between the plant's root ball and the sides of the new container

✗ Use old, grubby pots, with soil clinging to their interiors. Wash used pots thoroughly (see below).

✗ Press the plant down with your hands if it's sitting too high in the pot. The roots will get compressed. Instead, remove the plant from the pot and start again.

Hot tip

"Raid your kitchen cabinet for houseplant tools, or go to garage sales. You don't need to buy anything expensive. An old stock pot is great for mixing up potting soil. Stir it with an old fork. Dole the soil into pots with an old kitchen spoon. Use a chopstick to make holes for plant cuttings."
—*Mary-Fran McQuade, budget gardener*

Wash your pots

Anytime you use an old pot, scrub it out first to prevent diseases and bug eggs that may have been lurking in the pot from infecting your plant. Mix water with a bit of bleach—a cupful (250 mL) to a bucket or sinkful of water is a good ratio—and wear rubber gloves. (Long gloves that reach above the elbows are perfect for this job. They're sold in hardware stores, or by mail order from garden products companies.) Remove hardened bits of soil and decayed matter clinging to the sides of pots with a hard brush. Rinse the pots and let them dry before filling them with growing mix.

Potting soil or soil-less mix?

Those big, shiny bags at garden centers can be bewildering. It's hard to know which product to buy. Check the labels; there are now special formulas for many different kinds of plants—African violets, cactus, and orchids, for example—and it pays to pick an appropriate one. But bear in mind that the most expensive mix isn't necessarily the best. A garden writer who conducted tests found that mixes varied enormously, and in one test (on annual plants grown in window boxes) the most expensive mix performed the worst.

Potting soil: Also sometimes called houseplant soil, potting soil is heavier than growing mixes, and it works well for most houseplants. If you're repotting a big plant, pick potting soil instead of a lightweight growing mix—it will anchor the plant better.

Bagged potting soil varies enormously, but usually contains a mixture of organic and inorganic ingredients such as peat moss, compost, sand, and vermiculite. Some products have slow-release fertilizers added. You'll also see "sterilized" potting soil, which has been heated to over 180°F (82°C) to kill bacteria and weed seeds. It's fine to use this, particularly if you're worried about bugs and bacteria multiplying indoors. However, *don't* buy sterilized soil if you intend to stick to organic fertilizers, such as fish emulsion or seaweed extract. These products need the microorganisms found in the unsterilized stuff to work.

Don't start seeds in potting soil (it's too heavy), and never bring soil from the garden indoors—it may be full of bugs, which will multiply like mad in your pots.

Soil-less mixes: Lighter than potting soil, soil-less mixes are specially formulated for plants grown in containers. They usually consist of peat moss (lots of it), plus perlite and/or vermiculite, both of which look like nubbly bits of Styrofoam. Other organic materials, such as composted softwood bark, may be added, as well as slow-release fertilizers. The additives are all designed to improve drainage.

Most potted plants require good drainage. The best way to supply it is to add sand to your growing mix. Cacti crave a high proportion of sand. Herbs also seem to thrive in soil that's on the sandy side. You can sometimes find bags labeled "horticultural sand" at garden centers. But it's much cheaper to buy regular builder's sand at a home reno store or a construction site. Do not use beach sand from the ocean (it's too salty) or fine sand from around a lake. It should feel coarse and contain sharp particles. (Gardening books often use the rather mystifying term "sharp sand" to describe this stuff.)

Some of these mixes are "sterilized," some aren't. Both work fine, but the same rules regarding fertilizers apply to mixes as to potting soil. If you want to "go organic," don't selected a sterilized mix. Starting seeds is another matter. You *must* use a sterile mix (see page 71).

Generally speaking, short-lived flowering plants do better in a lightweight mix than in potting soil. But shop around and experiment, because the contents of those bags you see at garden centers can be very unpredictable.

Cheer your plants with charcoal

Add a small chunk of charcoal to your growing mix—it will help absorb odors and other impurities, such as fertilizer salts. It's especially good in the bottom of a container that has no drainage—an aquarium or a bottle, for instance. Charcoal can be hard to find in garden centers. Buy it at a pet store, where it's sold for use in aquarium filters.

A few fertilizer facts

The topic of fertilizers perplexes many people. Those funny groups of numbers—15-30-15, 20-20-20—what do they mean? Is it necessary to know all this scientific stuff?

No—and yes. Amateur indoor gardeners don't need to understand the complex technical aspects of fertilizers and how they work. But a basic understanding of plant nutrients (which is what fertilizers are) is helpful, because your potted plants require them to thrive. The fact is, most plants grown in containers do better if they receive occasional applications of fertilizer. This may pose an ethical dilemma if you're concerned about the environment (nowadays, many of us hesitate to do anything "artificial"), but there simply isn't sufficient nourishment in containers to leave everything to Mother Nature in the long term.

What the numbers mean

All fertilizers contain three basic nutrients:

* Nitrogen (N) promotes growth of green leaves and stems.
* Phosphorus (P) helps roots, flowers, and fruit grow.
* Potassium (K) assists flowering and fruiting, but also helps plants develop strong stems and resistance to disease.

The three symbols are always listed in that order on product labels. A bottle of plant food that says 5-10-5 on its label contains 5% nitrogen, 10% phosphorus, and 5% potassium.

What's best to use? It depends on your plants. A good all-round formula is 20-20-20 or 10-10-10. These work well with most houseplants.

Organic or chemical?

Both have merits. "Natural" fertilizers—often, composted manure, fish emulsion, bone meal, and/or blood meal—are more expensive, but they take effect slowly and generally won't harm plants. Chemical products get quicker results, but can burn leaves and roots if used incorrectly. Ultimately, the choice is a personal one. Look for a product that suits what you're growing and follow label instructions to the letter. More plants are killed by people being too generous with fertilizer than by anything else.

Caution: don't use organic fertilizers containing fish emulsion or blood meal if you have cats. Kitties are attracted to the smell of both, and the little devils will often dig up potted plants in search of a snack. The same rule applies if you live in an area that's plagued by raccoons and you plan to put your plants outside on a balcony or deck in summertime. These wild critters love blood meal and things that smell fishy, and they will go digging too.

Wet or dry?

There are many different fertilizers aimed at home gardeners nowadays. They have names like Granny's Jungle Juice and Bob's Therapy for Houseplants, and are divided into five basic types:

❀ **Liquid:** Some of these you mix into a watering can, others are ready to use, and you spray them directly on leaves or the soil. The latter may be called "foliar spray" or "nutritional spray" or "nutrient leaf spray" or simply "plant food." Sprays are certainly easy to use. However, they have drawbacks. It's easy to overdo the spraying by mistake, burning leaves, and the nutrients are quickly leached from the soil when you water the plant. Use them with caution. Most foliar sprays are designed to give a quick boost to plants that are looking lousy. Organic liquid fertilizers, such as seaweed extract (also called kelp), which you dilute with water, are a better bet. They won't burn plants and are a good source of micronutrients. But they tend to be expensive.

❀ **Soluble:** These usually come in the form of crystals (often a lurid shade of turquoise), which you mix into a jug of water. They are the most widely used fertilizers for potted plants, and are often simply labeled "plant food." You will see different concentrations, but 20-20-20 is a good all-round formula that works well for most houseplants. Use this stuff sparingly; don't be tempted to mix more crystals into your watering can than the directions indicate. And let the concoction sit overnight before you pour it on plants.

❀ **Spikes:** Little stakes of compacted fiber, impregnated with fertilizer, that you push into the soil. They are convenient for houseplants, but be sure to pick the right size or you may burn the plants' roots. Spikes also tend to be expensive. Soluble fertilizers give a bigger bang for the buck.

❁ **Teabags:** A new gimmick that's becoming hot. Basically, this is composted manure packed in "teabags" and sold in a pretty box. You soak the bags for twenty-four hours in water, then pour on plants. One product is called Barnyard Bounty. It's 100% organic and won't harm plants, but its nutrient concentration is very weak—only 2-3-2—and so it won't deliver much of a boost.

❁ **Time-release:** Fertilizers in capsule form, just like the vitamins we take. These release nutrients over an extended period of time, usually up to nine months—and they are designed to work their magic as the soil temperature rises. They are better used outdoors than on indoor plants.

Wise Up to Watering

Worried about when to water your houseplants? You're not alone. Gauging the right time to give indoor plants a drink is a justifiable source of anxiety, because it's unquestionably more complicated than doing the job outdoors. In a garden or on a balcony, it's usually a simple matter of hauling out the garden hose or watering can when plants (or the lawn) look thirsty. However, in the artificial environment of our homes, watering is not so straightforward.

Five factors to consider

1. **What kind of plant is it?** Generally speaking, the thicker the leaves, the less water the plant needs (because it can store moisture in the foliage). A rubber plant, for instance, is virtually indestructible. But thin-leafed tropical plants such as caladiums require more TLC. Most should be kept slightly moist, but not water-logged. Some, like *Ficus benjamina*, must never be allowed to dry out. Their thin, shiny leaves are incapable of retaining water. (Finicky ficus may die abruptly, with no warning signs like wilting, if you forget to water it.) Most cacti and succulent plants prefer their soil on the dry side. So do flowering plants, such as kalanchoe, once their period of vigorous growth and flowering is finished. Other bloomers, such as amaryllis and spring bulbs, shouldn't receive much water when they're in bloom. Confusing, isn't it?

2. **Where is the plant growing?** In a sunny window, plants will dry out much more quickly than in the interior of a room. They'll stay damp in a bathroom or kitchen. If the room is very warm, with the central heating going full blast, they'll probably require more frequent watering than what's considered normal for those types of plants. The proximity of heating and air-conditioning ducts, radiators, and fireplaces also plays a big role.

3. **What season is it?** During the winter, most plants have a slower rate of growth, so they require less water. Some go into semi-hibernation and need only a dribble of water now and then to stay alive. Most plants are at their thirstiest in spring, when they're putting out lots of fresh new growth, and summer. But there are exceptions. Winter-blooming tuberous plants, such as cyclamens, require plenty of water in winter, but none in summer, when they go dormant.

4. **What type of pots and growing mix have you used?** Pot up two identical houseplants indoors—one in a clay flowerpot, the other in plastic. You'll be amazed by how much quicker the clay container dries out. Growing mixes also influence how often you need to water. Potting soil retains water much longer than mixes containing peat moss, vermiculite, or perlite. If you add sand to your mix (a smart idea with some plants, like cacti and spring bulbs, that like good drainage) the pot will dry out faster.

5. **How old are your plants?** Plants that are established, with lots of roots twirling around inside their pots, need water more often than new plants.

> **Hot tip**
> "Choose a particular day of the week to water your plants. Then attach a word to that day to remind you. For instance, Moisten Monday or Wet Wednesday or Thirsty Thursday. That way, you won't forget."
> —*Anne Lockley, houseplant lover*

Check plant labels

Take the trouble to examine the information shown on plant labels; they usually provide the best guide to a plant's watering requirements. (But remember to take the factors listed above into consideration.) Look for one of three magic words on the label:

- 🏵 "Plentifully," or "frequently," means you should keep the growing mix consistently moist. Never let it dry out.
- 🏵 "Moderately" means give the plant a good soak, but let the top inch (2.5 cm) or so of the mix dry out before you water again.
- 🏵 "Sparingly" indicates that only an occasional watering is required. Never soak the plant so that water comes out the bottom of the pot. Let the growing mix get dry as a bone before watering again.

If the leaves wilt or the entire plant gets droopy, you're not watering enough. Some plants' stems may shrink, as well. But sometimes there are no warning signs. The plant will simply shrivel up and die from lack of water.

Overwatering: It's the biggest mistake beginners can make

We're so keen to cosset our plants, we often give the poor things too much to drink—and they drown. Plants will sometimes wilt when there's insufficient water, but this condition is also an indicator that you are wielding the watering can too often. Other telltale signs are leaves turning yellow, stems that are soft and transparent-looking (or turning black), and soil that is sodden, not simply moist. Turn an unhappy-looking plant out of its pot and examine its roots. If they look mushy and black, you're giving it too much water. Cut the mushy bits off and restore the plant to its pot with some fresh growing mix. It may recover.

Another common mistake is inconsistent watering. Most plants prefer a regimen. Yellow leaves are often a sign that your watering practices are not consistent enough. Put your plants on a schedule and stick to it. If you water once a week, for example, always water on the same day.

Hot tip

"If your houseplants are looking waterlogged, wrap a pencil in a piece of newspaper and insert it in the soil. The newspaper will absorb the water."

—*Deirdre Black, houseplant lover*

Who watered the broadloom?

You can always tell the homes of houseplant addicts: they're the ones with water marks on the coffee tables and stained patches on the carpet or hardwood flooring. But these folks aren't just sloppy. It's awfully easy to make a mess when watering plants indoors. Water comes out the drainage hole at the bottom, overflows from the saucer, and oops!

Here's how to give plants a drink without wrecking everything else in the process:

Do

✓ Buy a watering can that's designed for houseplants. It should have a long, slim curving spout that pokes right into pots—and it should not be too big. It's courting disaster to lug around heavy containers full of water.

✓ Aim the water at the soil, not the leaves.

✓ Move small plants to the kitchen sink or bathtub to water them.

✓ Make sure the saucers underneath pots are deep enough to hold the runoff.

✓ Place a layer of gravel in saucers to raise houseplants up, providing more space for the runoff.

> ### Hot tip
> "Plastic dinner trays sold at restaurant and hotel supply stores are great for putting underneath indoor plants. Spread a thin layer of aquarium gravel on the tray, then group plants together, without saucers, on top of the gravel."
> —*Priscilla Leung, houseplant fan*

✓ Water from the bottom, if you can, by filling the saucer and letting the plant drink up the water through its roots. For some hairy-leaved plants, like African violets, this is a must. Check plant labels.

✓ Be careful of potted plants crammed too full of soil. Spring bulbs are often sold this way. When you water, the overflow will dribble down the sides. There should be at least half an inch (1.25 cm) of space between the top of the soil and the pot rim.

✓ Do messy jobs—like mixing plant food into watering cans, or repotting plants—at the kitchen or bathroom sink, not on the dining room table.

Don't

✗ Use an outdoor watering can with a rose nozzle. It will spray water everywhere.

✗ Leave plants sitting in saucers of water and then keep adding more water on top. This will rot the roots of many plants. Tip the residue out after a few hours, or if that's not practical (as with big pots), suck it out with a turkey baster.

✗ Pour water onto long, pointy leaves that have an indentation running down their centers (those of amaryllis, for instance). The water will run straight down those leaves onto the floor.

✗ Leave decorative wrap around potted plants. It's not waterproof. Take the foil off (it looks tacky, anyway) and stand the pot in a saucer before you water.

Lukewarm is luverly

Most plants don't like being subjected to an icy cold shower any more than we do. Fill your watering can and let it sit overnight before giving plants a drink. Here's another advantage of waiting a while before watering: chlorine (which plants hate) gets dispelled from city tap water if it's allowed to sit in a container for a few hours. If you have lots of plants to water, keep a bucket handy under the sink or in the bath, then dip into that with an old yogurt container.

Gadgets and gizmos to water with

All kinds of gadgets are available now. Some are terrific, others a waste of money. Look for these in mail-order garden supply catalogs:

✿ **Telescoping hoses:** They look like concertinaed telephone cords and thus don't take up much space. You can attach them to a kitchen tap and stash them in a cupboard after use.

🌸 **The RainStick:** If you have lots of hanging baskets, this gadget—which is basically an oversized syringe—will be a godsend. Draw water from a bucket or kitchen sink into the syringe, then squirt it into the center of the plant. It's ideal for use indoors because you can direct the water where it's needed most, without splashing everything else.

🌸 **Automatic plant waterers:** The best ones come from Europe and are designed specifically for use with indoor plants. They have ceramic cones with lids, which are inserted into potting mix and connected to thin hoses plunked into jars of water. You fill the cone and the jar with water. More liquid is wicked through the hose as the plant needs it. They are effective, but you can get the same effect with a homemade wicking system.

How to wick water into plants

It's a smart idea to provide all plants with a wicking system when you plant them, in case you go away. Then you can simply stick the wick into a container of water during your absence. Here's a method that works:

🌸 Buy some 3-ply synthetic knitting yarn. Don't use wool (it rots). Old pantyhose, cut into pieces, or nylon cord from a fishing supply store are also fine.

🌸 Thread a long piece of yarn through the hole in the pot before you add growing mix. Then fill the pot with mix, making sure to leave a short length of yarn sticking out of the bottom and a longer piece hanging over the pot's side.

🌸 When you've filled the pot and positioned the plant in it, cut off the length of yarn sticking out the bottom.

❀ To wick water, simply place the long end of the yarn sticking out at the top into a water-filled container. (Put it in an unobtrusive spot, behind the pot. Strings of yarn and old pantyhose aren't exactly elegant.) Old cottage cheese tubs make good containers. Cut a hole in their lids. You can also give plants a gentle dose of fertilizer using this wicking system. Just mix the plant food crystals into the water container.

Get out the DustBuster

> **Hot tip**
>
> "Give your houseplants a bath once a month. Put them in the tub, then turn the shower on for a couple of minutes. Make sure the water is lukewarm. My plants love it."
>
> —*Richard Tawton, indoor condo gardener*

We've all been in homes full of dusty houseplants. Aside from being unattractive, dust isn't good for the plants—it prevents them from breathing. Wash your greenery regularly, and it will be healthier. The simplest method is to occasionally put your plants under the shower. If they're too big to haul into the bathroom, treat them to a sponge bath. Wipe leaves off with a damp cloth or sponge, dipped in clean water. Be sure to support big leaves with one hand while you wipe with the other. Wipe the undersides of leaves, too.

Some people swear by olive oil or beer to clean houseplant leaves. Others think milk is marvelous. Still others buy commercial leaf-shine products. The truth is, a glossy leaf isn't necessarily a healthy one. Plain, lukewarm water works best. Some of the other substances may make plants shine, but they block their pores and often leave residue on the leaves. Milk and beer may also turn sour and get smelly.

When you go on vacation

Group plants in the bathtub or kitchen sink, give them a shower before you go, and then leave them there. And stop worrying. Most indoor plants will survive well in that setup for a couple of weeks. For longer absences,

✿ Drape a length of self-wicking mat (sold at garden centers) on the kitchen counter, with one end of the mat dipped into a sink full of water. Stand pots on the counter, with the mat underneath them. Water will wick upwards by capillary action. Alternatively, use the homemade wicking system described above.

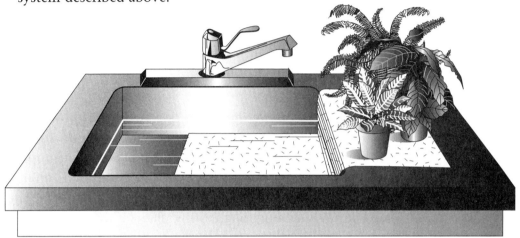

✿ Put transparent plastic bags over moisture-loving plants and seal them closed with elastics. (Be careful not to crush foliage when you do this. Use big bags.)
✿ Ask someone who knows about plants to come in and water for you. *Occasionally.* One of the biggest complaints of indoor gardeners is that, when they go away, well-meaning friends promptly kill their house-plants by overwatering them.

Mites, Mildew, and Other Nasties

We live in a buggy world, and there's no escaping it inside our homes. In fact, houseplants are quite vulnerable to attack by all kinds of infuriating insects and creepy-crawlies, partly because they live in what is essentially an artificial environment. Bugs may hitch a ride indoors on one plant, then multiply like mad on neighboring plants if the conditions are right. And unlike their cousins ensconced out of doors, these imported bugs don't get killed off in winter. It's pretty much the same story with viruses and fungal diseases. They may take hold and become hard to eradicate.

Another annoying fact of indoor gardening life is that most of the bugs that affect houseplants are tiny. So tiny you can't see the darn things without a magnifying glass. By the time you've noticed that something is laying siege to your poor peace lily, the culprit has had a chance to inflict major injury.

To keep infestations to a minimum,

- be meticulous about plant housekeeping (see page 116);
- make sure you maintain high humidity (see page 100);
- treat all your plants to the watering routine that fits their particular requirements (see page 110).

What are those disgusting things, anyway?

Aphids
Nasty little suckers (also called, appropriately, plant lice), aphids are the curse of gardeners everywhere. If they attack

your houseplants, be consoled: they inflict far more damage outside, in gardens. Aphids multiply rapidly and are cunning. They often change their colors like chameleons to match the plant they've chosen to munch on. However, their appearance hardly matters, because these trespassers are so small, you can't usually see them with the naked eye.

The telltale signs of an artillery attack by aphids are:

🏵 stems, leaves, or flowers that suddenly go limp or get sticky;
🏵 leaves that become puckered up, like pursed lips;
🏵 white blobs (like spittle) clinging to the plant;
🏵 whitish "skeletons" (aphids' outer skins, which they shed and regrow regularly as they go about their business).

Aphids can affect virtually anything grown indoors, but they are particularly partial to hibiscus, dieffenbachias, ivies (*Hedera*), hoyas, and basil.

Fungus gnats

These are little flies, a bit like miniature daddy-long-legs. They start out as larvae in potting soil. In most instances, you'll see a lot of them suddenly start appearing from nowhere (in reality, they're hatching out in your pots), then flying about the room. Fungus gnats are annoying, but they usually don't harm plants, although one kind can damage roots. They can appear in virtually any potted plant, but bulbs, geraniums, and poinsettia are particularly vulnerable. To avoid them, use sterile soil-less mix.

Mealy bugs

These fall into the "crawler" category. They don't fly, and they usually cluster on stems and leaves, or in leaf axils or roots, sucking the life blood out of plants. Mealy bugs' only good attribute is that you can actually spot them: they're oval, about an eighth of an inch (0.3 cm) long, with spiky bits sticking out all around their nasty little bodies. But they are often hidden (like spider mites) under a white, woolly overcoat that they spin. One telltale sign of mealy bugs is honeydew

dripping from plants. Other pointers are leaves turning yellow or the whole plant withering.

Mealy bugs enjoy munching on African violets, amaryllis, begonias, clivias, coleus, dracaenas, dieffenbachias, epipremnums, ficuses, hoyas, scheffleras, syngoniums, and various cacti and orchids.

What honeydew is

In the supermarket it's a tasty melon. But for houseplants it's not so nice. "Honeydew" is the rather inappropriate word that garden experts use to describe the stuff bugs secrete while sucking the sap out of plants. It's yellowish, orangey, or clear, and sticky. If you see blobs of honeydew on the floor or table where your plants are, or a liquidy substance dripping from leaves or flowers, the plant is under attack. It could be aphids, mealy bugs, scale, or whiteflies. Whatever the culprit is, act fast.

Red spider mites

Like most bugs, these start out on the undersides of leaves. But they can multiply—and move around—at an incredible rate, especially in hot, dry air. One condo gardener (who bought a lot of houseplants for her solarium but neglected to install a humidifier) wound up with spider mites in her sofa, her bed, and even, to her horror, in her nightdress. It took months of repeatedly washing everything in her unit to get rid of them.

Spider mites are pink or red, and so small you probably won't notice them. What you do see, however, is their webs. These are a whitish weaving (or coating) mostly on the undersides of leaves, but also on leaf tops or clinging to the stems. In bad infestations, these webs will wrap themselves around entire section of plants, distorting their appearance. Other telltale signs are "webby" foliage that has turned pale, or leaf tips that are stippled with dots, or twisted.

Organic solutions to spider mites abound because they are the number one problem plaguing houseplants. Old timers recommend this concoction: mix half a cup (125 mL) of buttermilk with 4 cups (1 L) of wheat flour, then stir this paste into a bucket containing 5 gallons (19 L) of water. Immerse the entire pot, plant and all, in the bucket. You can also spray or paint this gluey substance on stems and leaves. It is supposed to work by suffocating the mites and killing their eggs.

Plants that are particularly prone to red spider mites are African violets, azaleas, crotons, cyclamen, dieffenbachias, dracaenas, hibiscus, marantas, many ivies (*Hedera*), and palms.

Scale

Scale isn't crud found inside the kettle. It's alive: a horrid insect, with a hard, horny casing, that sucks sap from stems. If there's honeydew dripping from plants and their leaves are turning yellow and dropping, the problem could be scale. When
mature, these brownish or yellowish invaders encase themselves completely in a waxy suit of armor that coats entire stems of plants and is difficult to remove.

Scale typically affects bay trees, citrus trees, euonymus, ferns (but don't mistake ferns' spore-bearing organs for scale; they look similar), ficuses, jasmine, and various orchids and palms.

> **Hot tip**
> "Houseplant bugs can't swim. If you submerge your plants in a tub of lukewarm water, the bugs will drown."
> —*Charlie Dobbin, houseplant expert*

Whiteflies

If a cloud of insects rises from a houseplant when you touch it, it's probably whiteflies. These have pale, shimmery wings, and they cluster in vast numbers on the tops and undersides of leaves, where they lay larvae (which are greenish or transparent). Whiteflies suck sap from plants and excrete honeydew. The entire plant will eventually wilt.

Flowering plants are often affected by whiteflies. Their favorite victims are geraniums of all kinds and fuchsias.

How to battle the bug brigade safely

Gardening books—old and new—often advocate using a bewildering arsenal of chemical weapons against bugs and viral diseases on houseplants. But many of these pesticides—which have names like Chlorobenzilate, Diazinon, and Lindane—have been proven to be highly toxic to humans and pets. A few, such as Diazinon, have already been banned for use in gardens in certain municipalities. Who wants to have such products sitting around at home or sprayed into the air we breathe indoors? Not sensible gardeners, surely.

When bugs attack, try an environmentally-friendly way of getting rid of them first. Use pesticides only as a last resort. Organic methods are usually more fiddly than zapping nuisances with a shot of something lethal—and they take persistence. But they can work. Here are some tips:

Do

✓ Be careful where you buy plants. Avoid "fly by night" operations, which are often set up at roadsides during the summer. The plants sold in these temporary garden centers may be cheap, but they don't receive proper care—and they may have been acquired from dubious sources.

✓ When repotting plants, always use sterile mix (see page 105).

✓ Isolate plants immediately if you suspect something is wrong.

✓ Keep a magnifying glass on hand to examine plants. Turn leaves and pots upside down if you can. Pay particular attention to the undersides of leaves.

✓ If you detect insects, dunk the plant in a bucket of luke-warm soapy water. Immerse the entire plant, pot and all. Then rinse. Repeat this procedure three days later, then again ten days later.

✓ If only one stem of a plant is buggy, cut it off. Throw it away immediately, wrapped in a plastic bag. Then do the soap and water routine with the rest of the plant.

✓ Spray the soapy water on affected areas with a misting bottle if the plant is too big for the "dunk" approach.

✓ If you have a sprayer with your kitchen faucet, give the undersides of leaves a blast. This may wash bugs off.

✓ Dab individual insects that you can see (like mites and scale) with a Q-tip dipped in isopropryl alcohol. Watch them squirm—and feel triumphant.

✓ Scrape scale off stems with a fingernail or the blunt edge of a knife, if you can bear it. (It's yucky—and you have to be careful not to damage the stems.)

It's not necessary to buy expensive insecticidal soaps to wash plants. A mild dishwashing liquid such as Ivory will do the job just as well. But don't use detergent. Just put a few squirts of dishwashing liquid into a full sink (or pail) of lukewarm water, then immerse plants, pots and all. Be sure to rinse them thoroughly.

✓ Put infected plants in a see-through plastic bag. Seal the bag. Check again in a couple of weeks. If the bugs are back, consider getting rid of the plant.

✓ Sprinkle a bit of tobacco on the tops of pots. We all know how harmful nicotine can be to humans. It sometimes kills bugs too.

✓ With white fly infestations, buy a yellow sticky strip (sold at garden centers) and put it in a plastic bag, along with the plant. The flies will—you hope—get stuck on the strip.

Don't

✗ Try to salvage a badly infected plant. Throw it out. And if bugs or disease problems keep coming back, give all your plants the heave-ho and start again.

✗ Allow a new arrival to join your plant collection right away. Keep it separate for a few weeks until you're sure it's in good shape.

What is guttation?

Sometimes, honeydew isn't caused by insects, but by a curious phenomenon called "guttation," which occurs with some houseplants when they are watered incorrectly. Liquid starts dripping from the tips of their leaves, and it may feel sticky. Dieffenbachia is particularly susceptible. So is ficus. You can trigger guttation by allowing plants to completely dry out and then watering them too heavily. To find out if that's the problem, examine the leaves carefully. You should see white droplets of latex, especially on the main vein (and, of course, there won't be any bugs evident on the plant). To remedy the problem, don't let the plant get bone dry between waterings. Keep the soil a bit moist.

Mites, Mildew, and Other Nasties ❀ 123

✗ Don't bring houseplants indoors in fall without giving them a bath first (see page 129). There's a barrelful of bugs lurking out there in the great green world. Bugs (and bug eggs) hitchhiking a ride indoors, once the cold weather comes, are the most common cause of infestations on houseplants during the winter.

When plants look sick—but you don't see any bugs

The problem could be an infection or viral disease. These can affect any part of indoor plants—leaves, stems, flowers, or roots—and they are bad news because they can spread quickly to other plants. There are also no satisfactory treatments for many of these afflictions. Often, the best bet is to throw the affected plant out. The most common problems are:

- **Black leg:** The name fits because stems go black and rot at the base. It's mostly caused by overwatering.
- **Botrytis:** Leaves and stems develop a fluffy, raised, gray mold. It happens when the humidity is too high, and usually affects plants with soft leaves and stems (like coleus).
- **Leaf spot:** Brownish or yellowish blotches, often with damp centers, appear on leaves. These patches keep spreading and may eventually meet up. Or they become hard and brownish.
- **Powdery mildew:** This very common mildew is much whiter in appearance than botrytis mold and not as "fluffy." It often affects rosemary bushes brought indoors for the winter.
- **Stem and crown rot:** This looks very similar to black leg. The decaying part usually gets horribly slimy and soft.
- **Weird viruses with no name:** Humans get them. Unfortunately, so do plants. The symptoms may be anything from yellow streaking and mottling of leaves to distortion or stunting of the whole plant.

How to deter plant diseases

❀ Be careful about overwatering. It's one of the most common causes of disease. Soil shouldn't get soggy. Avoid letting water settle on leaves, and don't be a maniac with the misting bottle.

❀ Don't crowd plants too tightly together. Mildew often sets in when there's insufficient space between plants.

❀ Avoid damaging plants, or breaking stems, when you handle them. That's an invitation to infection.

❀ Set up a little fan close to plants and leave it on for a few hours a day to circulate the air.

❀ If you suspect a virus, cut the affected part of the plant off, using a sharp, clean knife, and move it to another room. If the problem keeps returning, throw the plant out.

❀ Avoid handling healthy plants after you've been tending to a sick one. Wash your hands first.

❀ Try treating mildew and leaf spot with baking soda. Mix a teaspoonful (5 mL) into a misting bottle and spray on plants. Repeat at three-day intervals. This sometimes helps—but you have to keep doing it again and again to get results.

Hot tip

"Spraying the undersides of houseplant leaves is always difficult. Try a misting bottle that's new on the market. Its nozzle is angled upwards, rather than downwards. I got mine from a company that sells garden products by mail—and I love it."

—*Gwen Farrow, condo gardener*

What To Do with Houseplants in the Summer

Should we put them outside? Leave them inside? Opinions differ strongly on this issue. Some experienced gardeners are vehement that houseplants should never go into a garden (or onto a deck or balcony) during the warm months. "It weakens the plants," argues one, "and it makes them vulnerable to infection—and attacks by insects." Other gardening experts are just as adamant that indoor plants benefit from a dose of fresh air. "After being cooped up indoors for the winter, house-plants like being outside as much as we do," says one nursery manager. "I always put mine out in the garden. They get lots of new growth, and that sets them up for the following fall, when I bring them indoors again."

Ultimately, it's a matter of personal choice. But if you are going to give your plants a summer vacation outdoors, it's important to break them into their new environment slowly. Houseplants are like residents of a northern city going off on a winter trip south. They've been used to low light levels inside, and suddenly they're plunked somewhere that's much brighter (light levels outside are invariably brighter than in our homes, even if we grow plants under lights). They may also have to cope with seesaw temperatures, wind, and rain. They need time to acclimatize or they'll get sunburned and out of sorts—and unlike humans, they may never recover from the shock.

> ## Hot tip
> "I always put my hibiscus and benjamina out of doors in summer, and by September they look fantastic."
> —*Mark Cullen,*
> *gardening show host*

Safe steps to take

Do

✓ Group plants together in a shady, sheltered spot in the garden (or on a balcony) where they won't receive *any* direct sunlight for at least a couple of weeks.

✓ Water all plants well after you put them outside.

✓ Be very careful about dappled shade. Tree leaves cast this kind of shade, and one problem with it is that it's not constant or impenetrable. The sun breaks through, particularly on a windy day when leaves are blowing to and fro, and it can be incredibly fierce. You may think you're giving houseplants a shady spot, but the reality is often different. The plants can actually get visible burn spots if piercing rays of sunlight sneak through the leaves.

✓ Whatever the location, if the indirect light is fierce, gently cover the plants with a light-colored sheet for the first week. This is particularly important if you've put them

 *If you've moved into a new condo and are strapped for cash, save money when summer comes by putting your houseplants outside on your balcony or terrace. The "tropical look" is all the rage nowadays in gardening—and that's exactly what many houseplants supply, in spades. Their big flamboyant leaves look great grouped together on a deck or balcony.*

on a balcony high off the ground, where they'll be exposed to wind, as well.

✓ Keep houseplants that normally thrive in low-light conditions—such as philodendrons, Chinese evergreens, spathiphyllums, and spider plants—in a shady area all summer. The same goes for amaryllis and clivias.

✓ Move cacti, rosemary bushes, bay trees, geraniums, and succulents such as jade plants out into the sun after an adjustment period—but do it slowly. Expose them to the sun's rays for only an hour the first day, then gradually increase their exposure. (If you have a trolley to move the plants in and out of the sun, this makes the job easier.)

✓ Cut houseplants right back if they developed growth that's pale and leggy over the winter. So long as you keep them well watered and nourished with plant food, they'll usually develop fresh new leaves quickly.

Don't

✗ Leave a houseplant sitting in the sunshine if it's obviously wilting. Move it immediately to a shady spot.

✗ Forget to water plants. They need more water than usual after their introduction to the great outdoors.

When winter rolls around

We often slow down. So do our plants. Generally speaking, plants grow much more slowly in winter—in fact, some go as dormant as hibernating bears. Cacti, for instance, will actually shrink in winter. Even if they don't lose weight, most plants require less of everything: watering, fertilizing, overall fussing. In fact, many of them like to be left alone, with just a drizzle of water now and then to keep them alive.

If you're bringing houseplants back indoors after a summer spent outside, take a crucially important step: give them all a "plunge bath" in lukewarm soapy water. Here's how to do it:

🏵 Use a mild detergent such as Dove. Put a few squirts of it into the kitchen sink, the bathtub, or a bucket, mixed with lots of water.

🏵 Prune any dead or straggly bits off the plant, then plunge the whole thing into the bath, pot and all.

🏵 Immerse it for a few minutes, until bubbles have stopped coming to the surface.

🏵 Rinse the pot and plant off thoroughly (under the shower works well) and leave it outside to dry on a sunny fall day. Then bring it into its winter quarters (preferably a cool room at first, so it can adjust to being indoors).

Giving plants a bath gets rid of bugs that may be lurking, unnoticed, under the leaves. It also kill eggs that creepy-crawlies and flying insects might have laid in the soil—and it washes away fertilizer salts that have built up in the container during the summer. Experienced gardeners say scheduling a bath day is always worth the effort.

Hot tip

"Before giving houseplants a bath, pick up a special mesh strainer that fits over the drainage hole of sinks or bathtubs. It stops soil and plant debris getting washed down the drain. You can find these strainers at hardware stores. They're only a few dollars."
—*Mary Wilkerson,
condo houseplant fan*

The Real Poop on Poisonous and Beneficial Houseplants

Can indoor plants kill us—or our kids and pets? Yes, it's undeniably possible, but the likelihood of this happening is *very* low. In fact, the poison potential of most houseplants is greatly exaggerated by the nervous Nellies of the world. In most instances, the benefits of having greenery around our homes far outweigh the drawbacks.

Which plants can harm us?

Some popular houseplants are definitely toxic, to varying degrees. They may make susceptible individuals sick with a variety of ailments ranging from stomach trouble to severe dermatitis. A few plants may also affect kids far more seriously than adults. And plants that don't bother humans can, in some cases, prompt poor Fido or Kitty to start barfing on the rug or showing other symptoms of poisoning. (Paradoxically, these problem plants often also do a good job of purifying the air. See page 134.) Here are common "baddies" to watch out for:

❀ **Aloe vera (*Aloe barbadensis*):** Often called the burn plant, this spiky, easy-to-grow tropical plant is a boon in the kitchen (see page 35). However, be sure to use only the jellified center of the aloe's "leaves," not the yellow juice that's immediately under its green skin. This liquidy stuff can give some people a bad rash. Note: use young plants. Older aloe plants contain lots of juice.

❀ **Amaryllis:** Don't ever mistake amaryllis bulbs for an exotic new onion. They cause diarrhea, nausea, and vomiting (but you have to gobble down huge amounts of them to get sick).

❀ **Angel's trumpet (*Datura arborea*):** This produces spectacular flowers, but if you have kids or pets, forget it. It's a relative of deadly Jimson weed (*Datura stramonium*) and shouldn't be grown indoors unless you're super careful. Sometimes called 'loco weed' because it makes cattle go crazy if they munch on it, *D. stramonium* is severely poisonous to humans and pets, and *D. arborea* is presumed to have similar effects. Symptoms include agitation, jerky movements, coma, drowsiness, hallucination, and elevated temperature.

❀ **Azalea (*Rhododendron sp.*):** Classified as "low toxicity," azaleas should nonetheless be kept away from kids and pets. In fact, experts recommend treating all rhododendrons as poisonous.

❀ **Caladiums:** If cats and dogs chew on these elegant houseplants with heart-shaped leaves, they'll get inflamed mouths and throats. Tummy upsets are another side effect.

❀ **Castor bean plant (*Ricinus communis*):** This plant is so deadly poisonous, terrorists have been caught attempting to transform its seeds into biological weapons. Enough said.

❀ **Crown of thorns (*Euphorbia milii*):** Many garden varieties of euphorbia exude an irritating sap. This one, often grown as a houseplant and sometimes called "Christ's thorn," is no exception. It can also cause abdominal pains and vomiting if eaten. Always wear garden gloves when handling euphorbias.

❀ **Devil's backbone (*Kalanchoe daigremontiana*):** Also called "mother of thousands" because young plantlets grow along its leaf edges. These new "babies" are potential troublemakers, because toddlers and pets often pull them off the mother plant to have a nibble or play with them. That's not a good idea because leaves and stems are quite toxic and can cause death in rare instances. Be careful of all kalanchoes.

- **Devil's ivy (Pothos, *Epipremnum*, or *Scindapsus*):** There's no evidence that this easy-to-grow trailing plant is poisonous to humans, but some people say it causes dogs' and cats' lips and tongues to swell up if they chew on it.
- **Dieffenbachia:** This distinctively leafed plant is nick-named "dumbcane" with good reason. Chew on it and you'll be struck dumb—a condition that can last for several days. (Fido's bark may be similarly zapped. Perhaps that's not such a bad thing.) The sap can also irritate skin.
- **English ivy (*Hedera helix*):** One of the most popular houseplants on the planet. But don't let pets nibble on its leaves or be tempted to use it as a garnish in cooking. Ingesting ivy may result in breathing difficulties, convulsions, paralysis, and coma. Some people also get a rash from the sap.
- **Flamingo lily (*Anthurium andraeanum*):** Sometimes called "painter's palette." Don't let pets play with this one or they'll get painful blistering of their mouths and throats. Further symptoms are gagging and difficulty breathing.
- **Hyacinth:** See page 86.

- **Hydrangea (*Hydrangea macrophylla*):** These shrubby garden plants are increasingly popular indoors. Eating the buds and leaves can cause vomiting, abdominal pains, diarrhea, lethargy, labored breathing, and coma. If you have sensitive skin, you may also get contact dermatitis when handling the plants.
- **Oleander (*Nerium*):** Increasingly popular as a houseplant in northern climates because of its pretty pink, red, white, or salmon flowers and graceful green-gray leaves, this shrub is so highly toxic, it's against the law to burn it on some Caribbean islands (oleander smoke can send susceptible individuals into convulsions). Don't let pets nibble on it, and avoid handling nerium with bare hands.

❀ **Swiss cheese plant (*Monstera deliciosa*):**
Unfortunately, there's nothing delicious about this plant (also called split-leaf philodendron). Its leaves are toxic to both humans and pets. Symptoms include loss of speech, blistering, hoarseness, mouth irritation, and raised watery lesions on the skin, accompanied by intense itching.

How to avoid hassles with problem plants

Do
✓ Wear gloves when handling anything that may cause a rash.
✓ Group potentially hazardous houseplants together in a separate area of the house that's not accessible to family members and pets.
✓ Contact a doctor, go to the emergency department of a hospital, or call a vet if you suspect poisoning. Some people keep syrup of ipecac or hydrogen peroxide on hand and administer a dose to induce vomiting.

> **Hot tip**
> "Cats get neurotic if they're constantly told to stop nibbling on houseplants. So I let mine munch on my spider plant. It doesn't really hurt the plant, and it keeps the cats happy during the winter."
> —*Barrie Murdock,*
> *cat and plant lover*

Don't
✗ Place houseplants on or near the floor, where they're more likely to be nibbled or played with by pets and young children.
✗ Buy anything lethal, like datura. It isn't worth the risk.
✗ Grow castor bean plants indoors. They should be restricted to the garden.
✗ Get too hung up on the issue of "bad" houseplants. Severe poisoning is very rare.

Don't point fingers at poinsettias

People insist that the "Christmas plant" is toxic, causing everything from tummy upsets to convulsions to death. In fact, some worry warts refuse to have it in their homes over the holidays on the grounds that it may make somebody ill. Experts say that's hogwash. Poinsettias are *not* poisonous. Period. They were once thought to be mildly toxic, but both the American and Canadian governments have concluded that they goofed on this point, and they recently crossed the pretty, harmless poinsettia off their poisonous plant lists.

However, since this much-maligned plant is a member of the rash-inducing euphorbia family, it may be wise to wear gloves when handling it.

Which plants absorb pollutants?

Astronauts whirling around in space on shuttle flights for NASA have conducted complex experiments on many common houseplants. Their primary interest was in testing the plants' capacity to purify air, but they made some other amazing findings. Houseplants are, in fact, true friends to humanity. They not only convert carbon dioxide to oxygen, but some of them also have the ability to trap and absorb many of the chemical pollutants that we introduce into our homes. These harmful substances include:

❀ formaldehyde emitted from foam insulation and soft furnishings (like padded sofas and armchairs);
❀ trichlorethylene from paints and glues; and
❀ benzene, found in tobacco smoke and some detergents.

NASA says certain plants are particularly beneficial to have around because they swallow up the bad stuff and regurgitate it as nice clean air. They recommend these:

❀ Aloe vera (*Aloe barbadensis*)
❀ Chinese evergreen (*Aglaonema*)
❀ Chrysanthemum (garden mums, sold as potted plants every fall)
❀ Dieffenbachia
❀ English ivy (*Hedera helix*)
❀ Golden pothos (*Epipremnum aureum*)

- Ficus
- Gerbera daisy
- Philodendron, especially the heart-leaf and lace tree varieties
- *Spathiphyllum* 'Mauna Loa'
- Spider plant (*Chlorophytum comosum*)

The astronauts found that aloes, epipremnums, and philodendrons were particularly good at removing formaldehyde from the air. Gerbera daisies and chrysanthemums worked similar magic with benzene.

> **Hot tip**
> "Don't grow miniature roses (*Rosa chinensis*) indoors if you have a cat. Mine loves nibbling on the rose buds. They haven't poisoned her, but it sure wrecks the roses."
> —*Joan Thomas, condo gardener*

Where To Get Help for Unhappy Houseplants

It's the middle of the winter, it's well below freezing outside, and suddenly your ficus has dropped all its leaves. What to do? You have several options:

Your friendly neighborhood florist

Establish a relationship with a local business that sells plants—it's worth it. When you have a problem, you can drop by and get their advice, which they are usually only too happy to supply. Many gardeners follow the "cheapest is best" formula: they stick to buying plants from big box stores out in the suburbs. This is certainly cheaper, but savvy souls buy from a local supplier—a florist, garden center, or even a neighborhood greengrocer (these folks are often surprisingly knowledgeable), because when things go wrong, there's a real live person close at hand to quiz about solutions.

Surf the Web

Use a search engine like Google, type in a few words such as "ficus houseplant care," and you'll find links to lots of Web sites related to that topic. Some of the information these sites supply is useful. A lot isn't. Many are created by companies selling products, and there's a ton of marketing hype to wade through before you get to the nitty-gritty stuff you need. Others are written badly, and the type is so small it's hard to read. If you're a techie, you can certainly track down valuable tips—there's so much information floating around in cyber-space nowadays—but if you want fast results, try these first:

- **http://rhs.org.uk/index.htm:** This is the site of the Royal Horticultural Society in London, England. It's laid out well, is easy to read, and contains useful information for indoor gardeners.
- **www.windowbox.com:** Down-to-earth gardening tips, supplied in a punchy style. Their houseplant expert is called the "Care Counselor," and you can leave your own tips at the site or pick up suggestions from other site users.
- **www.chestnut-sw.com:** This site, belonging to an outfit called the Weekend Gardener, offers advice on indoor plant care and starting seeds.
- **www.bulb.com:** Operated by the International Flower Bulb Centre, this super site has everything you need to know about growing all kinds of bulbs.
- **Web sites operated by universities:** Many dispense solid information aimed at gardeners—and while the writing is often dry and academic, you can pick up useful tips. Two good ones are:
  - **http://extention.oregonstate.edu.eesc:** Operated by an organization with a mouthful of a name (Oregon State University Extension and Experiment Station Communications), this has an excellent site on house-plant care.
  - **http://extension.umn.edu/topics.html?topic=5:** The University of Minnesota manages this one. It's strong on information about seed-starting.

Ask a Master Gardener

Master Gardeners are trained volunteers who take courses in horticulture. They spend much of their spare time educating the public about gardening, simply because they love it so much. Many of them are houseplant addicts—and they're a mine of information about the pleasures and pitfalls of indoor gardening.

You can find Master Gardeners in information booths at

flower shows and agricultural shows. In many cities, they also run gardening information phone lines, which provide free answers to questions about all aspects of growing things. Some MG groups operate advice clinics (usually during the summer months) at garden centers. You can take an ailing houseplant there and get some advice on the spot.

To find out if there's a Master Gardener group operating in your area, ask at your local horticultural society or garden center. Universities that offer agricultural or horticultural programs also know how to track down these knowledgeable and helpful individuals.

Get to know other gardeners

Join your local horticultural society. Local garden centers can usually find phone numbers and addresses for you. If you live in a condo or apartment building, get a gardening group going. In a high-rise, there are bound to be other people already growing things indoors—and they're often a treasure trove of information.

Acknowledgments

There are two things I love about gardening: plants (of course) and people. I've met so many delightful gardeners, from all walks of life. Whatever their particular passion in the great green world, they're always enthusiastic, knowledgeable, and fun to be around. When I get together with other gardeners, there's never a lull in the conversation. We find so many things to talk about! Indeed, it never ceases to amaze me how open-hearted gardeners are. There can be no other group of people who share their creative ideas, practical know-how, and the fruits of their labors (all those plants) so generously.

Many gardeners have assisted me in the preparation of this book. In particular, I want to thank: Janet Brothers, who gave me a lesson in transplanting seedlings at Cedar Springs Nursery in Elora, Ontario; Carol Cowan, of the Netherlands Flower Bulb Information Centre, who shares my passion for growing amaryllis; horticulturist Cathie Cox, who taught me everything I know about starting plants from seed; Mary-Fran McQuade, for her budget-minded savvy with houseplants; African violet aficionado Sandy Morgan; Conrad Richter, a repository of many fascinating facts about herbs; Richard Tawton, who claims to be a beginner with houseplants but is really a pro; indoor gardener extraordinaire Ida Weippert, who appears on the cover; and Paul Zammit, who introduced me to the charms of clivias.

I am also grateful for tips, ideas, and information gleaned from many other sources. One valuable reference guide I recommend for its in-depth information is *Success with House*

Plants, published by Reader's Digest. Another is *From Seed to Bloom*, by Eileen Powell. Two garden writers from whom I gained insights into the pleasures of amaryllis are Starr Ockenga, author of *Amaryllis*, and Veronica Read, author of a book on amaryllis to be published in 2004. Derek Read, of the Research Branch of the Biological Resources Program of Agriculture and Agrifood Canada, provided useful information on poisonous houseplants and the NASA research into beneficial plants. Other tips came from many friends and acquaintances, including: Trevor Ashbee, Deirdre Black, Dugald Cameron, Mark Cullen, Irene Day, Charlie Dobbin, David Eddy, Gwen Farrow, Marianne Fenner, Stewart Hamilton, Becky Heath, Sandra Henry, Lorraine Hunter, Alison Hunberstone, Sara Katz, Priscilla Leung, Anne Lockley, Douglas Markoff, Sue Martin, Barrie Murdock, Truc Nguyen, Catherine Pitt, Andrew Pepetone, Larry Sherk, Joan Thomas, Ann Travis, Mary Wilkerson, Karen York, and Tilly Zomer.

Finally, I wish to thank my editor, Sue Sumeraj, for her expertise in assembling this package of material into a readable (and, I hope, useful) book.

Index